Advance Praise for *The Gospel according to Disney*

"Mark Pinsky has done it again, a highly readable, entertaining, and important look at a major media icon. Bravo. This is must-reading."
—Ted Baehr, chair of the Christian Film and
Television Commission and publisher of *Movieguide*

"My highest recommendation. . . . *The Gospel according to Disney* will literally open your eyes and give you a fresh way to understand these important animated art treasures. So, sit back, read, and enjoy the journey, as Mark transports you to Disney's magical Wonderland."
—David Bruce, host of HollywoodJesus.com

"Here is both an entertaining tour and an educational read through Disney's world of animation. Disney's 'reel' faith is engagingly documented, as is the varying response of both church and synagogue to it."
—Robert K. Johnston, coauthor of *Finding God in the Movies*
and professor of theology and culture, Fuller Theological Seminary

"Parents and grandparents who want to share biblical values and memorable lessons with their children will find a wealth of opportunity in Disney-animated features—with the help of Mark Pinsky's new book. This easy-to-read book will get you started talking with your kids about good messages behind the movies. Pop some popcorn and let pop culture work for you for a change!"
—Connie Neal, author of *The Gospel according to Harry Potter*

The Gospel according to Disney

Faith, Trust, and Pixie Dust

Mark I. Pinsky

WESTMINSTER
JOHN KNOX PRESS
LOUISVILLE · KENTUCKY

Scripture quotations, unless otherwise indicated, are from the New Revised Standard Version of the Bible, copyright © 1989 by the Division of Christian Education of the National Council of the Churches of Christ in the U.S.A., and used by permission.

This publication was not authorized or endorsed by The Walt Disney Company.

Book design by Sharon Adams
Cover design by Mark Abrams/Jennifer K. Cox

First edition
Published by Westminster John Knox Press
Louisville, Kentucky

This book is printed on acid-free paper that meets the American National Standards Institute Z39.48 standard. ∞

11 12 13 — 10 9 8 7 6 5 4 3

Library of Congress Cataloging-in-Publication Data

Pinsky, Mark I.
    The Gospel according to Disney : faith, trust, and pixie dust / by Mark I. Pinsky. — 1st ed.
        p. cm.
    Includes index.
    ISBN 0-664-22591-8 (alk. paper)
    1. Walt Disney Company. 2. Children's films—Moral and ethical aspects. I. Title.

PN1999.W27P56 2004
791.43'682—dc22

2004050887

For
Paul G. Pinsky,
brother and hero;
and
Charlotte and Joe Brown,
supportive in-laws, wonderful grandparents, good Presbyterians

Contents

Introduction   ix
Methodology   xv

  1 The Disney Gospel: Secular 'Toonism   1

Part One: The Disney Years: 1937–1984   13
  2 Walt and Roy: The Christians   15
  3 *Snow White and the Seven Dwarfs* (1937):
     Sin and Salvation   22
  4 *Pinocchio* (1940): Prove Yourself   28
  5 *Fantasia* (1940): The Sorcerer's Mascot   33
  6 *Dumbo* (1940): Mother Love   40
  7 *Bambi* (1942): Man Is in the Forest   46
  8 *Cinderella* (1950): Prince Charming II   52
  9 *Alice in Wonderland* (1951): Take the Red Pill   57
 10 *Peter Pan* (1953): Faith, Trust, and Pixie Dust   61
 11 *Lady and the Tramp* (1955): Mixed Marriage   69
 12 *Sleeping Beauty* (1959): Not in Death   74
 13 *101 Dalmatians* (1961): Black and White   79
 14 *The Sword and the Stone* (1963): Knowledge Is King   83
 15 *The Jungle Book* (1967): Nature and Nurture   88
 16 *Robin Hood* (1973): Tax Rebates   94
 17 *The Fox and the Hound* (1981): Nature and Nurture Redux 99
 18 *The Black Cauldron* (1985): Contains Occult Material 104
 19 Shorts: Pagans, Jews, and Christians   109

Part Two: The Eisner Years: 1984–2004   119
 20 Michael and Jeffrey: The Jews   121
 21 *The Little Mermaid* (1989): Upward Mobility   138

22 *Beauty and the Beast* (1991): Feminism, Transformation,
    and Redemption   143
23 *Aladdin* (1992): Encountering Islam   148
24 *The Lion King* (1994): Karma on the Savannah   154
25 *Pocahontas* (1995): Animating Animism   160
26 *The Hunchback of Notre Dame* (1996):
    The House of the Lord   167
27 *Hercules* (1997): Superman, Samson, and Delilah   175
28 *Mulan* (1998): Woman of Valor   179
29 *Tarzan* (1999): Taming the Savage   185
30 *The Emperor's New Groove* (2000): Eminent Domain   189
31 *Atlantis* (2001): Adventure Capitalism   194
32 *Lilo and Stitch* (2002): Send in the Clone   203
33 *Treasure Planet* (2002): Mining the Father Lode   209
34 *Return to Neverland* (2002): Faith, Trust, and Pixie Dust II   215
35 *Brother Bear* (2003): Primitive Predestination   220

Part Three: Disney and American Culture   227
36 The Theme Parks: American Pilgrimage   229
37 The Baptist Boycott: Culture Clash   238
38 Conclusion: Questions and Answers   262

Acknowledgments   268
Bibliography   271
Index   274

Introduction

Mickey Mouse and faith? The world's most famous rodent and his animated friends say more about faith and values than you might think—they're not just postage stamps. Peter Pan taught us that "faith, trust, and pixie dust" can help you leave your cares behind. Jiminy Cricket showed Pinocchio (and millions of movie-goers) that "when you wish upon a star" dreams come true. *Bambi* stimulated baby boomer support for gun control and environmentalism. *Cinderella* became a syndrome. *The Little Mermaid* illustrated the challenges of intermarriage. *The Lion King* hinted at Hindu tradition in the "Circle of Life." Walt Disney wanted his theme parks to be "a source of joy and inspiration to all the world." Some have compared them to shrines to which American families make obligatory pilgrimages, parents reconnecting with their own childhoods while helping their kids experience a cartoon fantasy Mecca. Even Disney's detractors see tremendous symbolic value in his cartoon characters. As a boycott loomed in the mid-1990s, one Southern Baptist leader—denouncing the Disney corporation's human resources policies toward same-sex couples—asked his sympathizers, "Do they expect Mickey to leave Minnie and move in with Donald? That's Goofy!"

Like many baby boomers in the 1950s, I was raised on Walt Disney's animated features. And I imagine—although I am not certain—that, as with the generations that have followed, my first trip to a movie theater was to see one of these films. I recall more clearly seeing some of them again years later, introduced by an avuncular Uncle Walt, on Sunday night television in our suburban

New Jersey living room. Much later, at college in the late 1960s, I remember watching *Fantasia* in an altered state, but enjoying it no more than when I struggled to sit through it the first time.

This book, like my earlier work, *The Gospel according to The Simpsons: The Spiritual Life of the World's Most Animated Family*, begins with my children, Liza and Asher. While living in Southern California and writing for the *Los Angeles Times* in the early 1990s, I watched as the toddlers viewed the classic Disney features over and over. My wife, Sallie, and I took them to the theater to see new releases such as *The Lion King*. Some of the older films that we watched at home on video I had not seen for forty years; the newer ones I'd never seen at all. Now, with a parent's eyes, I tried to observe their impact in our tiny Long Beach den. There were lessons and values in the films that I supported and wished to encourage, such as the acceptance of differences in others and respect for the feelings of others. "If children could be 'entertained' into good behavior, then Disney is just the one to send them to for instruction," William I. McReynolds wrote in his groundbreaking thesis, "Walt Disney in the American Grain." Other aspects of the earlier films—such as dated racial, national, and cultural stereotypes—disturbed and embarrassed me, and required me to stop the tape and discuss these matters with the kids. "There is nothing innocent in what kids learn about race as portrayed in the 'magical world' of Disney," wrote Henry A. Giroux in *The Mouse That Roared: Disney and the End of Innocence.* "The racism in these films is defined by the presence of racist representations and the absence of complex representations of African Americans and other people of color."

As often happens with journalists (and academics, I soon learned), the personal led to the professional. In my case, I recognized in these films what I believed was a generally identifiable theology and ethical system. I sensed—correctly, I think—that millions of children around the world were having their values shaped by Disney's animated features. So, in my last days as a reporter for the *Times,* I began doing research on the role of religion and ethics in Disney's movies. Thus, the first story I wrote for the *Orlando Sentinel,* where I was hired as a religion writer, described what I called the "Disney gospel." That piece, carried on the Knight-Ridder–Tribune News Service in July 1995, was widely reprinted in newspapers around the country and posted on the Internet. In the decade that followed, I have returned to the subject of religion and animation more than a dozen times, reporting on this issue as it relates to Disney and other movie and television studios.

This newspaper reporting on religion and animation led to other stories about the Walt Disney Company's interaction with the faith community. Well over 50,000 people work for Disney in Central Florida, making the entertainment giant the region's biggest employer. The Southern Baptist Convention, the nation's largest Protestant denomination, is also the church of choice for the largest number of worshipers in the Orlando area. So it was inevitable that when, in the 1990s, the Baptists decided to boycott Disney for a variety of reasons discussed in chapter 37, I was consumed by the story and drawn even deeper into the company's involvement with, and relationship to, religion. Later, I was gratified when officials from both the company and the denomination told me that my coverage was fair and evenhanded.

The Gospel according to The Simpsons offered a counterintuitive thesis: *It's not what you think,* I argued, in analyzing that long-running, subversive television series. Contrary to conventional wisdom—widely held by people who do not watch the show—*The Simpsons* respects sincerely held belief and religious practice. As evidence for this thesis, I provided numerous, specific examples of the ways Protestant, Catholic, Jewish, and Hindu faith were portrayed on the show. With *The Gospel according to Disney,* I am saying something quite different about the company's animated features: *It is what you think, more or less, but here is how and why.* There is a consistent set of moral and human values in these movies, largely based on Western, Judeo-Christian faith and principles, which together constitute a "Disney gospel." This gospel reflects the personal vision of Walt Disney and the company he shaped in his image and, to a lesser degree, the commercial goals of the studio. Good is always rewarded; evil is always punished. Faith is an essential element—faith in yourself and, even more, faith in something *greater* than yourself, some higher power. Optimism and hard work complete the basic canon.

These animated features have drawn children and their parents—my family included—to theaters for releases and rereleases. Often these experiences have exposed the youngsters to the magic of the big screen in a darkened hall for the first time in their lives. Later, the animated features became an enduring staple, as Walt Disney himself became a regular weekly visitor to millions of American homes on the Disney television series, first on ABC and then on NBC, where the films reappeared in color. Yet this was nothing compared to the emergence of home video and later DVD technology, which enabled tots to watch both the classics and the newer releases over and over again.

Different readers will find different uses for this book. Parents and grandparents of young children may find it a helpful handbook, one that can provide guidance for which features to watch, and, more importantly, *how* to watch them. Serious students of film, religion, and popular culture may be more engaged by the analytical and historical chapters. In the interests of fairness and full disclosure, I offer several caveats.

First, among the credentials (and baggage) I bring to this work is a lifetime commitment to Judaism, informed by some years of formal and many more of informal study. Raised in an observant, Conservative home in the Northeast, I am now an active member of a Reform synagogue, the Congregation of Liberal Judaism in Orlando. But my interpretation of Disney is also shaped—perhaps equally—by the past nine years I have spent living and working among evangelical Christians in the Sunbelt suburbs. While total immersion might be overstating the case some, this period of my life has been the equivalent of an extended crash course in a culture I knew virtually nothing about. As a result, and with help of many sincere Christians, I find that I have developed "evangelical eyes" in analyzing popular culture, for me a kind of second sight.

Second, to be fair in analyzing Disney's animated features and religion, it is important to see these films in historical context, a persuasive insight impressed on me at the outset by my friend and colleague Jay Boyar, the *Orlando Sentinel*'s longtime film critic. Until the early 1960s, explicit portrayal of religion was largely off-limits and seldom attempted throughout the movie industry. The consensus in the early days of American cinema was that religion was sacred and movies were largely profane. There were notable exceptions—biblical epics such as *The Greatest Story Ever Told, The Robe, King of Kings, The Ten Commandments,* and *Ben-Hur,* as well as later versions of the story of Jesus, such as *Jesus of Nazareth* and *The Last Temptation of Christ.* Works set in more contemporary times, such as *Going My Way* and *The Song of Bernadette,* tended to give Catholics reverent treatment. Protestant clergy were represented by the Protestant Film Office, which was founded by the precursor to the National Council of Churches. But this office never had the clout of a well-organized lobby like the Catholic Legion of Decency, and seemed to fare less well in films such as *Cape Fear* and *Elmer Gantry.* But apart from films such as these, with religion at their center, there was little cinematic evidence of religion, except in passing—praying children, grace at dinner, and fighting military chaplains played by Pat O'Brien. "It would be a big mistake to automatically conclude, however, that Hollywood was anti-religious," said Boyar. "It's important to keep in mind that until universities and museums began embracing movies in the 1960s, movies were frequently viewed as trash. The idea of making a movie about religion was, in itself, likely to be seen as a little suspect or even disrespectful—even if the movie was strongly pro-religion."

In the case of Disney, the reluctance to make organized religion a significant part of the fabric of film mirrored Walt's early concerns: fear of offending and fear of excluding. At the same time, Disney was and is a studio with a unified artistic and corporate vision, and its animated features are designed for children and young teens. So, in my view, singling out the studio and its leaders for examination is fully justified. "The individual Disney films act as chapters in the Disney book on what the world looks like or should look like," wrote Annalee R. Ward, in her perceptive study *Mouse Morality: The Rhetoric of Disney Animated Film.*

Methodology

Some reviewers of *The Gospel according to The Simpsons* complained that there was not enough of my own analysis and interpretation in that work, and too much paraphrasing from the show's episodes, and material from academics, ministers, and theologians. These critics may be right. So in this book I have tried to remedy that, especially in the heart of the work, the appraisals of the individual animated features. To do this, I have chosen to view (or re-view) the animated features in the order that they were released, and to let my sense of each film form the core of the chapter. Some of these features I was watching for the fourth time—after screenings in the theater and on television as a child myself, and again on video as a parent. For others it was a first viewing. In either case, I took notes from the screen, with the help of closed captioning, stopping to play back action and dialogue as needed.

Only later did I consult academic papers, sermons, and books, and interview Disney experts and religious authorities. Unlike my study of *The Simpsons,* where I was relatively early to the academic field, there are nearly seven decades of literature on Disney. Where relevant and informative, I have included this material, even when these views clashed with my own. Most (but not all) of the academic critiques I cite come from the Left, where my own sympathies generally lie. However, much of what Marxist (and right-wing) observers have seen in Disney—the most sinister, malign, and conscious manipulation—I have not. This may be a matter of effect versus intent, or because it isn't there. To be sure, nothing significant on the big screen appears by accident, yet I have attempted throughout to guard against finding things in these features—"the text"—that are not there, and to avoid magnifying things that are there, simply to support my thesis.

These film essays vary in approach. Some are primarily critical readings of the narratives, highlighting elements of faith and values, and may provide a helpful guide for children's caretakers. Others probe deeper or take off in a different direction. On a key point, I have chosen not to dwell unduly on the differences between the Disney features and the source materials from which they have been adapted, a subject well covered by other researchers. It is true that the fairy tales, books, and stories on which many of Disney's animated features are based have had an independent influence on the larger culture. But it would be difficult to argue that, from the second half of the twentieth century forward, the printed word could in any way compete with images on the screen for impact. "At a certain time in history, before anyone knew what was happening . . . Walt Disney cast a spell on the fairy tale, and he has held it captive ever since," wrote Jack Zipes in *From Mouse to Mermaid: The Politics of Film, Gender, and Culture.*

There are, as you will notice, some gaps in my coverage of the Disney movies. Because they are so distinct and faithful to the originals, I have not included the *Winnie the Pooh* films. Neither do I discuss *Song of the South* and *The Three Caballeros*—considered among Disney's most offensive features—because they involve live actors and because they are episodic. And since they are so thoroughly modern and distinct (and were produced by another company and only distributed by Disney), I have not included the wonderful films of Pixar, such as *Toy Story* and *Finding Nemo*. Some of Disney's animated features from the period between Walt Disney's death and Michael Eisner's ascension, such as *The Great Mouse Detective, Oliver & Company,* and *The Aristocats,* do not appear at all, as they are in my view less relevant and less substantial to the subject of faith and values. Likewise, straight-to-video animated sequels appear only where they add significantly to the discussion of the features themselves. And, despite their early importance to the company's development, I have confined my discussion of Disney's many cartoon shorts to a single chapter. I also chose not to consider other significant elements in the Disney canon: the studio's nature and live action films.

In the current journalistic and academic environment, I have made every effort to avoid any inadvertent use of material not my own, without proper credit and citation. Unless otherwise noted, material quoted is from original interviews. Accounts of events and controversies involving the Walt Disney Company are based on reporting by myself and others writing for the *Orlando Sentinel*.

Chapter One

The Disney Gospel: Secular 'Toonism

*T*he old man needed a miracle, supernatural intervention to give life to his little boy, slumped motionless across the room. So the white-haired woodcarver did what might be expected under the circumstances: He knelt on his bed, folded his hands on the windowsill, and turned his eyes to heaven. Then, in his soft Italian accent, he did *not* pray. Instead, Geppetto wished upon a star. The transformation from puppet to boy that ensued in Walt Disney's 1940, Oscar-winning animated feature *Pinocchio* was indeed miraculous, but not traditionally divine. As the man slept, a winged, glowing spirit, the Blue Fairy, advised the marionette to "let your conscience be your guide," to "choose right from wrong" so he could earn the "gift of life." And Pinocchio is not an exception. Walt Disney did not want religion in his movies. "He never made a religious film, and churchmen were rarely portrayed in Disney movies," according to Bob Thomas, author of *Walt Disney: An American Original,* an authorized biography. In *Building a Company: Roy O. Disney and the Creation of an Entertainment Empire*, Thomas wrote that, throughout his career, Walt "had eschewed any film material dealing with religion, reasoning that portions of the audience would be displeased by the depiction of a particular sect." Thus, there is relatively little explicit Judeo-Christian symbolism or substance in seventy years of Disney's animated features, despite the frequent, almost pervasive use of a theological vocabulary: words such as *faith, believe, miracle, blessing, sacrifice,* and *divine.* It seems a contradiction, portraying consistent Judeo-Christian values without sectarian, or even a godly, context—the fruits without the roots.

The Disney empire, by its founder's designation, is a kingdom

1

of magic, almost totally without reference to any kingdom of heaven. It advertises Disneyland as the happiest place on earth—not the holiest. There are no churches on Main Street at Disneyland or Walt Disney World or chapels on Disney cruise ships. Walt's daughter Diane Disney Miller told one minister that there are no churches on Main Street because her father did not want to favor any particular denomination. It is an explanation repeated today by company officials—as if the company's genius for the generic did not extend to creating a one-size-fits-all church. Walt "didn't want to single out any one religion," according to Disney archivist David Smith.

"Pictures are for entertainment—messages should be sent by Western Union," the movie mogul Sam Goldwyn once advised his screenwriters, warning them against trying to telegraph a political position or a moral lesson. As a filmmaker, Walt Disney took a different view. His animated features were always designed to be "message" films in the broadest sense, and especially for children. Yet throughout his life, it was a decision he downplayed, steadfastly denying there was any particular theological perspective in his work. "We like to have a point of view in our stories, not an obvious moral, but a worthwhile theme," he told one interviewer. "All we are trying to do is give the public good entertainment. That is all they want." However, in an early draft of a 1962 article for the inspirational monthly magazine *Guideposts* that is filed in the Disney archives, Walt addressed this point more directly. "Children are people, and they should have to reach to learn about things, to understand things, just as adults have to reach if they want to grow in mental stature," Walt wrote. "Life is composed of lights and shadows, and we would be untruthful, insincere and saccharine if we tried to pretend there were no shadows. Most things are good, and they are the strongest things; but there are evil things, too, and you are not doing a child a favor by trying to shield him from reality. The important thing is to teach a child that good can always triumph over evil, and that is what our pictures attempt to do."

Few entertainment productions continue to have as profound an impact on young children as the full-length features that are the signature of the Walt Disney Company. Together, *The Lion King, Snow White and the Seven Dwarfs, Aladdin, Beauty and the Beast,* and *The Little Mermaid* have sold hundreds of millions of video-cassettes and DVDs, adding exponentially to viewings at movie theaters and readings of bedtime stories based on the films. These animated classics—which are reflected in all of the Disney theme parks—rely primarily on mythic tales and images, some pre-Christian, that are replete with witches and demons, sorcerers and spells, genies and goblins. Regardless, millions of children around the world know much of what they do about the practical application of right and wrong from Disney. In the Western world in particular, the number of hours children spend receiving moral instruction in houses of worship is dwarfed by the amount of time spent sitting in front of screens large and small, learning values from Disney movies and other programming.

For the past seventy-five years, through its films, toys, books, and theme parks, Disney has created a world of fantasy—based on a set of shared American beliefs—that both entertains and educates children in this country and around the world. What accounts for this enduring impact? For many parents, Disney's entertaining morality tales, from *Pinocchio* to the company's latest releases, have offered one of the few safe havens for children's viewing in modern popular culture.

But in the more than thirty-five animated features Disney has released since 1937, there is scarcely a mention of God as conceived in the Christian and Jewish faiths shared by most people in the Western world and many beyond. Disney's decision to exclude or excise traditional religion from animated features was in part a commercial one, designed to keep the product saleable in a world-wide market. In 1935, Walt and Roy were impressed to find that a theater in Paris was showing six Disney cartoons—and no feature, according to Thomas. Three years later, while visiting Paris without Walt to oversee the opening of *Snow White,* Roy arranged for the feature's dubbing into Arabic and Hindi, as well as into European languages. When *Pinocchio* was released in 1940, the studio spent $65,000 to dub it into seven foreign languages. "Walt wanted to communicate with a global audience," said John Culhane, an animation authority at New York University and author of two books on *Fantasia*. "He wanted to communicate with a multicultural audience." Thus, the choice was made to keep the films accessible and relevant to children from both inside and outside the Judeo-Christian tradition in order to pass through a minefield of conflicting sensibilities.

Yet since ancient times, dramatists have seen the need for a sometimes unexpected device to intervene and resolve plot conflicts. The Greeks had an actor portraying a deity descend to the stage in a basket to aid in the narrative, which they called *deus ex machina*, god from the machine. Magic, Disney apparently decided, would be a far more universal device to do this than any one religion. Clearly, this strategy has worked; Disney characters are arguably far more recognizable around the world than images of Jesus or Buddha. And this approach still works. "Magic never goes out of style," Kathy Merlock Jackson, president of the American Culture Association, told the *Orlando Sentinel*'s Jay Boyar in an article published on November 18, 2001. "We've never been without it. . . . Wish fulfillment is a key theme in many Disney movies," continued Jackson, author of *Walt Disney: A Bio-Bibliography*. "Magic becomes a way to empower the powerless."

In the same *Sentinel* article, discussing the *Harry Potter* phenomenon, film critic and author Leonard Maltin agreed: "Magic takes you away and shows you a better life. And then it allows you to apply it to your real life." Magic, wrote Boyar, "is often an agent of transformation, a way of changing an ordinary thing into some marvelous something else. Other films may feature these kinds of changes, but generally not to the extent that the Disney features do."

But there is also a key theological dimension to Disney's choice of magic over religion, as the evangelist and social activist Tony Campolo observed in the foreword to *The Gospel according to The Simpsons*, citing Bronislaw Malinowski's *Magic, Religion, and Science*. Magic, Malinowski said, "is an attempt to *manipulate* spiritual forces so that the supplicant gets what he or she wants, whereas in pure religion the individual *surrenders* to spiritual forces so that those forces (i.e. God) can do through him or her what those forces desire."

The case is easily made that, in selecting magic as its agent of supernatural intervention, Disney made a successful choice, both culturally and commercially, a phenomenon *Time* magazine writers have tracked since at least 1954. In a cover story that year, the magazine wrote, "Measured by his social impact, Walt Disney is one of the most influential men alive. . . . The hand that rocks the cradle is Walt Disney's—and who can say what effect it is having on the world?" Richard Schickel, in *The Disney Version: The Life, Times, Art, and Commerce of Walt Disney,* reached a similar conclusion, that Walt was "one of the most significant shaping forces in American culture in the middle third of the [twentieth] century."

A debate about Disney and the teaching of values broke out in the mid-1960s. Max Rafferty, the conservative educator then serving as California's superintendent of public instruction, wrote an opinion piece in the April 19, 1965, *Los Angeles Times,* calling Walt Disney "the greatest pedagogue of all," a more outstanding educator than "John Dewey or James Conant or all of the rest put together." This provoked a sharp response, reprinted in a variety of publications, from a librarian named Frances Clarke Sayers, who accused Disney of not being a good educator, of "making morals overly obvious so as to leave nothing to the child's imagination," according to Jackson's *Walt Disney: A Bio-Bibliography. Time's* Richard Corliss broached the subject in 1988: "Walt's entertainment edifice was a unique institution—a cathedral of popular culture whose saints were mice and ducks, virgin princesses and lurking sprites, little boys made of wood and little girls lost in wonderland. Virtually every child attended this secular church, took fear and comfort from its doctrines, and finally outgrew it. . . . For most American children of the past half-century, a Disney cartoon feature was the sacred destination of their first trip to the movies." Walt's credo, Corliss wrote, must have been the Jesuits': "Give me a child before he's seven, and he will be mine for life."

The animated feature was the financial rock on which Disney built its corporate church. Early hits enabled the company to expand and move to newer and larger studios, and, ultimately, made possible the construction of Disneyland in Anaheim, California. Even those classics that did not perform well in original theatrical release or rerelease have generated significant revenues when resurrected on videocassette as baby boomers began raising families and the cultural climate became more conservative. These features exalted the Calvinist paradigm of hard—sometimes unrelentingly hard—work, which was unfailingly rewarded with upward social mobility. In this sense, the model paralleled Walt's own rise to prosperity. Today the animated features have been able to advance Disney's interests around the world, raising synergy to an art form.

There are those who take a harsher view of Disney's magic versus religion marketing strategy. "There is an anathema against the New Testament in the Disney films," said the Reverend Lou Sheldon, head of the Washington, D.C.-based Traditional Values Coalition, an organization that later joined the religious boycott of Disney of the 1990s. "They're not fair to what the Christian message is of life, death, and eternal life." The Reverend Clark Whitten of Calvary Assembly Church, a megachurch in Orlando, said that "it is obvious that they sidestep and avoid what I would consider Judeo-Christian figures—literally anything that has to do with Christianity. They have a gospel—it's to make money," he said, while acknowledging that he has taken his children to see Disney films. Even critic Sheldon, whose organization began in a suite of offices in the shadow of Disneyland, sees the value in Walt Disney's early animated features. "They have a lot of good points, but they do not go far enough to truly reflect the deeply held Christian faith of tens of millions of Americans," he said.

In recent decades, such "culture war" debates between conservatives and liberals have unfolded in religious circles. One term in particular, *secular humanism,* emerged on the right as a pejorative term for the idea that universal values can be defined and communicated without a religious (usually Judeo-Christian) context. The 1954 *Time* magazine cover story, coinciding with the opening of Disneyland in Anaheim, noted that Walt Disney had been described as "the poet of the new American humanism" and that Mickey Mouse was "the symbol of common humanity in struggle against the forces of evil." For nearly seven decades, viewers of the com-

pany's animated features have been receiving a message with recognizable, if watered-down, religious values. I call this Disney
gospel "secular 'toonism." Some religious conservatives have complained that the animated features under Michael Eisner's regime
represent a betrayal of Walt's "family values" legacy. But in addition to the founder's humanism, as we shall see, the early films
strongly supported environmentalism, the theory of evolution, and,
arguably, a tolerant, even gay-friendly attitude that would doubtless
make today's conservatives uncomfortable, to say the least.

Many in the cultural debate insist that Walt Disney officials made
a wise and reasonable decision to finesse the touchy subject of religion and theology. Robert Schuller, a nationally known evangelist
and author, defended Disney's approach, saying he saw a strong and
consistent religious message reflected in the Disney animated films.
Disney's gospel is that "the bad news will never be the last news,"
said Schuller, whose *Hour of Power* television program is broadcast from the Crystal Cathedral in Garden Grove, California.
"Gospel means good news. In the culture that comes from Judeo-
Christian values, that is the theme: Ultimately, God will reward the
right and will never reward the unrepentant wrong."

Some see the movies in a more sectarian light. Disney films
"very much reflect Christian values in particular," said Robert
Knight, director of the Culture and Family Institute, an affiliate of
Concerned Women for America, a Washington, D.C.-based, conservative think tank. "The values in Disney films generally reflect
Judeo-Christian principles," said Knight, although "it is a little
troubling that Disney uses magic as a stand-in, essentially, for the
power of the Holy Spirit as a transforming agent of good. On the
other hand, with the moral ambiguity that Hollywood has been
dishing up, Disney's clear delineation between good and evil is
always welcome."

In the 1950s, Jewish moral philosopher Will Herberg wrote in
*Protestant—Catholic—Jew: An Essay in American Religious Soci-
ology* that we Americans, as a people, have a group of broadly
shared beliefs that constitute a "civic religion"—that is, a nonde-
nominational, nonsectarian faith, with an undergirding of uncon-
querable optimism, which I will argue is reflected in the Disney

gospel. Boiled down, American religion is "faith in faith," Herberg wrote. It is nontheological and nonliturgical, "secularized Puritanism. . . . It is not faith in *anything* that is so powerful, just faith, the 'magic of believing.'" Although he might just as easily have quoted Walt Disney to support this view, Herberg instead quoted President Eisenhower, who said in the early 1950s, "Our government makes no sense unless it is founded in a deeply felt religious faith—and I don't care what it is." (The former chief executive was a Disney admirer, describing Walt as "a genius creator of folklore [who] helped our children develop a clean and cheerful view of humanity," according to Kevin Maney, writing in *USA Today,* March 3, 2004.)

Tony Campolo echoes Herberg—and Eisenhower. "All of us have to believe in something transcendent," he says. "There is a sense in Disney that you have to believe in a transcendent power. Americans have faith, and if you have faith, things will work out well. Many in this country believe that people who don't have faith in something are really non-American. We're not really going to tell you what you have to have faith in, but you have to have faith in something beyond yourself. It's not *what* you believe in that makes the difference, it's the *believing* that makes the difference. Believing people are to be trusted; non-believing people are not to be trusted. So we don't care what you believe in, but if you don't have a faith, you're nothing in American society."

Of course, magic is okay, but for believers it always works best if *their* kind of God is in the mix somewhere, even implied or off-screen. "Americans believe, 58 percent to 40 percent, that it is necessary to believe in God to be moral," *New York Times* columnist Nicholas D. Kristof wrote on August 15, 2003, citing a 1998 Harris poll of more than 1,000 respondents. "Americans not only have faith in God," according to Campolo. "They have faith in themselves. Because with God on our side all things will work together for good"—what Campolo calls "the American value system spiritualized." Still, it only works if you do your part, just like Walt did in his own life. "In the Disney value system, success should always be competitively achieved. For somebody to inherit wealth is almost evil. . . . The answer communicated by the animated movies is that good people always triumph, get rich and succeed, and the poor people don't. Disney is a perfect embodiment of the Protestant work ethic, divorced of religious moorings."

Clearly the animated features have benefited from this approach—just as religion has, Campolo says. "The church does best when it picks up on the themes from the media and preaches on them. Jesus used parables. Are not the Disney movies parables? Are they not lessons? I'm not so sure that Disney creates the values as much as it reinforces values that are already operative in American society."

Take the one character that most epitomizes the Walt Disney Company—Mickey Mouse, "the most persistent and pervasive figment of American popular culture" in the twentieth century, according to novelist John Updike. "Mickey is a purely innocent creature," said Campolo. "There is no guile in him. He is the unfallen creature. And he's never done anything sinful in his life. He's Adam before the fall. There's a naiveté about him. And all of us are attracted to him. And we all cheer for him because he is 'so good.' And he calls people to goodness. And when you see him in the theme park parade, it's goodness wedded with joyfulness. Look at the fifth chapter of Galatians, where Paul talks about the fruits of the Holy Spirit. They are these: love and joy and peace and patience. All of these godly virtues are wrapped up in Mickey and his followers. Mickey is a wonderful, wonderful creature. He is innocence. And in a real sense, we all believe in Mickey."

More recently, others have questioned the way the studio has sanded away the sharp edges of traditional myths and has invented new ones. Martin Marty, emeritus professor of church history at the University of Chicago, said, "There's no question that Disney has been the most successful creator of a complete set of mythologies, that is, ways of telling stories that impart certain kinds of truths that people wouldn't listen to if they didn't come in that form." But while Disney's idealized values as presented in the animated features may work for moral instruction of young children, they may also be misleading in what they say about the real world. "Righteousness and right don't always prevail," continued Marty, "and I think that you have to learn that on your own after you've seen a Disney film. At the same time, Disney's prime—the '30s of the Depression, the '40s of World War II, the '50s of the Cold War—were times when people got a pretty heavy dose of reality, and their morale had been flagging. Disney's kind of stories said virtue does have rewards and it pays to endure. And many of his features were just that—endurance stories."

Phil Vischer, cofounder of the VeggieTales video empire, compared Disney's gospel to a bland, generic salad topping. "Like a house dressing designed to appeal moderately to almost everyone while offending no one, Disney created a sort of 'house religion,' absorbing much of the benefits of Judeo-Christian belief while leaving behind any 'unseemly' obligation to conform to the will of a higher authority. The Judeo-Christian tradition is all about God. His will. The 'Gospel of Disney' is all about me. *My* dreams. *My* will. 'When you wish upon a star, your dreams come true.' The Disney Bible has but one verse, and that's it. Walt's religion was built on the unfailing American belief that virtue and hard work will make all your dreams come true. But Walt's early reliance on European folktales for story fodder added an unusual twist to nineteenth-century American optimism: If your 'American dream' seems hopelessly out of reach, Providence will show up in the form of a fairy, wizard, talking willow tree, or some other folktale device to snatch victory from the jaws of defeat and ensure that American values never go unrewarded. Disney has wrapped up and sold America what people wanted to hear, which was 'Give us the upside of religion, without the obligation of religion.' And that's what's packaged in so many of the films. It's all the good stuff with none of the bad stuff. And it has sold very well overseas because in Europe the church is largely dying or dormant, but they still accept the values, because they are great. The future is going to be better than the past, if we all get along and use our God-given—without the God part—intellects in the human spirit."

With his partner Mike Nawrocki, Vischer has created a series of animated videos that use religious plots and elements to teach Christian values to young children while entertaining them. Their company has sold more than 33 million videos and DVDs. Their first full-length movie, *Jonah,* grossed more than $25 million at the box office, a crossover breakthrough for a Christian movie. A former Bible college student and puppeteer, Vischer has as legitimate a claim on Disney's personal mantle as anyone working today. Not surprisingly, he is a serious student of Walt Disney—his life and his studio.

Vischer thinks he knows why religious leaders have had such ambiguous feelings toward the animated features. "The reason religious leaders seem so variously drawn to and repelled by Disney's work may be the striking presence of Judeo-Christian values, juxtaposed with a complete absence of any call or need to submit to God's will. Walt's religion is at the same time selfless and selfish. 'Providence' at my disposal; the infinite obligated to make my dreams come true. Perhaps only the rampant optimism and ambition of turn-of-the-century frontier America could inspire a belief system simultaneously virtuous and self-absorbed, values Walt derived from that idyllic portion of his childhood spent in Marceline, Missouri."

Vischer continues: "Disney's target market—and it has proved to be a large one—is an audience of people who want to believe in something that doesn't require anything of them. That's the religion that we've all been dying for. So it's a powerful thing. It engages kids very deeply and it offends no one, except the intellectual elite. Amazingly, Christians were some of Disney's biggest fans because he held on to the values that were important to them. So they forgave the fact that God had gone missing somehow along the way, but that everything that God set up was still there."

However, the Reverend Michael Catlett, pastor of McLean Baptist Church in McLean, Virginia, is one who felt no need to forgive Disney for its sins, either of omission or commission. On June 22, 1997, he preached a sermon entitled, "Everything I Needed to Know I Learned from Watching Disney." Catlett, speaking as the father of a three-year-old daughter as well as a pastor, cited examples from a half dozen full-length cartoon features to make his points. "I have discovered the gospel from time to time within their celluloid frames of animation. I have heard the gospel pronounced by some unlikely characters. The gospel is not relegated to special places and times. If we will but listen we can hear it spoken all around us. Sometimes we hear the gospel through sermons and worship services, and sometimes it's through children's stories contained on VHS tapes with a mouse ears logo. I want to listen to the gospel wherever I can find it. Don't you?"

There is growing evidence, beyond the speculative and the theoretical, that the animated features can have a real impact on the lives of children. A study conducted by two Colorado State University researchers suggests that "Everything we need to know about parenting and family relations can be learned from watching Disney movies," according to a March 27, 2004, article in the *National Post* newspaper of Canada. "These films are likely to play a role in the development of children's culture and may influence children's and adults' information about families," wrote Toni Zimmerman, Shelley Haddock, Mia Adessa Towbin, and Lori K. Lund, of the university's department of human development and family studies, where the research was done. Given the large percentage of movie characters in families without both birth parents in the home, the features may be helpful to parents and children in "blended families," the study found. "Having a variety of families portrayed in the animated films is beneficial for children in two ways," the study found. "It presents children with images of families other than their own, helping children to realize that there are many family types they can choose from later in life. It also increases the likelihood that children will be able to see a representation of their own kind of family in at least some of the movies."

All of this is not to argue—and I will not—that Disney's animated features are a viable substitute for therapy, education, worship, or Sunday school. What I will argue in the chapters that follow is that they are useful tools in building a general, moral sensibility among children and in reinforcing parental and religious values. In some cases, where individual films parallel the situation children may find themselves in, the movies may be able to do more. But before we can understand the Disney gospel and how it came to be, we'll need to examine the religious background and practice of the men that created it: Walt and Roy.

Part One

The Disney Years: 1937–1984

Chapter Two

Walt and Roy: The Christians

A ccounts of the early lives of the Disney men are varied, and subject to editing and burnishing by the company's public relations apparatus—for good reason. "It may not be surprising that the story of Walt Disney seems to have special, almost sacred, meaning for Americans," Janet Wasko wrote in *Understanding Disney: The Manufacture of Fantasy*. "Not only does the Disney company actively present him in this special way, but the legends of Walt and Mickey Mouse have been picked up and repeated endlessly by journalists, historians and biographers." Alan Bryman, in his book, *Disney and His Worlds,* makes the same complaint, noting the "incredible similarity" among the Disney biographies published to date. "The majority of the facts are reproduced from book to book with very little added in each case, in spite of different informants being interviewed. There seems to be a constant recycling of the same anecdotes which are referred to in book after book."

This consistency is also true of the accounts of family members' religious and spiritual lives. All versions agree that this part of the story begins with Elias Disney, born in 1859. The father of Walt and Roy was a man greatly conflicted about faith, according to numerous books, articles, and recollections. As a child in Bluevale, Ontario, Elias attended Wesleyan Methodist Church and Sunday school, which adhered to an austere form of Methodism. "He came out of a period when they were very strict and stern," Roy Disney said of his father in 1967, in an interview in Bob Thomas's biography, *Building a Company: Roy O. Disney and the Creation of an Entertainment Empire*. In Canada, the family was so strongly opposed to music and dancing that Elias had to head for the backwoods to play his fiddle, and on one occasion his mother discovered him performing at a dance and smashed the instrument on Elias's head. "The devil was in the fiddle, to their notion," Roy recalled. "Dancing was just evil."

Living in Chicago with his wife, Flora, and working as a carpenter, the young father became quite religious and joined a Congregational church, a conservative denomination. Elias fell under the influence of the Reverend Walter Parr and became a deacon, He even built a wing of the St. Paul Church. Elias preached when the pastor went on vacation, and Flora played the organ.

Elias required strict, if inconsistent, observation of the Sabbath, forbidding his four sons from playing baseball, but requiring them to perform their newspaper delivery duties when the family lived in Kansas City. "When these boys were born, hell and damnation were preached from the pulpit," said Dorothy Puder, whose father, Herbert, was one of Walt's three older brothers. "It was very hard on the children. They weren't able to play or read a book on Sundays. Their parents were very deeply into the church."

The Disney family left Chicago for a farm in Marceline, Missouri. Elias said later that the move was to escape the evils of the city and to raise the children in a more Christian environment. Ironically, the family rarely attended church in Missouri, in part because there was no Congregational church, although they sometimes visited a Baptist or Methodist congregation. "We just sort of got out of the church habit," Roy explained. However, that did not save Walt's older brother Herbert from a parental whipping when he cut his initials in a church seat. Walt, who remembered the farm years fondly, was not immune from mischief. On one occasion he slipped off with his only sister Ruth to a local movie theater, where they watched a dramatization of Jesus' crucifixion and resurrection screened on a bedsheet, according to Thomas's biography of Walt. But successive crop failures turned Elias mean, and he took it out on Walt and his three older brothers, Roy, Herbert, and Raymond. "He railed at his sons when they failed to turn up at breakfast for early morning prayers or when, at night, he caught them reading 'frivolous books' instead of the Bible," according to Leonard

Mosley's biography, *Disney's World*. Elias's mother once paid a visit and, while on a walk with young Walt, they snatched some turnips from a roadside field. This provoked an off-the-cuff sermon from Elias on the subject of "thou shalt not steal" at the family dinner table. "Only Elias would be narrow-minded enough to get heated up over a thing like that," his mother recalled to Walt's daughter, Diane. When Herbert and Raymond took off, effectively dooming the farming operation, Elias claimed that they had sold their souls to the devil. From Marceline, the family moved to Kansas City, where Elias and his remaining sons went to work delivering newspapers. Before long, Roy also escaped his father's tyranny. Elias wrote in a letter that, in doing so, his son "has turned his back on us—and on God."

Elias and Flora maintained an eclectic relationship with religion. In the 1940s, when the couple's grandson, Roy Edward Disney, was visiting them in Oregon, they sent the boy to a Christian Science Sunday school. Dorothy Puder, another of their grandchildren, married a Presbyterian minister, Glenn Puder, who conducted the funeral service for Flora at Forest Lawn Cemetery in Glendale, California.

Most family historians agree that Elias's authoritarian and sometimes cruel nature—and his propensity for whipping and even beating his young sons—played a role in turning Walt and Roy against the church. The brothers' ambivalent relationship with organized religion is well documented, as is their strong, personal faith in God. Both brothers were married in the homes of relatives rather than in houses of worship. As an adult, Walt did not start attending church until he was forty, according to Marc Eliot, author of the critical biography *Walt Disney: Hollywood's Dark Prince*. Bob Thomas provides a different account in *Walt Disney: An American Original:* "Walt considered himself religious yet he never went to church. The heavy dose of religiosity in his childhood discouraged him; he especially disliked sanctimonious preachers. But he admired and respected every religion, and his belief in God never wavered." Walt regularly dropped his two daughters off at Hollywood Presbyterian Church for Sunday school and youth group. Other accounts suggest they attended a

Christian Science Sunday school for a time. In January 1943, according to biographers Katherine and Richard Greene in an essay written for the Disney Web site, Walt wrote his sister Ruth that "Little Diane is going to a Catholic school now, which she seems to enjoy very much. She is quite taken with the rituals and is studying catechism. She hasn't quite made up her mind yet whether she wants to be a Catholic or Protestant. I think she is intelligent enough to know what she wants to do, and I feel that whatever her decision may be is her privilege. I have explained to her that Catholics are people just like us and basically there is no difference. In giving her this broad view I believe it will tend to create a spirit of tolerance within her." In 1954, Diane and her fiancé, Ron Miller, were baptized at an Episcopal church in Santa Barbara, with Walt and his wife, Lillian, as witnesses, a week before they were married in the church.

Sharon, Walt's younger daughter, wed in a Presbyterian ceremony in 1959. Although he was not a churchgoer, Walt "was a very religious man," Sharon said, according to the Greenes. "But he did not believe you had to go to church to be religious. . . . He respected every religion. There wasn't any that he ever criticized. He wouldn't even tell religious jokes."

Like his brother Walt, Roy Disney also reacted to Elias's strict religiosity, according to an interview with Roy's son and namesake, quoted in Bob Thomas's *Building a Company*. "Dad's religion was absolutely inside his head. He didn't go to church, but I think he believed in a very strict moral code. I'm certain he believed in God, although I don't think anybody ever asked him to define God. I'm not sure he would have said anything beyond, 'Well, he's there, and we all know that, don't we?'" In 1958, Roy came to his brother Walt with a live action project adapted from the novel *The Big Fisherman,* which was based on the life of St. Peter. Walt rejected the idea for Walt Disney Pictures, citing his career-long aversion to religious movies, so Roy proceeded to back the $6 million project, which was released through the company's Buena Vista banner. The film was both a critical and a commercial failure and, according to Bob Thomas, Walt was secretly pleased.

Around the time of his sixtieth birthday, Walt told his longtime secretary, Hazel George, he was concerned about whether he was providing for an orderly transition of leadership for the company he had built. "After I die, I'd hate to look down at this studio and find everything in a mess," he said, according to Thomas. "What makes you think you won't need a periscope?" George asked. "Smartass," Walt replied.

Walt died in 1966, five days short of his sixty-fifth birthday. He was cremated, and a small family funeral was held at the Little Flower Chapel at Forest Lawn, a cemetery he once called a "sacred place." The animator Ward Kimball, one of the pioneering Disney animators known as the "Nine Old Men," said that there was a "secret" funeral service conducted in the chapel. That secrecy helped fuel a rumor that Walt's body had been cryogenically preserved in the tunnels beneath Disneyland, awaiting some future cure for cancer. Despite denials by the family and the company, the story persists as an urban legend and, as recently as 2003, it was the subject of a novel called *Waking Walt* by Larry Pontius, who worked as marketing director for Disney theme parks in Florida and California during the 1970s. The tale is so durable that Disney CEO Michael Eisner had to debunk it again when he appeared on CNN's *Larry King Live* on February 20, 2004.

The end of Roy Disney's life five years later was a marked contrast to Walt's. Young Roy's marriage in 1955 to Patricia Dailey, a Catholic, had a fundamental influence on his father—especially when grandchildren began arriving. Patricia's father-in-law recalled the days when he and his brother Walt were infected with a common Midwestern prejudice in the early 1900s. "When I was in Kansas City, we used to run around town throwing rocks at Catholics," Roy told Patricia. "Now I have four Catholic grandchildren." Roy Disney never missed a baptism or a confirmation, according to *Building a Company*. Like his younger brother, Roy died at the Catholic hospital across the street from the Burbank studio, tended by nuns. Unlike Walt's secretive service at Forest Lawn, when Roy died in 1971 the funeral was held in the Catholic church where his son and his family worshiped.

A 1966 Disney promotional brochure described Walt as "a

man—in the deepest sense of the word—with a mission. The mission is to bring happiness to millions." More specifically, the official view of Walt's philosophy of faith appears in several places. In bite-sized, undated nuggets, they are tucked in the back of *The Quotable Walt Disney*, compiled by Disney archivist David Smith. "Faith I have, in myself, in humanity, in the worthwhileness of the pursuits in entertainment for the masses," Walt wrote. "But wide awake, not blind, faith moves me. My operations are based on experience, thoughtful observation, and warm fellowship with my neighbors at home and around the world."

Twice, essays appeared under Walt's byline in *Guideposts*, an inspirational monthly founded by Norman Vincent Peale. In June 1949, Disney recalled the importance to his development of his Congregational church, where he was baptized and attended Sunday school. "I believe firmly in the efficacy of religion, in its powerful influence on a person's whole life," he wrote. "It helps immeasurably to meet the storm and stress of life and keep you attuned to the Divine inspiration. Without inspiration, we would perish. All I ask of myself, 'Live a good Christian life.' Toward that objective I bend every effort in shaping my personal, domestic, and professional activities and growth."

Walt's thoughts on prayer were outlined in a three-paragraph article published in *Guideposts* in 1962, entitled "Prayer in My Life":

> Every person has his own ideas of the act of praying for God's guidance, tolerance, and mercy to fulfill his duties and responsibilities. My own concept of prayer is not a plea for special favors nor a quick palliation for wrongs knowingly committed. A prayer, it seems to me, implies a promise as well as a request; at the highest level, prayer not only is supplication for strength and guidance, but also becomes an affirmation of life and thus a reverent praise of God.
>
> Deeds, rather than words, express my concept of the part religion should play in everyday life. I have watched constantly that in our movie work the highest moral and spiritual standards are upheld, whether it deals with fable or with stories of living action. This religious concern for the form and content of our

films goes back forty years to the rugged financial period in Kansas City when I was struggling to establish a film company and produce animated fairy tales. . . .

Thus, whatever success I have had in bringing clean, informative entertainment to people of all ages, I attribute in great part to my Congregational upbringing and my lifelong habit of prayer. To me, today, at age sixty-one, all prayer, by the humble or highly placed, has one thing in common: supplication for strength and inspiration to carry on the best impulses which should bind us together for a better world. Without such inspiration, we would rapidly deteriorate and finally perish. But in our troubled time, the right of men to think and worship as their conscience dictates is being sorely pressed. . . . To retreat from any of the principles handed down by our forefathers . . . would be a complete victory for those who would destroy liberty and justice for the individual.

As interesting as what appeared in *Guideposts* was what didn't make the published version. In an early draft, Walt said he was a student of Scripture and that he believed that religion "helps us immeasurably to meet the trial and stress of life and keeps us attuned to the Divine Inspiration." Because young Americans are "highly intelligent," he wrote, "lecturing to children is no answer to delinquency. Preaching won't keep youngsters out of trouble, but keeping their minds occupied will." Many times in the early years of his career, he recalled, he and Roy came under commercial pressure to "debase the subject matter" of their animation— which they refused to do.

On the *CBS Evening News* following Walt's death, commentator Eric Sevareid said that he "probably did more to heal, or at least soothe troubled human spirits than all the psychiatrists in the world." Walt Disney has become for many "an almost Christlike figure," wrote McReynolds. There is a "pseudo-religious aura that has come to surround his name before and after his death." If anything, Disney's stature has grown since his demise. "His disciples venerate St. Walt as a beloved purveyor of innocent imagination, uplifting fantasy and moral instruction," wrote Steven Watts in *The Magic Kingdom: Walt Disney and the American Way of Life*.

Chapter Three

Snow White and the Seven Dwarfs (1937): Sin and Salvation

Snow White and the Seven Dwarfs was, as the Walt Disney Company proclaims, "the one that started it all," the first and still one of the most popular of the company's full-length animated features. It also created a template for the Disney gospel, its cosmos and its value system, which remained intact for at least as long as Walt lived. In the beginning is the supernatural—the magic mirror and its ability to see all and know all within the realm. From this beginning there is also the introduction of sin, presented in a clear, unambiguous, and negative light. The queen, the written text explains at the start of the film, is Snow White's evil stepmother. She is driven by envy, since she "feared that someday Snow White's beauty would surpass her own." At first, Snow White is safe from the "vain" queen's "cruel jealousy." So, within the film's first moments the sins of envy, vanity, and jealousy are presented, with much worse soon to follow.

Banished to the scullery, Snow White bears the hardship of her lot with good spirit and, as a result, "rags cannot hide her gentle grace." She does want to change her situation, and so she turns to a wishing well, a benign form of the supernatural, singing her hopes for true love. Sure enough, a handsome prince hears her song and falls for her, despite her patched skirt and apparently low status. Her wish, at least for the moment, appears to come true. The wicked queen, informed that her stepdaughter is now fairest in the land, can bear the competition no longer. She orders her huntsman to kill the girl and, as proof, to bring her heart back in a small box. Deep in the forest, ostensibly for a picnic, the huntsman and the trusting youth begin to recreate what the Hebrew Bible calls the *Akedah*, the sacrifice of Isaac. In the book of Genesis, as a test of faith, a sovereign God orders the patriarch Abraham to take his beloved son Isaac to a mountaintop and to kill the boy. After Abraham binds Isaac to a rock and raises his knife, an angel stays Abraham's hand and provides a ram caught in a nearby thicket as a substitute. Snow White, backed against a large rock by the equally reluctant huntsman, watches another upraised hand clutching another knife. But she too is miraculously spared, as the man cannot go through with murder. The huntsman returns to the queen, substituting the heart of a wild boar in the box.

In the woods, after a terrifying escape from death and from sinister-appearing vegetation that seems to assault her, Snow White sings the Disney credo—that adversity can *always* be overcome with a song and smile, a combination that can fill the world with sunshine. Despite her dire straits, she is confident she will "get along somehow," a view of life that must have had deep resonance when first heard during the Depression. In the woods, Snow White soon befriends birds and small animals, another motif central to the animated features that will follow. Led to an empty cottage by her woodland guides, she assumes that the filth and disarray of the small residents may be because "they have no mother." She decides to clean the place in hopes that they will let her stay—not exactly a case of unalloyed altruism—as she sings "Whistle While You Work," a paean to the work ethic. Even with the help of woodland friends, dirt is *never* swept under the rug and dishes are always properly washed. Exhausted by her work, Snow White falls asleep in the upstairs dormitory.

The dwarfs are introduced at their mine, and they are likewise happy at their work. They sing that it "ain't no trick to get rich quick," as they pluck precious stones from the rocks. (This probably came as a disturbing revelation to real miners, who practiced then as now one of the most dangerous and backbreaking of occupations.) Yet these contented workers, too, have their foibles. One dwarf, trying to swat an irritating fly, inadvertently smacks the rump of the deer pulling his cart; he is immediately repaid for this cruelty with a swift kick from the animal. On the way home from work the dwarfs sing another happy song, "Heigh-ho, Heigh-ho," as they return to their transformed cottage.

Grumpy, the voice of skepticism, is immediately suspicious at the newly cleaned abode, attributing their apparent good fortune to a goblin, a ghost, or a demon. Fearful but armed, the dwarfs surround the covered, sleeping form sprawled across three of their beds. Just as their blades are about to fall on Snow White (again!), they are stayed as she emerges from her blanket. The dwarfs are mesmerized to see such a beautiful figure; "just like an angel," observes one. Although fully dressed, she modestly pulls the cover back up to her neck, surveying what she calls the "little men," terminology used at the direct insistence of Walt Disney, according to the film's DVD commentary.

Snow White does not see the dwarfs as in any way grotesque or comical. This establishes a key element of the Disney gospel, from the outset a gospel of inclusion and of concern for the feelings of others. (Some Disney staffers, according to Kathy Merlock Jackson, objected to the naming of Dopey, the last to be named, because it sounded too "imbecilic.") Snow White accepts the dwarfs for who and what they are, and for what they do. In life, as in Disney, this is not always an easy thing to do.

Initially at least, Grumpy is also the voice of misogyny, recognizing the intruder as a female, all of whom he says are poison and "full of wicked wiles." He orders Snow White out and warns the other dwarfs—correctly—that no good deed on her behalf will go unpunished by the queen. The monarch, full of black magic, is "bound to wreak her vengeance on us." Nonetheless, knowing the risks of sheltering an unjustly persecuted young woman (think Anne Frank in World War II Amsterdam), the dwarfs agree to provide refuge to Snow White. Their decision is eased as the princess begins to list the dishes she is prepared to make for her hosts. The prospective menu, perhaps in deference to her woodland friends, is strictly vegetarian. She also insists on cleanliness (next to godliness?), but there is no similar insistence, at least on the screen, of saying grace before the meal. According to story notes in the Disney archives, a sequence in which Snow White teaches the dwarfs how to pray was suggested but never filmed.

Back at the castle, the queen has discovered the huntsman's ruse, thanks to the magic mirror, and has embarked on a mission of revenge. In the lower reaches of the castle, she uses an ancient text to transform herself into a crone—from beauty to ugliness, in order to do evil—and she creates a temptingly beautiful, poison apple. One bite will cause a fall, a deathlike sleep so convincing that the dwarfs will likely bury Snow White alive and prevent the only antidote, "love's first kiss." The queen, now clearly a witch, carries the deadly apple into the Edenic paradise that Snow White and the dwarfs have made for themselves.

There is joy and mirth, but also longing, in the cottage in the woods. Snow White sings that someday her prince will come, thereby echoing and reinforcing generations of unrealistic expectations for American women and others around the globe. Snow White was written as a passive female character, Walt explained in a subsequent promotional film for television, "a kind, simple little girl who believed in wishing and waiting for her Prince Charming to come along." And praying. Snow White goes upstairs to what has become her exclusive sleeping quarters and kneels by her bedside with folded hands. There is no mention of God or Lord or Jesus. Yet as moonlight streams through the window, she asks for blessings on "the seven little men who have been so kind to me." Having prayed for others first, Snow White then prays for herself, asking that her own dreams come true. As an afterthought she asks, "Please make Grumpy like me."

The next day, as the dwarfs file out the door to work, there is evidence that at least part of Snow White's prayer has been answered. Like the other six, Grumpy presents his bald pate for a kiss from Snow White. "Why Grumpy, you *do* care!" she exclaims. After they are gone, she and her forest friends start making a gooseberry pie for Grumpy, only to be interrupted by an old lady with a basket of fruit. The birds and animals instantly sense danger, but Snow White evinces the traditional value of reverence for the elderly—alas, misplaced on this occasion. The witch tempts Snow White with what she calls a "wishing apple." One bite, the crone says, and "all your wishes will come true." Eden is about to be profaned.

Snow White wavers, wanting to be convinced. After all, she has already wished and prayed for true love. She repeats her wish for the handsome prince who will carry her away to his castle, where they will live happily ever after. She tastes the apple and falls away. Good may ultimately be rewarded, but in this instance, evil must first be punished. Alerted, the angry dwarfs and birds and animals pursue the witch to a craggy mountaintop. As she attempts to crush them with a huge boulder, lightning strikes her in what is clearly an act of cosmic, if not divine, intervention.

All of this comes too late for Snow White. Apparently dead, she is laid out lovingly in the forest by the grief-stricken dwarfs. She rests on a bed, enclosed in a glass coffin with candles all around, as organ music plays. The dwarfs kneel at the bier and their tears flow, even from Grumpy, as they keep "an eternal vigil at her side." A golden, heavenly light streams down onto the clearing. Then the prince arrives on a white horse, and with his kiss of pure love allows Snow White to return to life from her deathlike sleep. In *The Complete Fairy Tales of the Brothers Grimm* (translated by Jack Zipes), when Snow White opens her eyes, she says, "O Lord, where am I?" She doesn't speak those words in the Disney version, but according to Rudy Behlmer, in *America's Favorite Movies: Behind the Scenes,* there was a sequence, created in preproduction, in which Snow White and the prince dance in the clouds and board a celestial ship.

It did not take long for people of faith to see a religious dimension in *Snow White.* The Reverend Charles W. Brashares, of the First Methodist Church of Ann Arbor, Michigan, wrote a letter that appeared in the August 10, 1938, issue of *The Christian Century,* published under the headline, "Walt Disney as Theologian." Brashares asked if readers "did not see in the story a reprint of the Scripture? And can't we recognize moral and theological truth unless it is labeled?" He continued, "Did not the happy innocence of Snow White with her animal friends remind you of the original Eden?" In the biblical garden, "a serpent urged the eating of the apple. But in the play, a witch, skilled in the black arts of the past and the sciences of the present, prepares an apple so tempting that one does not even need to sin in order to taste it."

Yet sin is clearly present in the movie, the minister wrote. "Where can you find a clearer delineation of sin than in this tale?"

The queen's conversation with the magic mirror is surely sin. "Self upon the throne is the tap root of all sin. From it grows pride, jealousy, greed, murder and all the other sins." *Snow White* is not a flight from reality, Brashares wrote. "It is the retelling of truth as basic as sin and salvation. It might even tempt one to a sermon."

Richard Schickel recalled in *The Disney Version* that there was an outcry on the part of some parents who said that some of the more intense scenes prompted hysterics and nightmares on the part of young children—which they may do today. But he argued that it was not wrong "to introduce children to symbolic representations of evil, in restricted doses and the right context of course, in the hope that it will provide them with the imaginative tools to deal with it intelligently when they encounter it in its more dulling manifestations in life."

With *Snow White,* Walt Disney—leading his writers and animators—created a new genre of feature films. Visually, viewers were stunned and delighted, according to news accounts of the time. Despite the frightening aspects of the movie, most parents were equally pleased by the primary messages the story conveyed: Welcome the stranger, respect and accept those who are different, pray when you are in need. And avoid the temptation of the easy solution—eating a magic apple will never solve your problems. Mothers and fathers brushed aside critics who complained that Disney had tinkered with the Grimm original. A social contract was born. Parents could put their faith in Walt Disney, and he would not disappoint them or betray their values. The founder kept that pledge as long as he lived. In the decades following his death, the studio has tried to uphold that contract—with uneven results, as we will see.

Chapter Four

Pinocchio (1940): Prove Yourself

*O*f all the early Disney features, it should come as no surprise that *Pinocchio* is a favorite of parents of young children. It is a simple morality tale—cautionary and schematic—ideal for moral instruction, save for some of its own darker moments. From the opening song over the credits, "When You Wish Upon a Star," the dynamic is set. Faced with insurmountable odds, the lyrics advise, fate—not God—"steps in and sees you through." The Blue Fairy, approaching the woodcarver's bedroom as the wishing star, appears as a glowing ethereal figure, benign rather than divine. She explains to the sleeping Geppetto that his wish to bring life to the puppet is being granted because the toys and whimsical clocks he has created have brought so much happiness to others—surrogate salvation through another's works. Then, provisionally, the Blue Fairy gives Pinocchio life, setting the benchmarks for his promotion to human existence. The little marionette, shorn of strings, will have free will, and thus, she says, the outcome "will be entirely up to you." In order to become a real boy, he will have to prove himself to be brave, truthful, and unselfish—more works.

Help for Pinocchio is provided in the form of the first of Disney's comic sidekicks—Jiminy Cricket. The dapper insect is the puppet's designated conscience, to help him choose between right and wrong. (Note the insect's initials. After the movie's release, "Jiminy Cricket!" became a more acceptable substitute exclamation for "Jesus Christ!" in some parts of the country.) He represents, the cricket explains in a combination of cynicism and foreshadowing, that "still, small voice that people won't listen to." Rabbi Daniel Wolpe, of the Southwest Orlando Jewish Congrega-

28

tion, pointed out that the phrase "still, small voice" appears in 1 Kings 19:12. In that context, the words describe either the voice of God or of an angel. "It is fascinating that a conscience is described with the same words as God's voice," he said. When in doubt, Jiminy says, Pinocchio's conscience will advise him to avoid temptation and not depart from the straight and narrow path. The Blue Fairy reminds Pinocchio to let his conscience be his guide as she fades from the scene, spreading her arms in an image that, for an instant, could be a female crucifix.

The Blue Fairy may be a reference to the Virgin Mary, according to Michael P. Duricy, a researcher at the Marian Library at the University of Dayton, Ohio. "Her presence is anticipated by a luminous orb which approaches, fills the screen, then dissolves into circles of white light from which her figure appears. The Virgin Mary is said to have arrived in similar fashion for her apparitions at La Salette and Fatima. The fairy is clad in a light blue dress covered with shining white spots. She has wings that are colored in light blue or off-white. Blue and white have become commonly associated with images of the Virgin Mary. Beside the visual clues, there is thematic material that also suggests a Marian presence. The heart of the film is the need to accept responsibility for one's actions and to choose right over wrong. This sort of moral education is a very important facet of the Catholics (and other Christians, especially the Eastern Orthodox) who see Mary operating within the communion of saints." Steven Spielberg used a similar conceit, more specifically alluding to Mary, in his 2001 updating of the Pinocchio story, *A.I.: Artificial Intelligence.*

Jiminy Cricket explains to his charge that the world is full of temptation, which he defines as "the wrong things that seem right at the time." Pinocchio pledges to do right, and Jiminy promises to help him. Church bells sound as the puppet sets off for school, and a flock of white doves flies past a cross atop a building. But temptation is not long in coming, in the form of a sly fox named Honest John, who detours Pinocchio from school to "the easy road to success"—show business. Jiminy's warnings are ignored by the dazzled puppet. "It's great to be a celebrity," the fox advises—as true today as it was six decades ago. Sure enough, Pinocchio is a hit as an entertainer at Stromboli's traveling marionette show. Watching from the fringe of the crowd, even Jiminy is impressed by the cheers and applause: "They like him. He's a success. Gosh. Maybe I was wrong." Then "I guess he won't need me anymore. What does an actor want with a conscience anyway?"

Despite his Italian name, some see Stromboli as a caricatured Gypsy. After the show, locked in a birdcage in Stromboli's wagon, Pinocchio gets his first hard lesson in exploitation, one other Disney characters would also learn in the years that follow. "You will make lots of money—for me!" Stromboli tells him. Distraught and weeping, Pinocchio brightens with the arrival of his conscience. Jiminy admits that things look hopeless, that "it'll take a miracle to get us out of here." The two friends try to figure out what went wrong. Pinocchio says he should have listened to his conscience; Jiminy says he shouldn't have abandoned his charge. Of course, both are right. At this moment, the Blue Fairy returns. After hearing Pinocchio's outlandish and self-serving account of how he got himself in such a fix, she reminds him that he must tell the truth, suggesting that perhaps he hasn't been. But he compounds the offense in a way familiar to any parent or teacher, as his nose begins to grow. "A lie keeps growing and growing until it's as plain as the nose on your face," the Blue Fairy says.

Pinocchio promises never to lie again, and his conscience intercedes—for Jiminy's own sake—for the sinful, imperfect being in his charge. Like Jesus, the Blue Fairy believes in second chances. "I'll forgive you this once," she says, "but remember: A boy who won't be good might just as well be made of wood. But this is the last time I can help you." It doesn't take long for Pinocchio to stumble again before temptation; he is easily scooped up by another nefarious character. The Watchman is collecting "stupid little boys, the disobedient ones," and taking them to Pleasure Island, a place of no return. However, before they meet their fate they get to indulge in numerous juvenile sins and vices, beginning with gluttony—all the cakes, pies, candy, and ice cream they can eat. Along "Tobacco Row" they can smoke cigarettes and cigars, and chew tobacco. There is music (blues and jazz, naturally), beer, and amusement rides—all free, like everything else on the island—

along with a stained glass window and a model home, both ripe for vandalism.

As the island's gates of escape are silently closed and bolted, the Watchman observes, "Give a bad boy enough rope and he'll soon make a jackass out of himself." Pinocchio plays pool with a particularly unsavory young companion, Lampwick, and both begin the physical transformation to donkeys. The other boys, now fully donkeys, are driven off beneath cracking whips to their fate, unredeemed and irretrievably lost. Pinocchio grows a tail and donkey ears and brays occasionally, but the puppet escapes to seek salvation.

(Irony has never been a strong suit of the Walt Disney Company. Still, some mention must be made here of the company's decision to name its entertainment complex at the edge of Disney World "Pleasure Island." At this adult attraction adjoining the theme park, many of the same vices as those depicted in its *Pinocchio* counterpart are indulged in, although in this world they are not offered gratis. And here, young people also make jackasses out of themselves on a regular basis. In this venue, however, most ultimately recover their humanity.)

Returning to the woodcarver's home, Pinocchio receives a message (from whom is never made clear) borne by a glowing white bird. Geppetto has gone looking for his son, only to be swallowed by a whale. The allusion to the book of Jonah is just that, an allusion, since—unlike the Old Testament prophet—the old man has himself done nothing wrong. Pinocchio ties a rock to his tail and selflessly goes in search of his father. Through his wit and bravery he facilitates their escape from the whale, and he saves Geppetto from drowning, an act of filial piety that appears to cost him his life. Back in his bedroom, distraught, Geppetto is again on his knees, weeping. An ethereal light engulfs the lifeless puppet, and the voice of the Blue Fairy is heard: "Prove yourself brave, truthful, and unselfish, and someday you will be a real boy." Concentric circles of light signal the final transformation—resurrection. "Awake, Pinocchio, awake," the Blue Fairy commands, as a new verse to the film's theme song swells: "When your heart is in your dream, no request is too extreme." This is the first in a long line of salvations through acts rather than grace. "The essence of the Disney 'religion' is not theology, but 'morality,' and moral behavior; not 'thought' so much as action," according to McReynolds. "It is not Pinocchio's thoughts but his heartfelt actions that count in rescuing his father. The completed deed makes him worthy of being a 'real' boy."

Unlike Snow White, Pinocchio is an active character and, unlike the young woman, he is clearly flawed and imperfect. So much the better. The living marionette is a figure children can identify with and not merely idolize. Thus, small viewers are able to understand and to assimilate the lessons the puppet learns. In that sense, whether his salvation comes as a result of works rather than by grace through the intercession of the Virgin Mary is immaterial. And with *Pinocchio*, Disney expanded his storytelling palette rather than simply duplicating it with another version of *Snow White,* which would have been the safer course. And he was not finished with innovation and risk taking, as we will now see.

Chapter Five

Fantasia (1940): The Sorcerer's Mascot

Fantasia is one of the more problematic of Disney's animated features, as much for adults as for children. It was not what fans (and presumably parents) had come to expect from the studio after the first few full-length movies. It is episodic, experimental, abstract, and innovative. In collaboration with the famed conductor Leopold Stokowski and music critic Deems Taylor, Walt Disney took as his mission to make high culture accessible to a mass audience, both through explanatory narration and illustration— that is, "to bring classical music to the world by way of animation," according to his nephew, Roy Edward Disney, in a DVD commentary. A civilizing impulse, to be sure, although Walt would never have put it that way. For him, the purpose of animation was to "arouse a purely emotional response in the viewer," Roy said.

Despite the absence of a unifying "story" in *Fantasia,* there are along the way images and sequences with implications and messages—inspirational and disturbing, subtle and strong, scientific and pagan and Christian—all worth noting. Some are artistic departures for a Disney film; others are more familiar stereotypes. In an early section, based on Tchaikovsky's *Nutcracker Suite,* fairy spirits are transformed into dragonflies. They are nude, although nearly androgynous, and in some ways they foreshadow *Peter Pan*'s more voluptuous (and better-clothed) Tinker Bell. Dancing toadstools are presented as Chinese figures with conical hats, slanted eyes, and hands tucked into opposing sleeves, a caricature that for its time was probably intended to be more amiable than malevolent. In the same innocent spirit, flowers are transmogrified into dancing Russian Cossacks and peasant women.

The segment on "The Sorcerer's Apprentice," starring Mickey Mouse, presents *Fantasia*'s most clear moral message, at least for children. Deems Taylor, the film's narrator, explains that the story on which it is based took place 2000 years ago—conveniently, in pre-Christian times. Mickey is described as a bright young lad, very eager to learn the business from his master, in fact "a little bit too bright." Mickey observes the Sorcerer and his book of spells, but his attention is apparently focused more on learning magic tricks rather than on using magic in a controlled, responsible way. Ordered to fill the cauldron with water from a fountain at the top of a long set of stone stairs, Mickey has a brilliant idea. The apprentice decides that, rather than struggling himself with the two wooden buckets, making many trips to complete his work, he will use what he has learned to avoid this onerous task. After the Sorcerer retires for the night, the apprentice puts on the magic hat and brings a broom to life, adding arms and hands, and instructing it how to fill the cauldron. So, in order to avoid his work, Mickey usurps his master's powers and creates life. As if to seal this act of hubris, the apprentice does a happy dance and sits in the Sorcerer's chair. In the Disney universe of values, no good can come of this. Without discipline and self-control, supernatural powers can easily go awry.

After Mickey falls asleep in the chair, his spirit—or subconscious—leaves his body and enters a dream state. His shadow figure floats up and summons more powers from the stars, unleashing even greater cosmic forces, commanding the sea and the clouds. Suddenly he awakes and finds himself afloat in the Sorcerer's chair. The cauldron is overflowing, thanks to the unchecked actions of his creature, and the room is flooded. Mickey commands the broom to cease, but the effort is ineffectual; his nascent power fails, and the broom walks over him. Frustrated, the apprentice is moved to violence, using an ax to destroy what he has made, splintering the broom. Yet slowly the pieces revive themselves and become an inexorable legion of water carriers.

Mickey's efforts to thwart the brooms are futile. First he tries to hold the door against them, without success. Next he attempts to bail the rising, roiling waters out the window, using a bucket. For an instant, he sinks below the surface and seems in danger of drowning. He clings to the Sorcerer's large book of spells, frantically leafing through the pages in search of an incantation. The brooms mock his efforts by dumping their buckets onto him, causing him to surf the book down the staircase to the basement, into a whirlpool to certain death. Just then, the awakened Sorcerer comes down the steps, parting the turbulent waters and making them disappear. A chastened Mickey removes his master's hat and returns it with an ingratiating smile. The apprentice picks up the now inanimate broom, returns it to its place and takes his empty bucket. A small smile from his master produces a relieved smile from Mickey: no punishment, he assumes. But as the apprentice returns to his task, he gets a swat with the broom from the Sorcerer. The lesson is clear: Obey your superior, do your work, and do not trifle with the cosmos—until you are ready.

Over the years since *Fantasia*'s release, Mickey's image from the film has emerged as a "central icon" of the company's official faith, according to Bruce David Forbes of Morningside College in Sioux City, Iowa. "In fact, with his wand and his hat from *The Sorcerer's Apprentice*, he functions as the high priest of the Disney religion," Forbes wrote in his 2000 paper, "And a Mouse Shall Lead Them: An Essay on the Disney Phenomenon as Religion," delivered at a Disney conference at Florida Atlantic University.

For Stravinsky's "Rite of Spring," Disney decided to offer a lesson in elementary evolution, circa 1940. Controversial as a ballet, the composer said the ballet's purpose was to express primitive life. "Walt Disney and his fellow artists have taken him at his word," says Taylor, but in the process they have made it their own, as "a pageant, as the story of the growth of life on earth." The resulting work, he says, "is a coldly accurate reproduction of what science thinks went on during the first few billions of years of this planet's existence." To emphasize the seriousness of what follows, he says, "Science, not art, wrote the scenario of this picture."

In Taylor's words, and then in Disney's animation over Stravinsky's music, the earth's evolution unfolds. The planet emerges out of nothingness—no hint of a divine spark, no big bang—and, curiously, there are hints of the *Star Trek* musical themes at this point in the score. It is a hellish surface, pocked with erupting volcanoes and molten lava. The magma cools in water, giving way to what Taylor called "single-celled organisms, blobs of nothing in particular that lived under the water." This being Disney, it doesn't take long for dinosaurs, "Lords of Creation for about 200 million years," to emerge. While most are benign vegetarians, there are also "bullies and gangsters among them." The favorite prehistoric heavy, Tyrannosaurus rex, lumbers onto the screen to demonstrate survival of the fittest. There is no creationism here; according to the DVD commentary, some schools used this segment as an instructional tool in science classes.

Greek mythology—the Disney version—illustrates Beethoven's *Pastoral* Symphony, complete with Zeus, Bacchus, Vulcan, and Diana, characters that will reappear in a more fractured form more than half a century later in *Hercules.* There are also centaurs, satyrs, unicorns, and flying horses. Among the images are some atypical of the studio: topless female centaurs bathing, seen at a discreet distance; a pair of winged horses, one white and one black, with a black-and-white offspring; and a reasonably chaste bacchanal. "The girl centaurs were originally drawn bare-breasted," according to Richard Schickel, "but the Hays office insisted on discreet garlands being hung around their necks, a decision that satisfied Puritans." Ward Kimball, one of Disney's Nine Old Men, said that production notes to the artists were extremely specific on such touchy matters. On one occasion, for example, they were told to make the male centaurs less virile and threatening. In subsequent theatrical rerelease, offensive images of black female centaurs with braided, "pickaninny" hair, shining the hooves and grooming the tails of white centaurs, were removed. The cutting was done in 1990 by Disney animator John Carnochan, according to a story in the *Long Beach Press-Telegram* of November 28, 1991. "It's kind of appalling to me that these stereotypes were ever put in," he said.

The "Dance of the Hours" sequence, while poking fun at what had already become an old chestnut of the classical repertoire, has some ostensibly nice things to say about the overweight. There are sympathetic representations of gracefully dancing hippos and elephants in ballet slippers, and a romance between one of the hippos and a slender crocodile. Yet there is also a disturbing background to the animation, according to R. D. Feild's *The Art of Walt Disney,* written with the cooperation of the studio. In order to draw Hyacinth, the hippo prima ballerina, "a Negress weighing more than two hundred pounds was found who tripped with lumbering grace over the live-action stage while the cameramen recorded the least quiver of her flesh, noticing those parts of her anatomy that were subjected to the greatest stress and strain." Would a child viewing this segment assume the hippo is based on an African American woman? Probably not.

The most explicitly religious segment of *Fantasia*—and the most explicitly religious sequence in any Disney feature until *The Hunchback of Notre Dame*—is the finale, Moussoursky's "Night on Bald Mountain" paired with Schubert's "Ave Maria." It is, as Taylor says in his introduction, a struggle between the profane and the sacred. According to folk tradition, Bald Mountain is the gathering place of Satan and his followers for the medieval *Walpurgisnacht*—an occasion of nightmarish wildness. Satan gathers his evil minions to worship him and, under his spell, to dance furiously. Disney's devil is muscular and malign and as sinister as any image from the Middle Ages. Beneath a full moon, Satan's powerful hands fall over the village below. He attempts to uproot the church steeple but only tilts it. He is more successful in pulling souls from their graves, despite the crosses that mark the resting places as consecrated ground. With demon escorts they descend to hell. Nude women with flaming hair dance until they are transformed into grotesque animals and tumble into the fiery abyss. "Walt wanted this sequence to really give you the chills," said critic Leonard Maltin, on the DVD commentary. At the height of fury, church bells sound and, in Taylor's words, they "send the infernal army slinking back into their abode of darkness." The Prince of Darkness shrinks back, apparently defeated by the dawn.

With the light, the strains of Moussoursky's music are replaced by Schubert's "Ave Maria." The bells and the light herald the segment's "message of the triumph of hope and life over the powers of despair and death," according to Taylor's narration. Shafts of heavenly illumination shine down on a procession of the faithful, carrying candles into a natural, sylvan cathedral, as the trees create the outlines of Gothic church windows. Early sketches of the procession show the candles forming crosses of light, but in the final version they are circular orbs. Similarly, early sketches of the sequence's finale feature a stained glass triptych that, in close up, reveals the image of the Madonna and child. This, said New York University's John Canemaker in the commentary, was "a much more religious ending than what ended up in the film." Instead, towering trees create the appearance of a Gothic window through which an inspirational sunset concludes the film.

Disney commissioned Rachel Field to write special lyrics for the Ave Maria, according to John Culhane, in *Walt Disney's Fantasia.* All the verses were published in Field's *Ave Maria: An Interpretation from Walt Disney's Fantasia,* but only one was sung in the film's final version. It concludes:

> The Prince of Peace your arms embrace while hosts of darkness
> fade and cower.
> Oh, save us, Mother full of grace, in life, and in our dying hour,
> Ave Maria!

So Walt Disney, although raised with all the religious prejudices of early twentieth-century, middle-American Protestantism, produced a concluding segment with a distinctly Catholic sensibility. For Hollywood in this period, religion equaled Roman liturgy. For some, however, the effort was not seen as a compliment.

Perucci Ferraiuolo, in *Disney and the Bible: A Scriptural Critique of the Magic Kingdom,* dismissed *Fantasia* as "an almost total glorification of witchcraft, sorcery and Satanism set to classical music." In the final sequence, Chernabog—the embodiment of Satan—was "the complete antithesis of the God of the Bible," he wrote, and the presentation of "Ave Maria" was "an affront to Roman Catholics." Christians, he wrote, had no difficulty seeing the film for what it was. "Some family and church groups worried that depictions of characters like the Demon of Bald Mountain, Mickey Mouse as a sorcerer and the Pegasus Family [featured in the *Pastoral* Symphony] would conjure up nightmares for kids, or promote black magic."

This is a conservative, retrospective version of political correctness. *Fantasia* failed at the box office despite the best and most noble intentions of Walt Disney, who was deeply troubled by its reception. I think he was simply trying too hard to be innovative, sophisticated, and uplifting. Like young people's concerts, *Fantasia* might be an enterprising way to introduce children to classical music, but I still can't watch it without squirming in my chair. In his high-minded, consuming effort to educate, Walt violated his own first commandment: Thou shalt entertain. What the studio learned was that its strong suit with animated features was simple, narrative storytelling with a consistent theme. Disney would not deviate from that path for a long time.

Chapter Six

Dumbo (1940): Mother Love

Dumbo, like *Pinocchio*, was an early favorite of parents, built around clear messages of tolerance and acceptance for children. The film begins with a flock of storks bringing babies—the epitome of Disney sexuality. But the birds also arrive with a lesson—sung over the action—of universality, delivering children with equal respect to expectant parents of diverse nationalities, classes, and species. And all the babies are welcomed with love by their mothers; they are all wanted. None of the would-be mothers is more anxious than Mrs. Jumbo, an elephant in the circus's winter quarters in Florida, who scans the dark, stormy skies for signs of her delivery. When the bird does arrive with her baby, late, Mr. Stork reads the delivery papers: "Straight from heaven, up above, here is a baby for you to love."

The proud mother bathes the baby elephant with love and, at first, basks in the oohs and aahs of the other adult females. Then the baby's sneeze reveals his outsized ears, turning the admiration of the other elephants to ridicule. The baby is oblivious, but Mrs. Jumbo protectively slaps away the trunk of one of the pachyderms that attempts to examine the little one's large ears, and then she slams down a wooden slat, shutting out the unsympathetic elephant chorus. The mother cradles her baby, now dubbed Dumbo, with his ears serving as swaddling clothes.

When the circus train pulls into town, it is dark and rainy. Young Dumbo emerges from the elephants' car behind his mother, using a big ear to protect himself from the weather, and ready to do his part to set up the big top. Climbing out of another car are brawny, brown roustabouts—the first of several disturbing racial stereotypes to make their appearance in the film. The burly figures seem without discernible facial features and are dressed roughly, but they are clearly men of color, and their deep singing voices, although probably sung by Caucasians, are apparently meant to sound African American. The lyrics of their work song are representative of mid-century, middle-American attitudes toward the underclass. As they set up the circus, the men proclaim that they work all day and all night and, while they cannot read and write, they are happy. While other folks have gone to bed, they "slave until we're almost dead," but they remain happy. They don't know when they'll get their pay, they sing, which doesn't matter, since when they do they'll just throw it all away. No one questions this portrayal, and there is no interaction between any of the hard-working men and Dumbo or any of the other animals. On the other hand, the *Orlando Sentinel*'s Jay Boyar thinks that this sequence may be ironic, a subtle critique of how others view these men.

In the circus parade the following morning, Dumbo assumes his role as performer. He trips on his ear and is covered with mud, which leads to an endearing sequence of him being washed (restored?) by his mother. Again, the love between the mother and child is reinforced. Drying off, Dumbo is spotted by a boy who begins to make fun of his big ears. The boy has proportionally big ears of his own, clearly a signal to those who would mock the imperfections of others. Implicitly at least, it conveys the message of John 8:7—"Let anyone among you who is without sin be the first to throw a stone at her"—observed longtime Disney employee and fan Mark Matheis. At first, the innocent Dumbo does not see the ridicule for what it is. Mrs. Jumbo knows what is happening and tries to remove her child from the abuse. When the big-eared boy tries to drag Dumbo back, his mother spanks the boy with her trunk, and then she goes berserk. She is whipped by the ringmaster and subdued by the roustabouts, who confine her to a train car. Dumbo, separated from his mother for the first time, weeps.

The other female elephants gossip about Mrs. Jumbo's actions, attributing it to understandable "mother love" that went too far. The problem, one says, is "that little F-R-E-A-K." Dumbo cannot spell, but he knows they are talking about him, and it hurts. As a species—or race—elephants have always walked in dignity, they all agree. By extension, Dumbo's shame and disgrace is theirs. One haughty matron says that she would not eat at the same bale of hay with the little elephant. "I should say," chimes in another, with a distinctly white Southern lilt, as they close their circle surrounding the hay, excluding Dumbo. "The hugeness of the beasts contrasted gorgeously with the smallness of their souls," Richard Schickel wrote in *The Disney Version*.

All of this is too much for a feisty mouse named Timothy, who is dressed as a circus musician and speaks with a pronounced Bowery Boys, New York Irish accent. He thinks Dumbo's ears are cute and, more important, he is outraged at the way the adult elephants are treating the outcast. Since they are brave enough to pick on a little elephant, Timothy suggests they pick on someone small like him—and he proceeds to frighten them into a panic. Like Jiminy Cricket, the little mouse takes on the task of bucking up the innocent, offering to be a friend and a champion. He reminds Dumbo that, as an elephant, he "comes of a proud race."

Timothy takes a page out of another gospel. The Reverend Robert Schuller, the theological heir of the late Norman Vincent Peale and now the high priest of American optimism, often suggests that Christians "turn your scars into stars." By that, Schuller means convert whatever adversity life throws your way into some benefit. The mouse suggests that they build an elaborate elephant act featuring Dumbo. If successful, the effort might enable them to free Mrs. Jumbo, since the reason his mother is locked up is that she is brokenhearted, not crazy. Their first effort—a pyramid of seven adult elephants balanced on a large ball—fails disastrously. Dumbo again is literally tripped up by his ears—his disability—causing injury to the other elephants and to the circus itself. Because of his failure, Dumbo is made a clown and, for that shame, the other elephants declare that he is no longer one of them. For the little elephant, the next step is down—a humiliating routine with cruel clowns. Dumbo is perched atop a burning building and rescued by clown firefighters who dump him into a vat of water. Dumbo is left in tears, despite Timothy's effort to lift his spirits with flattery. The mouse directs the sad little elephant to a source of support that will not fail him: Mom. What follows is one of the most soothing and reassuring sequences in all of Disney's animated features, and includes one of the most touching songs. Even in chains, Mrs. Jumbo is able to comfort her child, cradling him in her trunk. Singers croon, "Baby mine, don't you cry," urging Dumbo not to be discouraged by what others may say about him.

That advice is soon put to the test. The clowns celebrate the success of their act with Dumbo, planning to raise the platform by hundreds of feet, in hopes of earning a raise. At least one critic suggested this sequence was a disguised jab at Disney artists and animators who were trying to organize a union at the studio. When one clown worries that a fall from such a height might "hurt the little fella," another snaps, "Elephants don't have feelings!" A bottle of the clowns' champagne, dumped accidentally into a water bucket, provides an opportunity for Dumbo and Timothy to unintentionally become drunk. The surreal sequence that results, "Pink Elephants on Parade," is enough to dissuade any young viewer from experimenting with mood-altering substances. The next morning, Timothy and Dumbo awake, hung over, at the top of a tall tree, where they encounter a flock of black crows.

Some critics—mostly white, such as the *Chicago Tribune's* Michael Wilmington and Disney expert Leonard Maltin—have argued that the portrayal of the crows (one named Jim) in this sequence is *not* racist. They maintain that the representation is, in fact, exuberant and positive, that the crows are not simply crude minstrels. "Far from being shambling, oafish Step 'n' Fetchit types—the boiling point for any attack on racial stereotypes—Jim Crow and his 'brothers' are the snappiest, liveliest, most together characters in the film," Wilmington wrote in *The American Animated Cartoon: A Critical Anthology.* "They are tough and generous. They bow down to no one. And, of course, it is they who 'teach' Dumbo to fly." Maltin is equally positive in *The Disney Films.* "There has been considerable controversy over the Black Crow sequence in recent years, most of it unjustified. The crows are undeniably black, but they are black *characters,* not black *stereotypes.* There is no denigrating dialogue, or Uncle Tomism in the scene, and if offense is to be taken in hearing blacks call each other 'brother,' then the viewer is merely being sensitive to accuracy."

The crows' dancing was patterned after African American dancers, according to Disney authority John Canemaker, in a DVD commentary; moreover, some of the background singing was done by members of the Hall Johnson Choir, an African American group. But the inescapable context is that they are characters, featuring a preacher and a jazz musician, written and drawn by white people. In the manner of the hit radio program "Amos and Andy," white actors speak and sing the lead parts in dialect, complete with improper grammar. One crow says to the other, "Ax dem what dey want." Ward Kimball, one of Disney's Nine Old Men, said the characterization was a result of "the climate of the times," and was in no sense malicious. "There were ethnic jokes everywhere you went," he told Michael Barrier in 1986, an interview that was posted on August 26, 2003, on michaelbarrier.com. (In a deft nudge in Disney's ribs, the African American actor-comedian Eddie Murphy sings several bars of the crows' song, in perfect grammar, while portraying a donkey in rival DreamWorks' hit *Shrek*.)

When Timothy addresses the crows, it is difficult to say whether he is saying "You boys" or "You boids." Having said all this, the crows *are* sympathetic and supportive, and one comes up with the idea to donate a "magic feather" to convince Dumbo that he can fly. And fly he does, even when he loses the feather during his circus act. He never needed the feather to fly, Timothy tells him, only the ability to believe in himself—another variation of the Disney gospel. Dumbo's huge, nationwide success enables him to free his mother from captivity and buy her a luxury car on the circus train. The movie was so successful that a cover story in *Time* magazine was planned, only to be bumped from the cover by the Japanese attack on Pearl Harbor.

The lessons for children in this sixty-four-minute film are more clear. Dumbo "learns to turn his hardship into an advantage and wins happiness along the way," wrote Kathy Merlock Jackson, in *Walt Disney: A Bio-Bibliography*. The moral, for William

McReynolds, "is that the little elephant earns his right to survive by his own efforts and . . . by listening to the instructions of his friends and making the best of what nature has given him: his big ears."

The Reverend Michael Catlett, in his sermon "Everything I Needed to Know I Learned from Watching Disney," suggested that members of his congregation, McLean Baptist Church, in McLean, Virginia, "ask a group of children about *Dumbo* and listen to what they tell you. . . . The mouse was willing to see that Dumbo's liabilities were actually his assets. . . . Just because someone is different does not make it right to make fun of them. No one should be ostracized because they are unique."

True, the price of these lessons is two arguably racist sequences—the roustabouts and the crows. An argument can be made that the roustabout scenes move so quickly that children, black or white, are unlikely to notice them. Similarly, the image of African Americans in contemporary life and culture is now sufficiently far removed from those invoked by the crows in *Dumbo* that many young viewers may not make the connection. Call it liberal guilt if you like, but when I first showed *Dumbo* to my son, I stopped the tape before the crow sequence and explained what he was about to see and why black people are no longer portrayed in that way—a teachable moment, as we used to say. Asher and his sister Liza did not let this interruption turn them against the loveable little pachyderm. The Dumbo ride at Disneyland was one of their early favorites.

Chapter Seven

Bambi (1942): Man Is in the Forest

Bambi did more to plant the seeds of support for gun control and environmentalism among the baby boom generation than any single piece of American popular culture. From the 1960s on, it has been difficult to have a lengthy discussion about the Second Amendment without someone—often a woman of a certain age—bringing up *Bambi*. Such is the enduring power of Disney storytelling, and it must drive members of the National Rifle Association nuts. "The politics of 'Nature vs. Man' in the film are such that the anti-hunting sentiment in America came to be called, perhaps fairly, 'The Bambi Syndrome,'" wrote David Payne, in *From Mouse to Mermaid: The Politics of Film, Gender, and Culture*, edited by Elizabeth Bell, Lynda Haas, and Laura Sells.

Yet the film at its core is not about hunting or an idealized and unrealistically harmonious portrayal of animal life. It is about family, acceptance, and love. "Love is a song that never ends," a crooner sings as the movie begins. *Bambi*'s opening sequence is—like that of *Dumbo*—a paean to mother love. From all through the forest the animals, mostly mothers with their children, rush to see the newly born Bambi. In what could be a gloss on the Nativity, they tell one another, "It isn't every day a prince is born." Although the Great Prince of the forest, a lordly stag and the presumptive father, stands apart from the event, other animals circle the young deer and his protective mother.

As Bambi makes his wobbly way to his feet, his first friend, Thumper the rabbit, begins to give him a tour of his forest world. In the process, Disney storytellers provide the kind of profound life lesson that has made them so beloved by parents. The fact that it is delivered fleetingly, almost in passing, in no way diminishes its power. Thumper is teaching the fawn the names of things as they wander into a patch of flowers, having Bambi repeat each term as they encounter it. Up from beneath some petals pops the head of a young skunk. Bambi mistakes fauna for flora and addresses the skunk as "Flower?"—sending Thumper into convulsive laughter, given the attribute for which skunks are best known. He's not a flower, the rabbit corrects. But before Thumper can say what he is, the skunk seizes the opportunity in the error: "That's alright. He can call me Flower if he wants to. I don't mind." Bambi agrees, emphasizing the point by saying, "Pretty Flower." Thus, an innocent accepts another being without preconceived notions dictated by nature, or by others. Without prejudging, Bambi looks for the best in the skunk—his sweet disposition—and finds it. Surely, by forest standards, a skunk qualifies as "the least of these" creatures, the same standard set by Jesus in Matthew 25.

Although Bambi forms a strong cohort with Thumper and Flower, his primary relationship is with his mother. She protects him from a storm's raindrops and introduces him to the wonders of the meadow. But there are dangers in the meadow as well. Bambi's headlong rush into the field is blocked with the same urgency as a human toddler's run toward the street. "You must never rush out on the meadow," his mother explains. "There might be danger!" The reason, she says, is that "out there we are unprotected. The meadow is wide and open and there are no trees or bushes to hide us, so we have to be very careful." She ventures out first to make certain it is safe, and, after demonstrating a caution born of experience, she calls to her son. Then the frolic begins.

The deer are not the only creatures enjoying the open space; others are out, also under the supervision of their mothers. Nor are Bambi and his mother the only deer in the meadow. There is another doe, a friend of Bambi's mother, and her daughter, Faline. She takes a liking to Bambi, demonstrating a boldness and level of interest that he finds disconcerting. Bambi is also disconcerted when a great regal stag passes him in the meadow, glancing at the young deer as he passes. This, implicitly, raises the issue of parentage. Bambi's mother describes the stag in glowing, almost reverential terms. "Everyone respects him," she says, "for of all the deer in the forest not one has lived half so long. He's very brave and very wise. That's why he's known as the 'Great Prince of the Forest.'" Yet his mother gives Bambi no inkling that this is his father, for a number of good, Disney reasons. In the 1940s, the nuclear family was still America's norm and, while some aspects of nature could be safely glossed, others could not. The great stag presides over a herd of females, a harem.

Crows and their harsh cries herald trouble for the creatures of the meadow. The Great Stag is the first to notice danger and returns to warn his subjects to flee. In the confusion, Bambi's mother and Faline's mother both search frantically for their offspring. It is the stag that reunites Bambi with his mother and leads them to the thicket and safety, as a shot rings out. Breathless, Bambi asks his mother why they all ran, and is told, "Man was in the forest." Thus is the enemy of harmonious nature, the land of the warm and fuzzy, introduced.

But nature itself can be cruel and capricious, as autumn and then winter arrive. Brown leaves flutter in the chilly wind and drop to the ground, their life cycle complete. Yes, Bambi also learns the fun and the wonder of snow and ice, thanks to Thumper. Soon, however, gnawing hunger becomes the deer's companion, as mother and son forage for vegetation, stripping the bark from the trees. At last, some early greenery pokes through the snow in the meadow, in what seems to be the arrival of spring. Bambi and his mother venture out into the open meadow to eat, yet there is danger in the air (and sinister music on the sound track). Bambi's mother urges her son to run for the thicket, and they both take flight. Offscreen, a single shot rings out—out of season, some have argued—and Bambi's mother tells him to keep running. Then, a second shot. Bambi makes it into the thicket, breathless again, but exalting in what he thinks is their narrow escape. Ominously, his mother is nowhere to be found, despite his increasingly desperate calls, which end in tears. Snow begins falling again; this is no spring. From the snow, the Great Stag appears and tells Bambi, "Your mother can't be with you anymore"—not, "Your mother is dead." The effect is the same. There is silence, and the reality sets in. "Come, my son," the father says. Bambi follows, but not without a mournful, symbolic look back at his carefree childhood.

Spring comes, although it is not clear how many years have passed before the three friends—Bambi, Thumper, and Flower—are reunited. Bambi is a mature young buck, with antlers, and his voice has changed. With spring comes the mating season, and it falls to the wise owl to explain the Disney version of the facts of life to the trio. Female sexual attraction is a matter of "twitterpation," the owl explains, and before it all males are helpless. The friends scoff at the notion, pledging that they will in no way succumb. Yet each in turn falls for the coquettish appeals of the female of the species. Flower shrugs his shoulders when his time comes, as if to say, "What can you do?"

Bambi's courtship is a little more complicated. He encounters a mature Faline and, after some uncertainty, pursues her. Suddenly an older, larger buck intervenes and attempts to claim the doe. Here Disney stands in opposition to Darwin. Bambi fights for Faline and, in this case, love and determination trump natural selection. Bambi fights and defeats his rival, surviving because he is the purer of heart rather than the fittest. The new couple dances in a starlit frolic. Their joy is short-lived, as Bambi notices that something is wrong, a sense confirmed by the arrival of his father and more cawing of crows. "It is man," the Great Stag says. "He is here again. There are many this time. We must go deep into the forest. Hurry. Follow me."

It is not enough that these creatures killed Bambi's mother. Now they threaten his home and habitat, another unspoiled Disney Eden. Separated, Bambi and Faline search for each other, as the hunters' indiscriminate gunfire begins. All the birds and animals of the forest flee in panic, and Faline is cornered by a pack of man's vicious hunting dogs. Bambi comes to her rescue but, in the course of saving his love, he is shot. At the same time, wind blows the hunters' carelessly untended campfire into a raging fire that threatens to engulf the entire forest. The Great Stag approaches Bambi's still body, commanding him to get up. With great effort he does, and father and son flee the flames, ultimately joining the conflagration's survivors.

The cartoonist Matt Groening, creator of *The Simpsons* and *Futurama* television shows, still remembers seeing *Bambi* in 1956 at the Paramount Theater in his hometown of Portland, Oregon. He was two years old, and it was his first trip to the movies, and he was with his older sister Patti. Groening recalled that he was less troubled by Bambi's mother's death than by the blaze. "I remember screaming my head off," he told Jeff Baker, of the *Portland Oregonian,* in a March 14, 2004, article. "That forest fire freaked me out for weeks."

Time passes. As the forest regenerates, the fruits of "twitterpation" are manifest. Thumper has a clutch of little Thumpers, and Flower has a son he has named for his friend Bambi, who respected him and accepted him for *who* he was, not *what* he was. In a reprise of the film's opening sequence, all the creatures of the forest stream to a clearing to see Bambi and Faline's twin fawns—presumably the fruit of a uniquely monogamous relationship between the two half siblings. The cycle is complete. The *New Republic,* then a magazine of the Left, wrote in its June 29, 1942, issue that the film was "too moralistic." But Kathy Merlock Jackson wrote that, in what was already becoming a familiar charge against the darker elements of Disney's animated features, "The biggest criticism of the film came from those who thought it too frightening for children."

Walt Disney knew exactly what he was doing in telling stories through idealized, anthropomorphous animals. It worked in cartoon shorts with Mickey Mouse and Donald Duck. It worked in *Dumbo* and in *Bambi,* and it would work dozens more times. "Sheer animated fantasy is still my first and deepest production impulse," he wrote in *Wisdom* magazine, in December 1959. "The fable is the best story telling device ever conceived, and the screen is its best medium. And, of course, animal characters have always been the personnel of fable; animals through which the foibles as well as the virtues of humans can best and most hilariously be reflected. . . . Fable animals are not real animals. They are human beings in the guise of bird and beast. From his earliest beginnings, as his cave drawings eloquently attest, man has been telling many of his experiences and dramatic conclusions and comments through animal symbols. . . . Animals which can be controlled, caricatured, exaggerated, are best for fable and morality tales—they have been since Aesop's day and before."

With *Bambi,* Disney initiated another theme that would weave in and out of his animated features and those produced by his successors: Nature undisturbed is good—if not ideal. Man disrupts and destroys. The crows that harshly herald man's entry into the forest in *Bambi* will return in future films. But nature, we are now led to understand by the film, also can be amoral, with few lessons to teach us, apart from the early and instinctive devotion to offspring featured in this movie. *Bambi* also suggests that patriarchy is another ideal, the natural order of things. Many Disney viewers would tend to disagree on that point as well.

Chapter Eight

Cinderella (1950): Prince Charming II

Cinderella is often recalled—in faded memory—as the tale of a poor scullery maid who rises to royalty. The song covering the opening credits reinforces this image, the lyrics an almost literal reprise from *Snow White*: "Though you're dressed in rags, you wear an air of queenly grace." This image is not entirely true, as the movie's narrated prologue makes clear. Cinderella was a child of privilege, the well-loved only daughter of an apparently wealthy couple, born in an elegant chateau in a tiny European kingdom and raised in "luxury and comfort." While not royalty, they are at least upper middle class. When her mother died, her kind, devoted father decided to remarry, because Cinderella "needed a mother's care." Although the stepmother was "a woman of good family," the match proved to be a disaster for Cinderella. It was "through the untimely death of her father that her stepmother's true nature was revealed," according to the narrator. Thus, Disney's stereotype of the "evil stepmother," first engraved on the popular consciousness in *Snow White,* was reinforced. This also cemented a trend in *Dumbo* and *Bambi*, that is, "the 'zero' of Disney mothers—absent, murdered or replaced," according to Elizabeth Bell, Lynda Haas, and Laura Sells, in *From Mouse to Mermaid.*

Cinderella mourns alone at her father's deathbed, her stepmother and stepsisters in the background. It soon becomes clear that the stepmother has betrayed the trust and purpose of Cinderella's father, "grimly determined to forward the interests of her own two awkward daughters." The chateau falls into disrepair, the narrator explains, as the family's fortunes are squandered on the vain and selfish stepsisters. Cinderella is abused and humiliated and, at last, compelled to become a servant in her own house, confined to an aerie garret. Yet, through it all, the beautiful young woman remained "ever gentle and kind," the narrator concludes, "for in each dawn she found new hope that someday her dreams of happiness would come true."

Here is the Disney formula for a heroine, a theory based in part on aesthetics. Cinderella is pretty, plucky, and without guile, echoing many novels of the nineteenth century. It is a description that has remained constant throughout the studio's history. The same is true for the presentation of evil. In *Snow White,* the queen has a cold, dark beauty that, through envy, curdles into evil as she transforms herself into a witch-like crone in order to kill her rival. Although less homicidal, Cinderella's stepmother has a dark, mature elegance that complements her icy malevolence. Yet her two daughters are merely homely and awkward—traits over which they have no control. They are indulged by their mother, at Cinderella's expense, and so become spoiled and petulant and thus objects of derision. Are they considered ugly because they are bad, or bad because they are ugly?

Cinderella, sleeping under a patched, threadbare blanket, is awakened each morning by her friends, the birds and the mice. Another song sets the scene for what is to come. "The potential for Disney to influence or shape moral identity, not only through the narrative, but also through the songs is tremendous," wrote Annalee R. Ward, in *Mouse Morality: The Rhetoric of Disney Animated Film.* "If you keep on believing," the singer explains, "the dream that you wish will come true." Her family can't order her to stop dreaming, she says, and perhaps some day the dreams that she wishes will come true.

Like Snow White, Cinderella's small animal friends help her wake up, dress, and clean her room. It soon becomes clear why the creatures care so much for the young woman, as she takes time to free a fat mouse from a trap, name him, and give him clothes. Cinderella is considerate of the household's ill-tempered and aptly named cat, Lucifer, insisting that even he has his good points. Before this lesson in interspecies comity can continue, the real world intervenes. Cinderella is summoned to bring breakfast tea to her mother and sisters. Each returns her cheerful morning greeting with a demand to do chores. Her stepmother suggests Cinderella has too much time on her hands, providing as a remedy another onerous list of housekeeping tasks: the carpet in the main hall, the tapestries, the windows, draperies, and gardening. All of this injustice Cinderella accepts without complaint. She sings sweetly, without visible accompaniment, as she works, while elsewhere in the chateau music lessons are wasted on her stepsisters.

At the castle, meanwhile, the king complains to his counselor about his son, the prince, who refuses to marry and have children. The monarch's solution is to summon every maiden in the small kingdom to a dress ball that very night. When the invitation arrives at the chateau, the stepsisters are ecstatic at the prospect that one might marry the prince, and they mock Cinderella's request to be included. Her stepmother says she can attend—if she completes even more chores and can find a suitable dress. At this point, the mice and birds are able to repay Cinderella's kindness. Like numerous Disney artists and animators and technicians, the little creatures work together to do the impossible, even as Cinderella is resigned to staying at home. The mice and the birds finish the cleaning and transform her late mother's dowdy old dress—adorning the outfit with the stepsisters' discarded cloth and accessories. Alas, all this is not enough. Cinderella's beautiful dress is ripped apart by her jealous siblings, and she is forbidden to join them at the ball.

Her hope raised and then dashed, Cinderella faces the Disney equivalent of a crisis of faith—in faith. Heretofore an indomitable true believer, her optimism is finally shattered, leaving her distraught and weeping. "It's just no use," she declares. "I can't believe—not anymore! There's nothing left to believe in." At this moment, much like in *Pinocchio*, hope materializes from above. Stars gather from the sky and configure themselves into a cloaked fairy godmother. Walt's production notes describe the appearance of the fairy godmother as "the miracle," according to Bob Thomas, in *Walt Disney: An American Original*. Even Perucci Ferraiuolo, in *Disney and the Bible*, grudgingly calls the apparition "a curious half-pagan, half Christian conception." The kindly old woman tells the girl that she couldn't have meant what she just said. "If you'd lost all your faith, I couldn't be here," she says. "And I am!" They must hurry if Cinderella is to make it to the ball, the magical godmother says, because "even miracles take a little time." In short order, accompanied by a bouncy production number, household friends are transformed into a coach-and-four with driver and footman. Cinderella is clothed in a beautiful dress and glass slippers, leading her to exclaim, "It's all a dream—a wonderful dream come true!" With her godmother's blessings, and the warning that the dream ends at midnight, Cinderella leaves for the castle.

Naturally, when the prince sees Cinderella and waltzes with her, it is love at first sight. She sings that "this is the miracle that I've been dreaming of." There is still the business of the flight at the stroke of midnight, and the glass slipper, which calls for Cinderella to stand up for her right to try it on and prove that she deserves the prince. As wedding bells ring, the closing song restates the film's moral—and Disney's theology: "If you keep on believing, the dreams that you wish will come true."

Cinderella is one of those few stories that has given its name to a syndrome, a shorthand expression to describe otherwise intelligent women who passively wait to be whisked away by Prince Charming. This was not the intention of the creator of the tale's movie version. In a promotional short made for television, Walt Disney explained how Cinderella differed from the earlier heroine, Snow White, on the assertiveness scale. Cinderella was "more practical. She believed in dreams all right, but she believed in doing something about them. When Prince Charming didn't come along she went right over to the palace and got him." Maurice Rapf, a screenwriter on the movie who was a member of the Communist Party at the time, said, "I structured it to make her a rebel who fights for what she wants, as a result of which she is locked up in the tower and is never going to be able to try on the glass slipper when the guy comes around," according to *Tender Comrades: A Backstory of the Hollywood Blacklist* by Patrick McGilligan and Paul Buhle.

These recollections are subject to debate, and others disagree. The story has produced scores of magazine articles and at least two books, *The Cinderella Complex: Women's Hidden Fear of Independence* by Colette Dowling, a feminist interpretation, and *The Cinderella Syndrome: Discovering God's Plan When Your Dreams Don't Come True* by Lee Ezell, which takes a Christian view. Yet both books attempt to address the damage done to young girls by the story.

Despite the best intentions of Walt Disney and Maurice Rapf, and some excellent songs, *Cinderella* remains a pale copy of *Snow White*. Both in its story and its animation, it lacks the verve of the original. The messages of good cheer in the face of adversity and ill will, and of determined optimism are overshadowed by the heroine's passivity. The redemption provided by the intervention of the fairy godmother, while it conforms with the Disney gospel, rings false. It is difficult for a middle-aged adult male to put himself into the mind of a four- or five-year-old girl watching this film for the first time—much less for the tenth or twentieth time. Still, I don't think I'd want to allow my daughter much repeat viewing of *Cinderella* without some serious discussions with Mom. Or perhaps with Prince Dad.

Chapter Nine

Alice in Wonderland (1951):
Take the Red Pill

Alice, Walt Disney explained in a promotional film made for television, "is curious about anything and everything. To me, Alice is a great deal like children today: Bright, eager, curious about places and people. It's this curiosity that gets her into all those fabulous adventures in Wonderland." To some degree, it is also about boredom with a conventional form of learning—a book—that leads to a disorienting detour from reality. In this sense, any parent lobbying for schoolwork over the video screen or the CD player can sympathize. The film, based on the Lewis Carroll classic, begins with Alice in the park as a governess reads to the girl about early English history. Petulant and inattentive, the young student complains that it is difficult to pay attention to a book with no pictures. In her world, Alice says, books would be nothing but pictures. In fact, she tells her cat as she dozes off, everything would be nonsense if she had a world of her own.

Enter the vehicle of her transformation and wish fulfillment: a distracted white rabbit on the way to a tea party. Alice knows that she shouldn't go where she isn't invited, and that curiosity can lead to trouble, but she pursues the rabbit down his burrow anyway. Immediately Alice enters a distorted world where, as she wished, everything appears to be nonsense. Animals and objects speak, often peremptorily and rudely. Drinking an unknown substance, which she acknowledges might be poison, she shrinks and grows and shrinks again—an experience that leads to tears. She meets the brothers Tweedle Dee and Tweedle Dum (progenitors of several dynasties of politicians), who give her lessons in manners. They also tell her a cautionary tale, about the Walrus and the Carpenter, who lure gullible young oysters from the safety and security of their home and native habitat to the stew pot. In this case, the moral is unspoken but obvious. If you leave your mother and the world you know for the temptations of the unknown, you will encounter danger—or worse. In this sense, the episode echoes, reinforces, and foreshadows the unfolding theme of the film itself.

Alice next meets a patch of singing flowers who teach her another lesson, this one about ego. Each different blossom wants to sing a song about itself, but in order to satisfy the needs of the diverse group, they decide to sing a song about all of them—together. As if to underline the lesson, they sing, "You can learn a lot of things from flowers," in this case, about harmony. Yet there is a harsher aspect to this exercise as well. When Alice hits an embarrassingly discordant note, she is accused by the flowers of being a weed—and is expelled. "We don't want a weed in our bed," they tell her.

By the time Alice meets a caterpillar smoking a water pipe, which exudes intoxicating fumes, the girl is beginning to weary of this world she has wished for. Everything is so confusing, she says. Yet in the midst of the accumulating absurdity, she gets some more advice: Keep your temper. An encounter with the Cheshire cat directs Alice to the White Rabbit's tea party with the March Hare and the Mad Hatter. (The name of the latter is said to be taken from real life, in the belief that hat makers who used mercury in their work often went insane.) Now that she has arrived at her destination, Alice has second thoughts. "I don't want to go among mad people," she says. "You can't help that," she is told. "Most everyone's mad here." In the midst of the riotous gathering, Alice continues to accumulate good advice, even when it sounds contradictory, for party manners. If you don't think, you shouldn't talk. If you don't like what is being served, you can at least make polite conversation.

But Alice has just about had her fill of the absurdity she wished for. No more nonsense, she tells birds wearing spectacles—she wants to go straight home. If she does, she thinks she could write a book about this place (a sly joke from Lewis Carroll?). Alice is increasingly desperate to get back to familiar surroundings and to her cat, yet Wonderland is not ready to let her go. She remembers another piece of good advice, perhaps from her mother: When you are lost, it is sometimes a good idea to stay where you are until someone finds you. But who would ever think to look for her in this strange place? Now the big lesson for the willful, curious girl who didn't want to pay attention to her history book: "If I listened earlier I wouldn't be here," she laments. "But that's just the trouble with me. I give myself very good advice, but I very seldom follow it. That explains the trouble I'm always in." Alice admits to herself that the good advice to be patient makes her furious. "I went along my merry way, and I never stopped to reason. I should've known there would be a price to pay some day. I'm through with rabbits. I want to go home, but I can't find my way."

Before Alice can go home, she must first encounter the Disney view of totalitarianism in the person of the Queen of Hearts. The sovereign is loud and large, a grotesque figure who will become a stock, female character in the studio's gallery of villains. She terrorizes everyone, beginning with the king, her diminutive, henpecked husband. Her playing-card minions prepare for a royal garden party as if it were a Potemkin village, painting the white roses red, her favorite color. The Red Queen, as she is sometimes called, has a Stalinist propensity for ordering executions. "Off with their heads!" she cries with disturbing frequency. Oddly, the occasion of a subject being dragged off for such a punishment is treated with humor, cheers, and a song heralding the execution.

The queen has some bracing advice for Alice when encountering a monarch: Look up, speak nicely, don't twiddle your fingers, curtsy, and always say, "Yes, your majesty." The girl also gets an informative lesson in realpolitik. The queen's way is always the right way, beginning with a friendly game of croquet that is rigged for her to win. If the queen loses her temper, someone loses his head. And so, when the inevitable happens and Alice runs afoul of the queen, the outcome is foreordained. "Sentence first, verdict afterwards!" the Red Queen bellows, a result familiar to those who read about or watched the Soviet purge trials of the late 1930s. Unlike the docile, resigned defendants at the Moscow proceedings, Alice is emboldened to speak out by a magic mushroom that turns her into a giant. She tells the queen, "You're just a fat, pompous, bad-tempered old tyrant!" Shrunk back down to size, she is forced to flee the enraged queen. As chaos ensues, Alice awakes from her dream, as her governess commands her to recite the same lesson that has put her to sleep.

In a candid interview reproduced on the DVD for *Peter Pan,* Walt Disney grappled with *Alice in Wonderland*'s disappointment at the box office and came to a different conclusion than his effusive analysis in the promotional short. He "came to think of Alice herself as a prim and prissy little person, lacking in humor and entirely too passive in her role in the story," according to Richard Schickel in *The Disney Version.* One problem was that there were too many different interpretations of the girl, that her portrayal was too intellectual. There wasn't enough heart or pathos to make the film work. Yet the governing metaphor of Alice as a seeker endures in popular culture. The Jefferson Airplane put her story to acid rock music in the 1970s, with the classic "White Rabbit." In the pretentious 1999 blockbuster film *The Matrix,* the character Morpheus offers the character Neo a choice of two pills. If he chooses the blue pill, "the story ends, you wake up in your bed and believe whatever you want to believe. You take the red pill . . . and I show you how deep the rabbit hole goes." Neo does what Alice does.

For all the complaints about Disney's tinkering with and sanding down the edges of fairy tales, *Alice in Wonderland* demonstrates the pitfalls of fidelity to the original, of illustrating a classic story rather than transforming it and making it your own. Lewis Carroll was a genius quite different from Walt Disney, and in this case they did not mesh. The charm of the film's original songs and the brilliance of voice actors such as Ed Wynn and Jerry Colonna notwithstanding, Disney's Alice is essentially a spectator, a tourist in Wonderland. Still, there may be some lessons to be learned from the movie. The Internet, it seems to me, is the modern rabbit hole. Boredom can lead unattended children—and adults—down unexpected paths and around blind curves and, sometimes, into trouble and regret. As Alice says, there is a price to pay for such explorations.

Chapter Ten

Peter Pan (1953): Faith, Trust, and Pixie Dust

*A*t its heart, *Peter Pan* is a tribute to the transcendent value of the traditional middle-class family—and especially to the civilizing power of mother love. Ironically, most of the narrative takes place in the absence of both. Notwithstanding, this is in sharp contrast to previous (and future) animated Disney features, where mothers are dead or crazy and fathers are absent or distant. As the film opens, London's Darling family is loving, affluent, and intact, settled in their home in the Victorian city's Bloomsbury district. The parents, Mary and George, are preparing for an elegant evening out as their three children get ready for bed. A song plays under the tumult about yet another Disney star in the heavens. This time it is the second one from the right—there to tell you that "the dreams you plan really can come true" and that we'll be thankful when they do.

The narrator explains that the eternally adolescent Peter Pan has chosen the Darling household to visit "because there were people there who believed in him." Wife Mary believes that Peter is the spirit of youth, although George is skeptical, calling the subject poppycock. The husband is a blustery, buffoonish authority figure, angrily issuing orders: Sister Wendy must move from the nursery she has been sharing with her younger brothers John and Michael, and the beloved St. Bernard named Nana must give up her job as nursemaid and move to the doghouse outside. Sooner or later, the patriarch snorts, people have to grow up. Mary does not disagree directly, but tactfully suggests reasons why her husband's orders may not be the wisest. Wendy declares she does not want to grow up.

In contrast to the way I felt in my previous viewings of *Peter Pan* over the decades, when I watched it more recently I was unsettled by Peter's first appearance at the Darling household. True, he is based on the Greek demigod Pan—a mischievous, goat-legged satyr—complete with pointed ears and flute. Yet now I noticed a certain hint of meanness in his face that I hadn't seen before, especially in a scene outside the house, when the streetlight gives his countenance a sinister cast. It is almost equine or mulish, though, rather than goat-like. (In a DVD commentary, Walt admits that even he couldn't warm to Peter.) Also, I found Peter's speech coarser than I recalled. As Wendy is sewing his lost shadow back to his foot, he snaps peremptorily, "Get on with it, girl!" He asks Wendy what a mother is, and she says it is "someone who loves and cares for you and tells you stories." Good, Peter replies abruptly, Wendy can become Neverland's mother. Notes of jealousy and vanity are introduced, as tiny fairy Tinker Bell interrupts an incipient kiss between Peter and Wendy—just after Tinker Bell inspects the width of her hips by standing on Wendy's hand mirror. (The fully rounded sprite was not, as rumor had it, patterned after Marilyn Monroe, according to Disney animator Marc Davis.)

Despite the abundant comforts of their safe and happy home, the girl and her brothers seem instantly willing to abandon it and accept Peter's offer to go to Neverland. However, the only way to get to the island is to fly. Peter informs the siblings that all it requires to take flight is to think a wonderful thought and then add faith, trust, and pixie dust. If there ever was a recipe for the Disney gospel, this is it. As Sammy Fain's song explains under the action, thinking happy thoughts is just like having wings, enabling you to bid your cares—and, it would seem, your parents—goodbye. "Think of all the joys you'll find," the song goes, "when you leave the world behind."

Neverland is also the home of Captain Hook—a cruel, foppish, Restoration dandy—and his happy, multinational crew of pirates. (Early drawings include a Sambo-like African pirate who does not appear in the film.) A buccaneer's life on the island can be nasty, brutish, and short, as Hook demonstrates by using his pistol to cavalierly dispatch a crewmember because he finds the man's singing infelicitous. The pirate chief, the narrator informs us, lost his hand in an earlier sword fight with Peter, who tossed it to a large crocodile. Also on the island are cannibals, who are never seen in the final cut, and a village of "redskins." Hook—who here, as traditionally in the theater, is voiced by the same actor who portrays George Darling—bemoans the fact that he does not know the hideout of Peter and his young band of followers, so he cannot eliminate them.

Peter's Lost Boys, by their harsh features, disheveled appearance, and grammar, are lower-class children without parents—urchins out of Dickens. On Tinker Bell's orders, which she claims come from Peter, they attack the Darling children as intruders. Peter intervenes, banishing Tinker Bell and informing the Lost Boys that Wendy will become their new mother. Minus Peter and Wendy, the enlarged group of boys sets out to fight the "Injuns." John Darling assumes command, by dint of his age, class, and, apparently, his glasses. The story of *Peter Pan* is set in the age of European colonialism, when white men assumed their superiority over darker peoples, which makes the satire that follows so acute. John tells his troops that a footprint they encounter belongs to an Algonquin—in reality, Pocahontas's North American people—who, he pronounces authoritatively, are quite savage. Since the Indians are cunning but not intelligent, John proposes that the English boys surround their quarry. But as the camera pulls back, it becomes clear that it is the Indians who have in fact surrounded the Europeans and captured them, thereby turning the stereotype on its head. John, the pompous Englishman with his notions of superior Western civilization, is taken down a peg, much like the British redcoats in the Revolutionary War.

The boys are taken to the Indian village, where John learns that this is part of the normal give-and-take of life in Neverland. Indians capture boys, boys capture Indians. Everybody is eventually freed—except that this time the game has changed, and the captives are in peril. The chief's daughter, Tiger Lily, has been kidnapped by Captain Hook, in hopes of forcing from her the location of Peter's hideout. She has been bound and set on a rock in the middle of a cove where the tide is rising. The pirate warns her that she will drown if she does not give Hook the information he wants. Apparently an expert on Native American theology, he cautions her, "There is no path through water to the Happy Hunting Grounds." That is, she risks losing the afterlife in Indian heaven for her loyalty. She is resolute, and is shortly rescued by Peter and returned to her family.

At the Indian village, almost every demeaning cliché about Native Americans is rolled out—peace pipe, drums, whooping, ridiculously fake sign language, pidgin English (the suffix *um* attached to every verb), women referred to as "squaws." The braves are slightly stoop-shouldered, with big noses, wearing war paint, headbands, and feathers. Grateful for the safe return of his daughter, the heavyset, deep-voiced chief makes Peter a chief and pledges to "teach our paleface brother all about red man." John Darling, now dressed like an Indian, muses that this should be an "enlightening" experience. He and the others ask what are, for them, obvious questions. What makes the red man red? When did he first say "ugh"? Why does he ask you "how"? The red complexion, the boys are told in a song-and-dance production number, comes from blushing when a brave kissed an Indian maiden "a million years ago." "Ugh" comes from an ugly mother-in-law. And, they sing, you can learn a lot from asking "how?" Marc Davis, one of the Nine Old Men, admitted on the DVD commentary that the portrayal of the Indians in this segment might have been done differently in light of contemporary views of Native Americans.

Throughout the film, Disney's Peter is the object of affection by most of the females on the island: Wendy, Tinker Bell, a group of mermaids, and Tiger Lily, who dances for him and with him, and gives him a kiss that makes him blush and bowls him over. He enjoys the attention, but takes no more than an adolescent interest in any one of them—unlike his Greek namesake. Yet, like some modern twelve-year-old girls, the females evince varying degrees of petulant jealousy. Tinker Bell's jealousy is most pronounced and most malignant. Captain Hook realizes how destructive such feelings can be, observing that "a jealous female can be tricked into anything." So he has the tiny fairy snatched and brought to his cabin, where he attempts to charm her with his sympathy. Wendy has come between her and Peter, Hook notes, taking the best years of Tinker Bell's life—a turn on the classic complaint of abandoned wives—and casting her away like an old glove. The pirate offers a solution: He will kidnap Wendy and take her from the island, freeing Peter from his "mad infatuation." All that is necessary is for Tinker Bell to provide him with the location of the Lost Boys' hideout. She agrees, in exchange for his promise not to harm Peter, a pledge he has no intention of keeping. When Tinker Bell agrees to the betrayal and gives him the information he wants, she is imprisoned.

At the hideout, beneath Hangman's Tree, Peter is baffled by Wendy's disapproval. "Everyone else thinks I'm wonderful," he says. Wendy diagnoses the Lost Boys' problem: They need a mother. The boys want to know what a mother is, and Wendy first speaks and then sings them an answer, in the form of an explanation that becomes a lullaby. "A real mother," she says, "is the most wonderful person in the world, the angel voice that bids you goodnight and kisses your cheek." As she sings, she takes away her brothers' signs of undisciplined "savagery" by removing their war paint and discarding their feathers. Mothers provide a helping hand, Wendy says, and are a source of unconditional love, guiding you, whether you are right or wrong. In other words, a mother is a civilizing agent.

Even the Lost Boys are listening, rapt, wiping away an occasional tear. How precious is a mother, Wendy asks? You might as well ask a star, she replies. Her worth? "Heaven on earth." Mother, she says, is just another word for "divine." At this, even Hook's motley pirate crew, poised above the hideout to attack, listen wistfully. In their own way, they too are Lost Boys. The attraction of the wild life on Neverland, once so attractive to the Darling brothers, instantly recedes as they recall their mother and their home. Reminded of what they left behind, Michael and John propose to return home and to bring the Lost Boys with them (an offer that is wholly unrealistic, knowing what we do about the Darling parents). Peter predicts disaster should they accept, and warns his followers that if they leave Neverland they will not be able to return. Having lost the argument and been abandoned, Peter takes to his flute and his hammock.

The young Darlings and the Lost Boys are taken prisoner by Hook and his men and brought to the pirate ship. They are offered a choice: Join the pirates for a life of crime or walk the plank. The boys clamor to sign up for service under the black flag, until Wendy stops and upbraids them, telling Hook on their behalf, "We will never join you." Besides, she is confident that Peter will rescue them. That won't happen, Hook informs them, since he has left a gift-wrapped bomb for him. Hearing this, Tinker Bell is horrified at the consequences of her jealous act, and she flies to try to save Peter. Her betrayal is redeemed as she risks her life to save Peter, her love. Near death, Tinker Bell hears Peter tell her that she means more to him than anything in the world.

Back at the pirate ship, Wendy is ever the resolute and principled Englishwoman. She would rather die than join the pirates and, as the oldest in the group, is willing to be first to walk the plank. Bravely marching forward to certain death, she turns her eyes to heaven and steps off into the air—but there is no splash. Peter Pan has come to the rescue. Before their final duel, Peter tells Captain Hook to say his prayers—apparently even heartless villains should pray when they face death.

Back in London, the Darling parents are returning home just as their children are arriving back at the nursery. Time has been compressed. Despite all that has happened in Neverland, only three hours have passed in London. Before the family is reunited, the dynamic between the husband and wife is made clear in a familiar way. Over the course of the evening, Mary has managed to reverse George's earlier, angry edicts: Wendy may remain with her brothers in the nursery, and the dog Nana may return to the house. "I'm so glad you changed your mind," Mary says sweetly. Her husband replies, "You know I never mean those things." As the Darling family gathers in the nursery, Wendy announces that she is ready to grow up. "All in good time," her father says, recalling that what looks like a pirate ship sailing into the cloud seems vaguely familiar.

"*Peter Pan* suggests the importance of faith, the need to see the world with a child's eyes," wrote Susan Lochrie Graham in "Some

Day My Prince Will Come: Images of Salvation in the Gospel according to St. Walt," a paper delivered to a panel of the American Academy of Religion meeting in Orlando in November 1998. But in this case, "the images of a boy rescuer from the sky who leads an unruly group of male followers parodies the biblical image of Jesus and his followers." Rather, Peter Pan is simply an antiestablishment figure whose tale argues that "the delinquency of young people is a phase that must be rejected; those who refuse to do so are Lost Boys."

Here, in the amplification of what has come to be known as the "Peter Pan Syndrome," the boy refuses to accept adulthood and domesticity. Graham argues further that Peter also rejects the notion that salvation is mutually dependent, that "one's own salvation is intimately linked with the salvation of others." Similarly, he wants no part of the traditional bargain in which adult male heroes are expected to rescue female heroines, providing them with a home and protection in return for a traditional family—that is, one in which the wife "indulgently mothers the husband as well as the children." As much as he might like to, this is something Peter cannot give the Lost Boys. What is the alternative? Graham asks: "the Darling family, where George Darling has clearly given up the boyish fantasies of pirates and treasure, but has moved into a different fantasy of the wife who will mother him."

The Darlings, like many long-married couples through history, operate on what, in its modern incarnation, I like to call the "Southern Baptist model." That is, where the wife *pretends* to submit to her husband's authority while effectively subverting it. In 1998, the Southern Baptist Convention voted to add to its denominational statement of belief that wives should "graciously submit" to their husbands. Ruth Graham, the wife of the world famous evangelist Billy Graham, retorted that, as a Presbyterian married to a Southern Baptist, "there's a time to *sub*mit, and a time to *out*wit."

But Peter Pan or George Darling shouldn't be the only two alternatives for boys and young men to consider. The past three decades have seen the emergence of an egalitarian model of marriage that many have welcomed, as I do, although it is a development others have found troubling or threatening. A man need not give up all his boyhood fantasies when he joins in a committed, lifelong partnership with another. This is the commentary I would provide any boy watching *Peter Pan*. I'd also add a short, simplified history lesson on why real Native Americans are nothing like those in Neverland—or maybe I'd just fast forward through the whole repulsive village sequence.

Chapter Eleven

Lady and the Tramp (1955): Mixed Marriage

*F*or all its romance, adventure, and memorable music, *Lady and the Tramp* is a gritty fable about class, breeding, authority, immigration, and social mobility—and the making of modern America. This populist story is set in the early twentieth century, an era of lingering innocence and emerging technology. Gas lamps coexist with telephones, horse-drawn wagons with motorcars. European immigrants still speak with accents and still get along with one another. America is busy becoming the country it will be. Animals, mostly dogs, are at the center of this story, and the various breeds reflect the national and geographic stereotypes that were current— though at a somewhat later period—when the feature was made. So the Scottish terrier hoards his bones in the backyard. The Southern bloodhound is slow-witted and often befuddled. The mournful Russian wolfhound quotes Maxim Gorki and makes jokes about red flags. The Siamese cats are "wily Orientals." But it is the raffish Tramp, the thoroughly mixed "American breed" straight out of Damon Runyon, who stands at the center of the movie. The gray dog is jaunty, resourceful, and irrepressibly optimistic. Accordingly, the nineteenth-century Yankee humorist Josh Billings provides the first words that appear on the screen: "In the whole history of the world there is but one thing that money cannot buy . . . to wit, the wag of a dog's tail." This is followed by an addendum: "So it is to all dogs—be they Ladies or Tramps—that this picture is respectfully dedicated."

It is Christmas Eve, and snow is falling on a prosaic town. There are carolers in the neighborhood of large, two-story houses on spacious lots, with the camera featuring a lighted church on a nearby hill. As often in Disney's animated features, the words of the theme song set the groundwork for the plot. It is a Christmasy number, with references to an evening that is peaceful, joyful, and calm: "holy is the spirit of this night" and "love unending that shall not cease." However, the words *Jesus* or *Christmas* are not heard. In one of these upper-middle-class homes, a couple opens a gift beneath the tree: a brown-on-brown, female cocker spaniel puppy they name Lady. The dog grows up pampered, but good natured. She chases off rats from the backyard and brings in the morning newspaper. Lady is also free to roam the Victorian neighborhood and spend time with her older friends, a Scottie named Jock and a bloodhound named Trusty. In the evening, she sits by the fire with her owners. "Jim Dear" says that the dog makes their life complete. His wife, "Darling," agrees: "I can't imagine anything could ever take her place in our hearts."

Across the tracks, literally, is another America. The dog Tramp, with no collar, snoozes in a barrel in a rail yard. He rouses himself, then drinks and washes from a water cistern. Tramp may be foot-loose and feral, as well as a freeloader, but he keeps clean and watches his diet—deciding to forgo begging at a French bakery because the fare is too starchy. He is both good-natured and clever, assuming a different identity at different businesses, ethnic restaurants, and homes in order to be fed. After cadging a bone from Tony's Restaurant, Tramp notices a sign of encroaching civilization: a notice posted by the dogcatcher that all unlicensed dogs are to be impounded. Undaunted and dismissive of authority, he unlocks the pound wagon in the street, freeing an English bulldog and Peg, a female of indeterminate breed whose tousled, blondish appearance and world-weary speech suggest a good-hearted floozy who has been around the block several times.

Tramp ensures his friends' escape by leading the dogcatcher on a wild chase, which takes the mutt to a tony part of town he calls "Snob Hill." He surveys the territory with the class-conscious eye of a canine Woody Guthrie, the great American folksinger whose songs include "This Land Is Your Land." Tramp observes that this is the kind of inhospitable neighborhood where there is a lid on every trashcan and a fence around every tree. That is, for outsiders and underdogs like him, there is no food and no place to relieve himself. He wonders what the "leash and collar set" does for excitement.

This is, of course, Lady's neighborhood, where her daily life appears suddenly less idyllic than it has been—for a reason she cannot comprehend. When Jim Dear walks home from work at five o'clock, he seems to ignore her. Inside, Darling doesn't want to walk her or play, preferring to sit in her rocking chair, knitting booties. It is left to Jock to explain to Lady what is about to happen in the household, but before he can get through to her about "the birds and the bees" and "the stork," Tramp arrives to give her a less varnished version about babies. However they get here, he tells her, they are home wreckers; Lady is destined to be pushed aside and to lose her place at center stage. Such low-class agitation is too much for the protective Jock, who tries to drive Tramp off, saying, "We've no need for mongrels and their radical ideas!" Tramp is undeterred and instantly (and overly) familiar, addressing Lady as "Pigeon" or, simply, "Pidge." He warns her that a human heart has only so much room for love and affection, and that when a baby moves in, a dog moves out.

Tramp's predictions are prophetic. Lady is moved from her customary sleeping place on her owners' bed upstairs to a box downstairs. She is perplexed by the inattention, as well as by her loss of status, but she is not jealous. When she is first permitted to look at the baby boy she smiles and wags her tail. But a short getaway for the new parents turns into a disaster for Lady. The babysitter, Aunt Sarah, brings her Siamese cats with her, and the Asian felines with slanted eyes and whiney voices are bent on mischief and destruction. It is all Lady can do to save the pet fish and bird from their predations, an effort that leads to unintended mayhem in the living room. Aunt Sarah assumes the dog is to blame and takes her to the pet shop, where she is fitted with a muzzle.

Lady breaks loose and flees the store, only to be pursued through the poor side of town by three vicious dogs. Tramp, though smaller and outnumbered, heroically drives off Lady's pursuers. "What are you doing on this side of the tracks?" he asks, without malice. After freeing her from her muzzle, Tramp gives Lady a tour of his footloose and collar-free world of generous immigrant families willing to feed him. The ramble concludes with an elegant, romantic spaghetti dinner in the alley behind Tony's. On a night "when the heavens are right," the words of the song "Bella Notte" explain, enchantment will weave its magic spell. Sensing he is on a roll, Tramp extols his life of adventure and excitement, while disparaging "life on a leash." Lady, the voice of practicality, wants to know who would watch over her owners' baby if she joined Tramp's world.

Misadventure and darkness separate Lady from the Tramp, landing the spaniel in the pound. There the consequences of life outside human protection, without collars and licenses, are stark. After the dogs mournfully sing "There's No Place Like Home," one of their companions is led off to be euthanized. Lady, clearly out of place, is greeted by the other dogs as "Miss Park Avenue" and "debutante" and asked if she has landed in the lockup for "putting fleas on the butler." Tramp's female friend Peg sticks up for Lady, saying, "You're too nice a girl to be in this place." Sure enough, her collar and license provide her a "Get out of jail free" card, and the next morning she is returned home. But she is mortified by the experience, further banished and chained to a backyard doghouse, inconsolable despite the best efforts of Jock and Trusty.

Tramp arrives to apologize to Lady for their separation, asking how things are among the "kennel club set." This prompts Jock to brand him a mongrel once again. Yet after Tramp risks his life and freedom by saving the baby from a rat that has invaded the nursery, the pure-blooded terrier admits that he badly misjudged the mixed breed. But Tramp is mistaken for an intruder and turned over to the dogcatcher—saved only through the heroic efforts of the bloodhound Trusty. The matter is resolved by Christmas. Lady and Tramp—now with his own license and collar—are the parents of a litter of puppies. There are three females identical to Lady, and one mischievous, Tramp-like male. The savage is tamed, civilized, and domesticated. Tramp has joined the middle class.

"Images suggesting the saving work of Christ shape the hero of *Lady and the Tramp*," according to Susan Lochrie Graham in

"Some Day My Prince Will Come." The mongrel "protects several characters from danger and releases them from bondage," but, unlike Jesus, "he rescues rather than redeems them. . . . [T]his story, with multiple examples of release from bondage, suggests that true heroism requires not only the desire to help others in trouble, but the willingness to risk one's own safety. But true freedom and love are not found out in the streets, or on the road in search of adventure; the best things in life are found in home, family, and order. . . . These pleasures, although they seem to have something in common with the virtues commended by the story of Jesus," in fact hold up "the value of risky self-sacrifice by rewarding it."

I prefer a more earthbound interpretation of the movie. Tramp represents the best of what America is, or once thought it was— that is, the guy from across the tracks, poor but game, who is not intimidated by anyone. In fact, he has a healthy disdain for the privileged, the pureblooded, and the haughty. Yet, in the end, he no more holds the circumstances of their birth against them than he would have his own mixed blood held against him. In America, with luck, we can be what we make of ourselves. I think Walt Disney saw a lot of Tramp in himself, and in that sense Tramp represents Walt's better angel.

Chapter Twelve

Sleeping Beauty (1959): Not in Death

Sleeping Beauty is yet another piece of evidence—if one is needed—in Disney's case for one of its most enduring themes, namely, that true love conquers all: undiluted evil, class differences, and medieval notions of marriage. It is also an undisguised, if oblique, argument for the eternal promise of resurrection, made in both *Snow White* and *Pinocchio*. In *Sleeping Beauty*'s opening theme, singers croon about finding love in a dream, while acknowledging that "visions are seldom all they seem." The familiar, ornate storybook opens with both the text and the narrator explaining that long ago there lived a good king and queen who hoped for a child for many years until at last their "wish" was granted and a baby girl was born. To celebrate the momentous event, the royal couple invites all in the kingdom, "of both high and low estate," to the celebration. King Stefan invites his friend from the adjoining realm, King Hubert, whose young son, Phillip, is betrothed to the infant princess, Aurora. Three good fairies, older women (perhaps the counterparts of wise men), arrive with their gifts for the blessed princess. Each of these gifts is illustrated by a moving constellation of stars. The first gift, of course (this being Disney), is beauty. The second is the gift of song. But before the third can be announced, the evil witch Maleficent arrives uninvited. Green-skinned and dressed in black, she wears a cowl shaped into demonic horns. She tells the terrified king and queen that she is insulted by her exclusion, especially in light of the fact that even the "rabble" has been included in the festivities. Maleficent's disdain for the feudal lords is based on their benevolent regard for their subjects, regardless of status, a characteristic that leads viewers to identify with them. The witch's "gift" for Princess Aurora is that, on her sixteenth birthday, she will prick her finger on the spindle of a spinning wheel and die. As the curse is pronounced, the image on the screen is the body of a young woman, laid out on a slab in the dark, illuminated by a shaft of light from above. The third fairy, her gift undelivered, tells the distraught king and queen that she cannot undo the witch's curse. However, she can ameliorate it. "Not in death, but just in sleep," the good fairy pronounces, "the fitful prophecy you'll keep. And from this slumber you shall awake, when true love's kiss the spell shall break." True love, the singers emphasize, conquers all. But in the meantime, evil must be combated. The three good fairies agree that the king's order to destroy all the spinning wheels in the kingdom is a futile gesture. What can be done about Maleficent? Reason with her, one suggests. After all, the witch can't be all bad. Oh yes she can, replies another fairy; this witch knows nothing of love, kindness, or the joy of helping others. Some evil is irredeemable, but the good fairies are limited in what they can do, since their magic can only do good. Turning Aurora into a flower would be as ineffective as burning the spinning wheels.

The trio finally hatches a plan to save the princess, albeit at considerable cost to her parents. The fairies decide to give up their magic powers and raise the child as mortals in a peasant cottage deep in the forest, spiriting the baby from the castle in the dark of night. For the king and queen, sad and lonely years follow, although they know the reason for their sacrifice. Maleficent, in her evil domain, rages with frustration as her prophecy goes unfulfilled. She berates her beastly soldiers for their inability to find Aurora. In the woods, the princess grows into a beautiful, blond young woman with a melodious voice and a sweet disposition, happily cleaning the house in which she is raised. On the eve of her sixteenth birthday, the three peasant women want to prepare a surprise party for their charge, so they send the girl off to pick berries. Like modern parents approaching high school graduation, the fairies are wistful. "Why did this day have to come?" asks one.

In the woods, another kind of magic spell is being woven. Aurora is singing with the birds and other woodland creatures, telling them about a dream she has had again and again in which a handsome prince appears. Phillip, the real prince, riding a white horse, hears the singing but, while trying to locate its source, falls from his mount. Aurora sings, "If you dream a thing more than once, it's sure to come true." The young man and woman meet and, of course, he appears to be the man of her dreams. Aurora admits, "I'm really not supposed to speak to strangers—but we've met before." Neither knows that the other is both a royal and their own betrothed. So when they dance and fall in love, it is a love match of independent choice—reinforcing the American paradigm of marriage. Still, the princess modestly flees the prince, saying that if he is indeed the man of her dreams, he should come to meet her that evening at her house.

Things are beginning to unravel at the cottage and the castle. A spat among the fairies has revealed Aurora's presence to Maleficent, and the three good fairies inform the princess that she has been promised in marriage to another. The girl is first reduced to tears by the news, and is then drawn away by the evil witch. At her parents' castle, where preparations are beginning for Aurora's sixteenth birthday and her arranged marriage to the young prince, King Hubert is trying to give his bad news to King Stefan. But before he can reveal that his young son has fallen in love with a peasant girl he met in the forest, Aurora meets her fate. Mesmerized by a mysterious green light, the princess pricks her finger on a spindle and falls into a deadly sleep. All the efforts of the fairies and the sacrifice of her parents are for nothing. Maleficent is not surprised. She cannot be defeated. "Me? The mistress of all evil?"

This turn of events requires a new plan, the fairies agree, especially after they learn that the boy Aurora met in the forest was her intended prince. Needing some time, they put everyone in the castle to sleep—literally, a case of suspended animation. Meanwhile, at their cottage in the woods, the smitten prince is captured by Maleficent's minions and taken to her dungeon. "Why so melancholy?" the witch asks him, taking a sly page from other Disney fairy tales. "A wondrous future lies before you—you, the destined hero of a charming fairy tale come true." She tortures him with the image of his beloved "in ageless sleep." The prince will be an old man by the time he is finally freed from Maleficent's castle to wake Aurora with his kiss. Yes, the witch says with a sarcastic laugh, true love conquers all.

The three fairies come to the rescue, freeing the prince and arming him with an enchanted shield of virtue and a mighty sword of truth. These weapons of righteousness that will enable him to triumph over evil are also heavy with symbolism: The sword looks like a cross, and it glows. The long shield is emblazoned by another large, raised cross. In this scene, my *Orlando Sentinel* colleague Mark Andrews sees a parallel with Ephesians 6, where the apostle Paul urges Christians to "take up the whole armor of God, so that you may be able to withstand on that evil day" against "the spiritual forces of evil." Later in the chapter, they are called on to don "the breastplate of righteousness" and to take up "the shield of faith, with which you will be able to quench all the flaming arrows of the evil one." Notwithstanding these weapons, it is magic that helps cover Phillip's escape from the witch's castle.

The fairies turn boulders hurled at him into bubbles, and arrows into flowers. Maleficent hurls lightning bolts, which the prince fends off by his sanctified shield. In the climax, the witch transforms herself into a fire-breathing dragon, warning the prince that now he will have to contend with "all the powers of hell." What follows is a literal and instantly recognizable reenactment of the battle between St. George and the dragon. Repeatedly, the shield and its cross protect the prince, even after he is thrown from his horse. When he loses his shield, the fairies chant, "O sword of truth fly swift and sure, that evil die and good endure." The prince hurls the sword and strikes the dragon's heart. With Maleficent gone, the young man seeks out his beloved and kisses her. She wakes and, yes, they live happily ever after.

This is the third—and, thankfully, the final—time Disney made what is essentially the same movie. *Snow White, Cinderella,* and *Sleeping Beauty* are all archetypal female rescue fantasies with essentially passive heroines. Each girl is particularly skilled at house cleaning, often with the assistance of small animals. In *Sleeping Beauty,* magic is the moving force, for both good and evil, although Christian imagery and symbolism appear at critical moments. Since the heroine's fate at the hands of Maleficent is in no way altered by her stay in the forest, the girl's sixteen years lost to her parents are wasted years. Aurora, the morning star, is raised from her death-like sleep by true love's kiss. For Disney, this is the final time the classic resurrection motif will be used.

Chapter Thirteen

101 Dalmatians (1961): Black and White

*I*f animal rights activists ever wished for a movie that would help enlist generations of children to their cause, *101 Dalmatians* is it. A woman whose first name literally embodies cruelty, and whose last name forms the word *devil,* wants to kill innocent little animals and turn their hides into fur coats. Although it prefigured the organization by decades, this movie did for People for the Ethical Treatment of Animals (PETA) what *Bambi* did for gun control.

The story takes place in London, "not so very long ago," according to the narrator, a male Dalmatian named Pongo. In terminology PETA supporters would love, Pongo refers to his owner, an unmarried composer named Roger, as *his* "pet." Pongo surveys the cluttered bachelor pad, just off Regent's Park, and decides that what Roger needs is a mate—with a dog. After surveying the field from his upstairs window, Pongo discards a number of candidate pairs of owners and dogs (all of whom resemble each other) as too intellectual, too stodgy, too fancy, too old, or too young. Finally, he spots a female Dalmatian he declares to be the most beautiful creature on four legs. Fortunately, her "pet" is an equally attractive woman. "I'd never find another pair like that, not if I'd looked for a hundred years," Pongo says. The Dalmatian, in life a breed not noted for its intelligence, contrives to have the four parties "meet cute" in the park that afternoon. Six months later, Roger and Anita are seen holding hands beneath a stained glass window, where a Church of England vicar is presiding at their wedding. Outside the church, Pongo and the female Dalmatian, Perdita, consider themselves mated as well, and they are soon expecting a litter of puppies.

Ensconced in their new digs, the family receives a visit from one of Anita's school friends, Cruella De Vil. Unmarried, witty, and worldly, she immediately sets off the alarm of the canine couple, who refer to her as "that devil woman." Not yet an obvious harridan (stay tuned), Cruella blows into the house like a tornado, sporting a luxurious, white fur coat. This new purchase, Cruella tells Anita, represents "my only true love. I live for furs. I worship furs. Is there a woman in all this world who doesn't?" She is a loveless woman and a materialist, all in one villainous package. Anita acknowledges that she too would like to have a fur coat, but there are other things with a higher priority. Cruella asks when the puppies are due, and admires a picture of Pongo and Perdita. Her cigarette smoke wreathes the frame in a patchwork pattern of pelts that is a harbinger of what Cruella hopes will be the future. She comments, admiringly, "Such perfectly beautiful coats." Roger, like the dogs, is no fan of Cruella. He senses the evil and writes a song with her name in the title, with lyrics that compare her to the devil, a vampire bat, and an inhuman beast. Perdita calls her a witch, and wonders what she wants with her puppies. During a late night thunderstorm, fifteen puppies are born, welcomed with much joy. Cruella comes to buy them, but she is rebuffed, and when she is, she declares herself finished with Anita and Roger and vows to get even with them.

101 Dalmatians "offered a defense of family virtue under threat from an evil, greedy villainess," according to Steven Watts, in *The Magic Kingdom*. William McReynolds, in his paper, "Walt Disney in the America Grain," saw something deeper in the character. "Representing ultimate depravity, Cruella bears a foreign name and is meant to be a threat to homely American virtues, such as innocence and good-heartedness. A dissipated member of the Jet Set, with her Tallulah Bankhead voice and her death-skull's head, she is out to disrupt wholesome family life. Her meaning is unmistakable, since she wears a seductive low-necked black dress and carries a big cigarette holder."

The new family is a happy one, made even more content by the presence of a black and white television set. For Disney, this is a fascinating acknowledgment of an emerging competitor for its animated features. The puppies and their parents are nearly mesmerized by the new entertainment medium, watching intently a Western starring a dog, an Alsatian obviously patterned after the 1950s live action hit, "Rin Tin Tin." In an inside joke, the young dogs analyze the action and predict the outcome of the episode, and discuss among themselves how their actions should emulate that of the show's heroic star. Later, while the human couple is walking the canine parents, two dim-witted thugs hired by Cruella break into the house, terrorize the nanny and make off with the puppies.

Roger and Anita are devastated by the loss, which generates tabloid headlines. They contact Scotland Yard for help, but there are no leads. Even Cruella calls, feigning concern. Pongo and his friends decide that in the face of human failure it is up to the dogs to find their own. "The humans have tried everything," says a Great Dane. "Now it's up to us dogs." This self-reliance entails an "all dogs alert," communicated through the "midnight bark" network, in which the message is passed along each evening from dog to dog, throughout London and beyond. The puppies are located in the countryside by a brave but befuddled English sheepdog—a retired British army colonel—in the old De Vil manor house, "Hell Hall." Although down at the heels and believed to be "bewitched," it is where Cruella's two thugs have brought the fifteen puppies and eighty-four other Dalmatian puppies purchased from pet stores. Plaster falls from the ceiling at the least disturbance, but here too there is a functioning TV set. The missing puppies are watching *Flowers and Trees*, a 1932 Disney cartoon (the first in Technicolor) that earned the studio its first Academy Award. Later, the two thugs are watching a quiz show called "What's My Crime?" patterned after the contemporary hit "What's My Line?" hosted by John Charles Daley. Like the puppies, the two malefactors are hypnotized by the television, making it almost impossible for them to respond to Cruella when she arrives to give them orders. She wants them to kill all the puppies, any way they choose, and then skin them for use as fur coats. One thug responds by asking if she has no pity, but he soon makes plain that the pity he asks for has nothing to do with mercy for the puppies. He simply wants to wait until the show he is engrossed in is over—another subtle commentary on the growing hold of television on Western minds.

The puppies—the kidnapped and the purchased—are rescued, and, led by Pongo and Perdita, they begin a long trek back to London. Along the way, other dogs and animals, from a Labrador retriever to a barn full of milk cows, help them through the snowy countryside. Frustrated by her loss, Cruella completes her standard Disney transformation from threatening but subdued woman into an enraged harridan, and gives chase. Sequences that are equal parts frantic and antic ensue, until Cruella and her hirelings are left behind and all of the dogs make their way back to Roger and Anita, who are celebrating Christmas around the tree. Roger's song about Cruella has become his first hit, providing the couple with enough money to adopt all the dogs and establish them on a "Dalmatian plantation."

This is another dog lover's movie, following in the paw prints of *Lady and the Tramp*. Once again the four-footed beings are smarter than the two-footed ones. But in the earlier film, there were bad dogs as well as good dogs, nasty cats and murderous rats. In *101 Dalmatians,* the embodiment of evil is human—and female. While Cruella's sin is covetousness, what makes her grotesque is that she wants to treat pets as if they were wild animals, or domesticated creatures raised for consumption. Anita would never be accepted by PETA because she admits she too would like a fur coat, but not one made from lovable pets. Presumably, by the movie's end she has enough money to afford one.

One of the messages of the movie, released at the dawn of the 1960s, seems to be that an independent woman with no apparent desire to marry and settle down is probably both bad *and* crazy. Cruella represents an alternative role for women in society, a role that at that time was still a caricature.

Chapter Fourteen

The Sword and the Stone (1963): Knowledge Is King

While most dramatic interpretations of T. H. White's *The Once and Future King* (the popular and durable version of the legend of King Arthur, Camelot, and the Round Table) focus on chivalry and combat, Disney's film chooses the first volume of the quartet, *The Sword and the Stone*, in order to focus on learning. In this way the movie becomes more of a children's story, emphasizing study, knowledge, and wisdom as the route to nobility and civilization. But dramatically, it is more of a lesson than a story. In a promotional short accompanying the video of *The Sword and the Stone*, composer Richard Sherman explains that there is a "magic key to the entire picture." He sings from a song written with his brother, Robert, but cut from the final production: "A noggin full of knowledge is the magic key." The reason for this approach to the story may have been strictly commercial. Or it may have had something to do with the lingering effect of the 1957 launch of the Soviet space satellite Sputnik, which provoked a drive for American education to catch up with its Cold War rival.

At the time of *The Sword and the Stone,* the storybook and narrator explain, England was living through a dark age and a time of Darwinian strife. There was no king on the throne to provide order and justice, so the strong preyed on the weak. Only the promise of a miracle—signaled by a shaft of heavenly light in a London churchyard—could save the day. A king and savior would one day remove a sacred sword driven through an anvil and into the stone. Many had tried, but all failed, demonstrating that the miracle had not yet happened. In the forest, the magician Merlin, who can see into the future, grumbles over the absence of plumbing and electricity. The wizard, soothsayer, and prognosticator knows that very important company is coming. Sure enough, young Arthur, a scrawny, eleven-year-old orphan, stumbles into Merlin's cottage, where he is invited for tea. Before much conversation passes between them, the old magician tells the illiterate lad, "You can't grow up without an education."

The boy explains that he has responsibilities at Sir Ector's castle, so Merlin proposes to pack up and follow him in order to be his tutor. Gathering up the cottage, even with the help of magic, provides another opportunity to press home the movie's primary lesson. "Books first," the wizard tells Arthur. Why? Study is important, he explains as the books sort themselves in the air and fly into a carpetbag, followed by everything else in the dwelling. Lest the boy get the wrong idea from the demonstration, Merlin tells him, "Don't you get any foolish ideas that magic will solve all your problems, because it won't." The problem with the period they are living in, the wizard says, is that the world is "all muscle and no mentality." Arthur is uncertain how to reply, since he has little to offer in either category. The real power, Merlin insists, is in higher learning: "Even in these backward, medieval times, you have to know where you are going." The magician orders a full course of study, beginning the next day, at Sir Ector's castle.

Merlin introduces himself to the lord of the manor as the world's most powerful wizard, causing Sir Ector to inquire fearfully whether he indulges in black magic. Not at all, Merlin assures him. "My magic is used mainly for educated purposes." Exhibit A to illustrate the magician's view of feudalism and the present world order is Sir Ector's son and heir, a dim-witted, muscle-bound lout named Kay. It is Kay who will go to London for a jousting tournament to determine England's next king—naturally, a trial of strength. Sir Ector proclaims that jousting is a science. Merlin retorts that it is nothing more than "one dummy trying to knock off another dummy with a bit of a stick." Even so, Merlin tells Arthur, it would be cheating to use magic to win in a tournament.

Entranced by the idea of slaying dragons and griffins, the boy is not yet sold on his mentor's dedication to knowledge. Merlin, having made no headway with traditional learning, proceeds with some magical life lessons. He turns Arthur into small creatures: a fish, a squirrel, and a bird. Through each experience, the magician tries to show the boy how to use his wits to succeed against larger opponents. At one point, Merlin sings, "The strong will try to conquer you, and that is what you must expect—unless you use your intellect." But between these experiences, Arthur also has a day job. He feels a responsibility for his kitchen cleaning duties at the castle, where Sir Ector took him in. Like his female counterparts in earlier Disney films, the boy does not bemoan his lot, and sings while he scrubs and cleans. He even manages to turn the tables on Merlin and teach him about responsibility.

Impatient to move on to the next life lesson, the wizard tells Arthur he will use magic to finish the boy's chores. The boy reminds Merlin of his earlier caveats, that this is the very kind of intervention that sorcery should *not* be used for. "*I'm* supposed to do it," Arthur says. No one will know the difference, Merlin assures him: "Who cares, as long as the work gets done?" But when the pair returns from the woods, where Arthur—as a squirrel—gets a taste of animal attraction, they learn just what can go wrong when such bad choices are made. In a reprise of Mickey Mouse's experience in *Fantasia*'s "Sorcerer's Apprentice" segment, the magic has gotten out of hand and turned the kitchen into chaos. Sir Ector is furious, denouncing Merlin and asserting his authority in his home and castle. "I'll decide what's right and wrong around here!" he thunders, calling Merlin an "old devil." Although his mentor was in the wrong in this instance, Arthur comes to Merlin's defense. "Just because you can't understand something, it doesn't mean it's wrong," the boy says, bursting into tears. Sir Ector can be a petty tyrant, Arthur snaps: "You make all the rules, and nobody can say anything."

Merlin returns to his primary theme: Arthur needs an education. The plan is for the boy to begin with formal lessons, learning to read with the help of the wizard's owl, Archimedes. But formal education—perhaps because it is not very cinematic or very interesting to children—gives way to another lesson from nature, as Arthur becomes a bird and escapes his studies. This time, however, the adversary he encounters in the woods is an evil but daffy witch, and he cannot save himself. Merlin risks his life in a successful battle with the crone, only by dint of his own knowledge and study. The wizard tells Arthur that the effort was worth it, if the boy can see the power that knowledge conveys. While he agrees, it doesn't take long for the prospect of action to turn his young head once again.

As the snow falls, Sir Ector taps Arthur to be squire for his son Kay, now Sir Kay, in the grand tournament in London to determine England's new king. Arthur proudly shows off his new clothes, but Merlin only harrumphs, "A fine monkey suit for polishing boots." He should be using his brains instead of acting as Kay's stooge. The boy is crushed by the wizard's disapproval. "What do you want me to be? I'm a nobody." He is much more than a nobody, as he soon learns. At the tournament, Sir Kay needs his sword, which has been left behind in their room. Arthur rushes back, but finds the inn locked. He spies the sword embedded in the stone in the nearby churchyard, and as he attempts to pull it out he is bathed in a heavenly light, as a choir sings. The sword is clearly enchanted, since the celestial light fades when Arthur lets go of the hilt and returns when he grabs it again.

Arthur removes the sword and takes it to the tournament ground for Sir Kay. But the glowing sword and the fabled inscription cannot be ignored. The crowd rushes to the churchyard to verify that it is the sword that identifies the new king. Both Sir Ector and Sir Kay try to claim the crown for themselves, but when the sword is replaced, they cannot remove it. Arthur is given a chance and, under a shower of starry snowflakes, pulls it from the stone. A voice shouts, "It's a miracle, ordained by heaven. This boy is our king!" The narrator affirms, "So at last the miracle had come to pass in that far off time upon New Year's Day."

Arthur is not so sure: "I can't be a king. . . . I don't know anything about ruling a country." That statement speaks to the film's great weakness. Drama succeeds best when characters are transformed by the action around them. This is especially true of children's literature and nowhere more true than in Disney's animated features. Yet for all of Merlin's hectoring and cajoling, Arthur is never transformed by knowledge or wisdom. He is a questioning—

if not querulous—boy when the movie begins, and not much different when it ends. There are occasional hints of his sense of what is right, but older viewers who know the story of King Arthur are forced to supply their own outcomes. Children who don't know about the monarch and his round table are likely to be left wondering why this boy is so special.

Chapter Fifteen

The Jungle Book (1967): Nature and Nurture

*R*udyard Kipling was the poet laureate of British imperialism and herald of "the white man's burden," the patronizing, racist notion that Europeans and North Americans had the obligation to colonize and "civilize" darker people around the world. Yet he sincerely loved the Indian subcontinent and those, like him, who lived there. Kipling's *Jungle Book* was the last animated feature Walt Disney himself was involved in, and that influence is obvious, according to his nephew Roy. "It is because he was there almost to the very end of it. [He] certainly influenced everything about it," the younger Disney said in a DVD commentary included with *Jungle Book 2*. "It has a kind of milestone quality to it in our own memories and our own history. With *Jungle Book,* he obviously got hooked on the jungle and the characters that lived there."

When Walt put his hand to *The Jungle Book,* most of Kipling's patronizing tone was excised. Inspired by the Mowgli stories, the movie begins with a shot of a village of thatched-roof houses on the edge of a jungle, as slightly ominous music of indeterminate, Eastern origin plays. The tone of the music lightens as the scene shifts into the tropical forest, with shots of ancient stone ruins. Bagheera, the panther and narrator, recalls how a baby's cries and laughter drew him to a riverbank and wrecked wooden boat. The infant is safe in a basket, like Moses. With his parents obviously dead, "man cub's" chances for survival in the jungle are nil. As Bagheera notes, the nearest village is days away and, "without a mother's care, he would soon perish." Still, the panther's first impulse is to walk away and let nature take its course. However, this depicting a Disney view of nature, Bagheera rescues the baby and deposits the basket in front of a den of nursing wolves, somehow confident that these are not predators that would make a quick meal of the young offering. "I knew there would be no problem with the mother, thanks to the maternal instinct," the panther says. The wolf father presents a different issue, given the baby's obviously different parentage, but the mother wordlessly convinces the father to accept the new addition. All adjourn to the den, where any cross-species suckling takes place discreetly offscreen, as with the mythical Romulus and Remus.

Ten years pass, and Mowgli has adjusted well to the jungle. He is gentle and sweet natured, nothing like what the scientific literature indicates about various children raised in the wild. He is also brown, with vaguely Asian features. There is no explanation for why he now walks upright rather than on all fours like his canine brothers and sisters, why he wears a loincloth, or who cuts his hair. "No man cub was ever happier," Bagheera says with a shrug, "yet I knew that someday he would have to go back to his own kind." That day—or night—arrives with a meeting of the wolf pack. Although led by an elder, it is evidently a consensus democracy. The elder explains that the feared tiger, Shere Khan, has been seen in the area. A hater of all things human, the big cat will surely kill Mowgli and, more to the point, all who try to protect him. The wolves nod unanimously in agreement, and the decision is ratified. The good of the group, even in Disney's version of nature, must prevail. Only the unpleasant duty of informing Mowgli's adopted father remains. The wolf objects to the council's decision, which is effective immediately. Mowgli is "like my own son," the wolf insists, and the boy cannot survive alone in the jungle. Alas, he is told, "the strength of the pack is no match for the tiger."

Again, it is Bagheera who comes to the rescue. The panther decides to escort the boy to the nearest village, where he will be safe. As Mowgli rides Bagheera, the panther explains why the boy must leave the jungle. Shere Khan has sworn to kill him because the tiger "hates man," and the big cat will not permit Mowgli to grow into "just another hunter with a gun"—by now a familiar Disney motif. In this sense, given the history of tigers on the Indian subcontinent, Shere Khan is acting rationally and without any evil

intent. But Mowgli says he wants to explain to the tiger that, having grown up in the jungle among animals, he is without predatory
human nature and thus will act differently. No one explains anything to Shere Khan, the panther retorts, which likely accounts for
the fact that the tiger is still alive. Under the circumstances,
Mowgli wouldn't last a day in the jungle, Bagheera says. Yet
Mowgli does not want to leave the jungle, danger notwithstanding.

A tiger is not Mowgli's only foe in the jungle. Kaa, a boa con-
strictor with a hypnotic stare, is kept from consuming the boy by
Bagheera's timely intervention. Mowgli is undeterred by the
brush with extinction, and his stubborn resistance to leaving the
jungle provokes the panther to stalk off, telling the boy that he is
on his own. Naturally, Mowgli falls into bad company, in the person of a large, amiable bear named Baloo. (What a large, furry
bear is doing in the tropical jungle is not explained.) Baloo takes
to the boy and, in the interests of self-preservation, decides that
what Mowgli needs is fighting lessons. These include learning to
roar fiercely, an exercise that brings Bagheera running. Since
Baloo is voiced by the white, Southern actor Phil Harris, it might
not have been surprising to original viewers that the panther
describes the bear as "a shiftless, stupid, jungle bum." If the character had been voiced by a black actor in 1967, such a description
would never have been acceptable; a lazy, white Southerner was
still an acceptable stereotype. The laid-back, good-natured bear
supports Mowgli's determination to avoid the village. "They'll
ruin him," Baloo says, by making a man of him. When Bagheera
asks the bear how Mowgli will survive the tiger, Baloo pledges to
"learn him all he needs to know." After all, the bear boasts, "he's
with me, ain't he?" Baloo explains his laissez-faire philosophy in
a song: "Don't spend your time looking around for something you
want—that can't be found." Nature is abundant, providing all
manner of food with little effort. Learned behavior is fine. If you
hurt your paw on a prickly pear, beware, and don't do it again.
Relax, and don't work too hard. Bagheera is again frustrated, and
abandons Mowgli once more, with the hope the boy can survive
with such a slacker.

"Racial stereotypes in particular organize certain key charac-

ters, including Baloo, the scat-singing, bebop bear," according to
Susan Miller and Greg Rode, in *From Mouse to Mermaid.* "This
racial stereotyping . . . finds its fullest expression in a scene in King
Louie's Jungle kingdom, the decaying abandoned remains of some
now extinct, supposedly 'primitive' culture." Captured by monkeys and chimps, Mowgli now meets a role model even more problematic than Baloo. In a nod to Darwin, the king greets the boy
with an outstretched hand, saying, "Shake, cousin." Louie explains
to Mowgli that his goal is the opposite of the boy's. "I want to be
a man, I want to be like you," the orangutan sings in a jazzy production number. "An ape like me can learn to be human, too."
Louie believes the key to humanity is the ability to make fire, an
arguable point. Baloo and Bagheera team up to rescue Mowgli
before the fire-making skill can be transferred, but not before the
battle with the apes further destroys the ruins.

The portrayal of King Louie and the monkeys, appearing at the
height of the American civil rights movement and a time of fiery
urban unrest, was troubling to some theatergoers and academics,
a controversy that persists. In the turbulent 1960s, when traditional values were under assault, many Americans looked to Walt
Disney for support, Richard Schickel wrote in *The Disney Version.* "The confused middle class expect him not merely to cater
to their values but to articulate them as well," he wrote. Coming
in 1967, "after years of the civil rights movement, the scene in the
Jungle Book is at worst a display of retrograde racist rhetoric
coded as a children's tale, or at best, an insensitive throwback to
earlier standard cartoon stereotypes," wrote Alex Wainer, in the
spring 1994 issue of *Sync: The Regent Journal of Film and Video.*
King Louie's part was voiced by Louis Prima, an Italian American from New Orleans, but to some his voice sounded "black."
The *Orlando Sentinel*'s film critic Jay Boyar agreed that the primates could be perceived as representing African Americans in a
time of turmoil, but he saw no racism in the portrayal. Rather, he
saw King Louie voicing the aspiration of his species to be
accepted as equals. While some might disagree, I think that in the
current environment, a child watching *The Jungle Book* is
unlikely to assume a racial dimension.

After Mowgli's escape, Baloo declares that he wants to adopt the boy. The panther is certain this is a bad idea; the boy must return to his own kind. "You wouldn't marry a panther, would you?" he asks, using another familiar construction from the civil rights era. Bagheera also understands that the bear's lackadaisical approach can be fatal in the wild. "Can't a guy make a mistake?" the bear asks. "Not in the jungle," the panther says. Baloo has no conception of the threat posed by Shere Khan. "He hates man with a vengeance," Bagheera says, "because he fears man's gun and man's fire." Mowgli can't protect himself, the panther argues, and as long as he remains with the bear the boy is in danger. Baloo says he loves Mowgli as if he were "my very own cub."

Bagheera stalks off again, unable to compete with the bear for the boy's affection—reminiscent of a child who prefers the company of an indulgent uncle or grandmother to that of a stern but loving parent. But even Baloo understands that the panther is right about what is best for Mowgli, and, in his own stumbling way, breaks the news that he must go to the village. Betrayed, the boy runs away, into the forest, not far from where Shere Khan has his eye on a young deer. Mowgli, distressed by his predicament, finds himself in the company of four vultures, who are similar in some ways to the crows in *Dumbo*. But, this being the 1960s, the vultures have English accents and sound like the Beatles. They ask the boy if he is sad because, like them, he has no friends or parents. Mowgli says that no one wants him around, and the vultures commiserate. They have hearts and feelings too, and they know what that feeling is like; creatures don't like it when they show up, for obvious (if unstated) reasons.

Finally, Shere Khan confronts Mowgli, who bravely refuses to back down. With the help of his friends Bagheera and Baloo, and his own quick wits, the boy drives the tiger off. But Baloo appears to have died in the battle, and Mowgli is shattered. The panther, without citing the source, consoles the boy, saying, "Greater love hath no one than he who lays down his life for his friend," as organ music plays in the background. The words are from Jesus, in John 15:13, another rare instance of Scripture citation in one of Disney's animated features. As Bagheera goes on to say that the memory of

Baloo's sacrifice and bravery will make the spot a hallowed place, the bear revives, and asks him not to stop such a beautiful eulogy. Although Shere Khan is gone, the issue of where Mowgli belongs still must be resolved. The two animals and the boy make it to the river at the edge of the jungle, where a young girl about Mowgli's age is filling a jug with water. We see that she is Hindu, from the red dot called a bindi on her forehead, and she sings a song about domesticity. Mowgli is curious and creeps toward the bank, attracting the girl's attention. He is smitten, and he follows her as she sashays up the dock toward her home—another classic Disney case of "twitterpation." Although Baloo begs him not to succumb, Mowgli just gives that familiar Disney shrug and goofy grin that acknowledges the inevitability of sexual attraction. Where romance is concerned, nature appears to trump nurture.

Given the source material—Kipling—and Walt Disney's relatively unenlightened views on race, it is surprising that *The Jungle Book* isn't more offensive than it is. There are several reasons for this, I think. The songs, both the music and the lyrics by Richard M. Sherman, Terry Gilkyson, and George Bruns, are transcendent. And the exuberant performances of Phil Harris and Louis Prima are peerless. Beneath and between these classic numbers, there is a serious discussion about what constitutes "human nature." Mowgli thrives in the natural state, and it is only Shere Khan's "evil" nature that threatens the boy. But evil is a human construction. This seems to turn *Bambi*'s premise, that in the wild it is man who equals menace, on its head. In the end, Mowgli accepts that he must return to his own species. Keeping to your own kind is a theme the studio would often revisit in the next three decades.

Chapter Sixteen

Robin Hood (1973): Tax Rebates

*F*or moral filmmakers aiming at a young audience, the Robin Hood story presents a particular challenge: How to present a situation where it is justified to take up arms against an unjust authority. It seems to be the opposite of Jesus' admonition, in a similar situation, to "render unto Caesar what is Caesar's," voiced at a similar time of incipient rebellion. Viewed in a certain light, Robin Hood makes the Judean Zealots' case for revolt against Roman tyranny and oppression. One way Disney gets to navigate this theological thicket is to make the characters in its version of *Robin Hood* animals, providing at least one degree of separation, and to have the creatures speak in both English and Southern accents, the former mostly villains, the latter mostly heroes. Also, the moral deck is stacked as decisively in Robin's favor as it is in the traditional story. There is no opening song, just words on the page of the traditional storybook explaining (for those old enough to read) that King Richard is away and his evil brother, Prince John, is on England's throne. "Robin Hood was the people's only hope. He robbed from the rich to feed the poor." It is the social gospel in action, with a member of the clergy playing a crucial role.

Robin, a fox, and Little John, a bear, are relaxing in Sherwood Forest when they are ambushed by the Sheriff of Nottingham, another bear, who wants to hang them. After they escape, Little John wonders whether their robbing of the rich to feed the poor means they are good guys or bad guys—which is another way of asking whether or not the ends justify the means. Robin recoils at the word *rob*, calling it naughty. The way the outlaw leader sees it, they are just "borrowing" a bit from those who can afford it.

94

Although not the brightest bear in the woods, Little John stumbles into the sophistry in that rationale by replying, "Boy, are we in debt." The pair spots a royal caravan passing through the woods and Robin rubs his hands: "Sounds like another collection day for the poor!" Little John agrees: "Sweet charity!"

Prince John is an insecure, mother-obsessed thumb-sucker, a male lion with no mane, and a crown too big for his head. But even when it is slipping, the prince says, the crown gives him a sense of power. The coach is gilt, and the prince is playing with sacks of gold coins, lauding his "beautiful, lovely taxes." They are en route to the city of Nottingham, "the richest plum of all." His flattering councilor, a snake, compliments his "absolute skill for encouraging contributions from the poor." Prince John agrees, enunciating a philosophy directly opposite of Robin Hood's; he takes from the poor to feed the rich. Although Little John is not so sure about the assault, noting that there is a law against robbing royalty, he and Robin dress as female fortune-tellers and artfully hustle the vain prince. Prince John is easily relieved of his tax receipts and left in his underwear by the two brigands.

In Nottingham, the consequences of Prince John's confiscatory tax policy are evident and dire. Tax dodgers are in stocks and, according to the rooster acting as troubadour and narrator, the people of the town are starving to death. Amid the misery we see Friar Tuck, obviously well fed but wearing patched clothing beneath his brown robe. The "old do-gooder," a badger, goes door-to-door surreptitiously, distributing small amounts of Robin's booty to the needy. "God bless Robin Hood," says an injured blacksmith. However, the sheriff, who is also the prince's enforcer, has been trailing the monk. He shakes down the blacksmith, which enrages Friar Tuck, who denounces the tax collector as "evil" and a "skinflint." The sheriff replies, "Save your sermons, preacher. It ain't Sunday, you know."

Next stop for the sheriff's villainy is the cottage of a poor, widowed rabbit with a house full of children. A seven-year-old boy is having a meager, family birthday party. Inside a single, wrapped box is a farthing coin, all that his mother can afford. The sheriff takes the coin and wishes the weeping boy a happy birthday on behalf of Prince John. On his way out of the cottage, the lawman pauses to take coins from a blind beggar who has come to the door. The beggar is welcomed into the cottage, demonstrating that the poor often have compassion for those worse off than themselves. Their generosity is rewarded, as the beggar turns out to be Robin Hood in disguise, bringing his own birthday gift for the boy, a small bow and arrow. The outlaw brings another gift: hope. He tells the family to keep their spirits up, and promises them that happiness will one day return to their town. The mother rabbit blesses Robin and thanks him for risking so much to keep their hopes alive. Running with his new bow, the birthday boy shouts, "Death to tyrants!"

Prince John's claim to the throne is soon called into more direct question, when he lays a trap for Robin with an archery contest. The prize is a kiss from Maid Marian, the outlaw's highborn, childhood sweetheart. Robin wins, and is then seized by the prince's soldiers, although he manages to proclaim his love for Marian before he is sentenced to death. When Prince John declares him a traitor to the crown, the outlaw retorts that the crown belongs to Richard, raising support from the other animal spectators. A wild escape brings Robin and his followers back to Sherwood Forest, together with Maid Marian, his true love. As they stroll together through the woods, a song plays, noting that life is brief, but when it's over, love lives on. At the encampment, however, it is insurrection that is in the air. "A pox on a phony king of England," shouts one animal. Another song complains that while Prince John taxes the people to pieces and robs them of their bread, "King Richard's crown keeps slipping around that pointy head." Even in his castle, the prince senses he is being humiliated.

Still, Prince John continues to turn the screws, trebling the taxes and jailing all those who cannot pay. In prison, too, the poor try to comfort one another. Outside, Friar Tuck decides to toll the church bell, to the same end. "We must do what we can to keep their hopes alive," he tells the mouse who serves as organist and sexton, even though the prince is taxing the heart and soul of the people. The church is like the alms box, Tuck says—empty. At this, the sexton's wife goes to their bed and, from beneath the mattress, retrieves a farthing coin for the poor. Friar Tuck is touched by the gesture from the poor church mouse. "No one can give more than that," he says. "Bless you, little sister." If this sounds familiar to those who know their New Testament, it should. In Mark 12, a few verses after Jesus tells the Pharisees to "give to the emperor the things that are the emperor's," he denounces those who "devour widows' houses." Later, in a scene at the treasury, Mark writes, "Many rich people put in large sums. A poor widow came and put in two small copper coins, which are worth a penny. Then [Jesus] called his disciples and said to them, 'Truly I tell you, this poor widow has put in more than all those who are contributing to the treasury. For all of them have contributed out of their abundance; but she out of her poverty has put in everything she had, all she had to live on.'" Naturally, this is the moment the sheriff chooses to stride into the sanctuary and confiscate the coin. Tuck denounces the sheriff—and Prince John—and orders him out of the church. This provokes a warning from the lawman that the priest is getting so preachy that he is in danger of "preaching yourself into a hang-man's noose." In the land where Thomas Becket and Thomas Moore had and would forfeit their lives for their beliefs, this is no idle threat. Still, Tuck is uncowed. Outside the church he attacks the sheriff with his staff, which is no match for the sheriff's sword. The friar is arrested for high treason and led away in chains.

Tuck's arrest presents Prince John with an opportunity. He will hang him in the town square, certain that Robin Hood will attempt a rescue. But there will be no execution. Little John frees Tuck from the cell where he is shackled. "Thank God," he says. "My prayers have been answered." While Little John has been freeing prisoners, Robin has been stealing Prince John's treasure. Fleeing the prison, Tuck exclaims, "Praise the Lord and pass the tax rebates!" *Robin Hood* ends at the front door of Tuck's church, where the outlaw and his true love have been joined, pardoned, and blessed by a returned King Richard, wearing a white doublet featuring a large gold cross.

I never watched this film before beginning to research this book. It may have been because of the timing of its release, roughly coinciding with the Watergate scandal and the subsequent impeachment hearings. The idea of a cartoon version of Robin Hood, using animal characters, must have seemed hopelessly insipid to me then. What I found watching *Robin Hood* thirty years after its release was a small revelation. The explicit portrayal of Christianity's social gospel and radical class politics, the venality of the rich and the nobility of the poor, were striking. All of these may have been a result of Walt Disney's absence from the film's production, since in these respects they run counter to his guidelines. The source material may have provided the narrative roadmap, and it may have been released three years after the decade ended, but this is the studio's '60s movie.

Chapter Seventeen

The Fox and the Hound (1981): Nature and Nurture Redux

A parable of friendship struggling against natural law, *The Fox and the Hound* begins untraditionally for Disney, without a storybook flipping open or a narrator or theme song setting the stage or outlining the plot. Instead, the camera pans through a misty forest, with only the sounds of the wild. A fox with a small kit in her mouth is being pursued by baying hounds, which seem to be gaining on their prey. After breaking from the woods onto farmland, the fox pauses at the base of a fence post. She licks her offspring one last time, and heads off over a hill to draw off the hounds. Two shots are heard—signaling the same dire fate as Bambi's mom.

Observing the action from above is an old owl, Big Mama. In nature, the helpless kit would be a quick meal for such a predatory bird, but in this case the owl sees the situation as an opportunity for a therapeutic intervention. She takes the baby fox to a lonely farmwoman, the Widow Tweed, who adopts it as a pet, naming it Tod, feeding it with a bottle, and giving it a collar. Although soon domesticated, the young fox has difficulty suppressing some instinctive urges, as when he eyes some chicks in the barn in a way that enrages a protective mother hen and sets off a wild pursuit. At about the same time, in a hunter's cabin next to the farm, a new puppy arrives to join an older dog, named Chief. The young bloodhound, named Copper, is completely inexperienced, but his sense of smell is already superior to Chief's. Copper follows his canine instincts and tracks his way to Tod, who is chasing a butterfly. When he locates the fox, he makes a feeble, immature attempt to howl. Tod asks why he does that, and the puppy replies that it's because he is a hound dog. "We're supposed to do that when we find what we've been tracking."

The two young creatures have no notion that they are natural enemies, so they act as if they should be friends. Tod suggests that Copper would be good at playing hide-and-seek, and that they tussle. The owl observes the interaction with amazement, and sings a song called "Best of Friends." For the funny pair, she sings, life is a happy game; their friendship blinds them to their natural boundaries. "If only the world wouldn't get in the way, if only people would just let you play," Big Mama sings, as the two animals are breaking all the rules. When these idyllic moments pass, she wonders, will the young animals' friendship last? Tod and Copper think so, pledging to be best friends forever. But Copper's owner doesn't like the idea of the puppy running free, so he ties him up next to the older dog. A visit to the hunter's spread by Tod, looking for his friend, sets off a chase after the young fox by Chief and the hunter, named Amos. The hunter assumes the fox is following his own nature, trying to eat his chickens, and he chases the animal back to his neighbor's farm, threatening to blast the widow's pet with his shotgun the next time he sees him. The issue is moot for the moment, since Amos is about to take both his dogs on a long hunting trip, where Copper will learn to fill his role in life.

The next day, Tod wonders whether the two animals will still be friends when Copper returns in the spring. Big Mama asks, in a Socratic way, if the fox learned anything from his brush with death at the hands of Chief and the hunter. His friend would never hunt him down, the fox insists. The owl sings a song that advises that the fox's choices are "education or elimination." Lack of education about his natural enemy will lead to the fox's death, she informs him. Tod resists the notion that Copper will become his enemy, even after the owl and other birds open the door to the hunter's shed and Tod sees that it is lined with animal pelts—which could include that of the fox's own mother. Because of his nature, Copper is sure to return as a trained hunting dog, a real killer, Big Mama warns. Tod persists in his idealism and naïveté; Copper will never change. The owl says she hopes he is right, but it is clear that she is certain he is wrong. The two animals will be friends forever,

Tod says. "Forever is a long, long time," Big Mama says, "and time has a way of changing things."

Meanwhile, Copper *is* changing—and growing—and he soon supersedes Chief in the open fields. Where the old dog smells nothing, Copper flushes quail, which are blasted offscreen, leaving a shower of feathers. When the dogs and the hunter return, it is Copper who rides in the front seat of the car with Amos. Tod, now also grown into a young adult, comes to pay his friend a visit. The hound says he is glad to see the fox, quickly adding that Tod shouldn't be there, that he's going to get them both in a lot of trouble. The fox wants reassurance that they are still friends, but Big Mama seems to be right. Those days are over, Copper tells him. "I'm a huntin' dog now." Tod should go, Copper says, gesturing to the Chief, sleeping next to him. "You're fair game, as far as he's concerned."

Chief does wake, setting off a chase after the fox, this time involving Copper as well as Amos. It is a sequence that nearly replicates the film's opening sequence in which Tod's mother dies. While the fox is able to give the older dog the slip, hiding in a stack of railroad ties, he is not able to elude his old friend. Copper is torn at his discovery, and hesitates. He doesn't want to see the fox killed, he tells him, so he decides to let him go "this one time." Chief is not so charitable when he stumbles onto Tod, chasing him onto a train trestle. But the unexpected arrival of a train sends the old dog off the bridge, in what seems like a fatal fall. Copper discovers Chief in the creek below and realizes the cost of the favor he did for his childhood friend by going against his nature and his kind. The hound looks up at Tod, still on the trestle, growls, and then vows, "If it's the last thing I do, I'll get you for this!" Chief only has a broken leg, and is basking in the attention it engenders, which does nothing to relieve the guilt Copper feels. "It's all my fault," Copper tells his hunting companion. "I shouldn't have let Tod go." The fox "almost killed Chief, and I'm going to get him."

The Widow Tweed understands how irrevocably things have changed for Tod, and decides that the only way her pet will survive her neighbor's wrath and his dog's nature is to return the fox to the wild. She removes his collar and frees him in a nearby, fenced-off nature preserve. At first uncomprehending and disoriented by this abandonment, Tod soon becomes acclimated and, in short order, falls for a female fox named Vixey. But it is too soon in the movie for them to live happily ever after, for the vengeful hunter has figured out where the woman has taken Tod. Armed with his shotgun and leg traps, and accompanied by an equally vengeful Copper, the hunter disregards the "No Trespassing" sign and barbed wire fence that protect the game reserve.

When the inevitable confrontation occurs, Tod sends Vixey to their burrow for safety, and faces Copper. The two old friends square off, baring their teeth, snarling, biting, and chasing one another as if they had never met. Tod flees to Vixey in their burrow, trapped by Copper at the front entrance and Amos at the back, who is setting a fire. (Like *Bambi*, *The Fox and the Hound* will not do much to enhance the image of hunters.) A frantic breakout leads to a chase and a waterfall. There the foxes are spared from their tormentors when a huge, fierce black bear attacks Amos. Although overmatched, Copper instinctively comes to his master's aid, only to be tossed aside by the bear. From a safe place, Tod hears the pained cry of his old friend and hesitates only for an instant before coming to his rescue. The two smaller animals' assaults on the bear allow Amos to escape, but when the bear turns on Tod, the two crash down a long, rocky waterfall. Later, Copper discovers Tod, bedraggled but alive, in the shallows. Before he can thank him, however, the fox is looking up at the barrel of Amos's shotgun. But friendship and gratitude will not be denied this time. Copper interposes himself between his master's weapon and his friend. Amos lowers the barrel and says, "Let's go home." The fox and the hound smile at one another; they may not be friends, but they won't be enemies.

For anyone—black or white—who grew up in the American South in the pre-civil rights era, *The Fox and the Hound* must have a particular poignancy—and relevance. In this rigidly segregated region, especially in rural areas, it was not uncommon for black children and white children to be friends and to play together. These relationships often lasted until the approach of adolescence, when the mores of the time wrenched them into separate and inherently unequal worlds. True, they were not, like the fox and hound, predator and prey. Yet the two races often existed in a dynamic that made them economic and political adversaries; white superiority required black inferiority. More critically, it required a white monopoly of force, including lynching, to ensure black powerlessness. In *The Fox and the Hound,* I believe it is no coincidence that the puppy, Copper, speaks with the accent of a white Southerner, and that the wise owl, Big Mama, is voiced by Pearl Bailey, a popular African American entertainer. Yet this movie's message of hope in the face of adversity is not exclusive to the American South in the first two-thirds of the twentieth century. The lessons of nurture trumping nature would be equally clear—the parable equally applicable—to a child or parent from any bicultural environment that is freighted with historical grievance and inequality: the Balkans, South Africa, Northern Ireland, Cyprus, or the Middle East. As human beings, the film says, our better selves can triumph.

Chapter Eighteen

The Black Cauldron (1985): Contains Occult Material

*T*he occult is unvarnished and front-and-center—dark, evil, and creepy—in *The Black Cauldron*. Its heady brew bubbles with spells, witches, griffins, gremlins, an enchanted sword, a clairvoyant pig, people who used to be frogs, and a furry, forest creature who speaks in the third person and seems to have been lifted from J. R. R. Tolkien. The Judeo-Christian construct that frames most of Disney's animated features is wholly absent in this pagan fantasy, rated PG and without any saccharine songs. For once, conservative critic Perucci Ferraiuolo had something real to work with beyond his fervid imagination, although as usual he managed to overdo it. "*The Black Cauldron*," Ferraiuolo wrote in *Disney and the Bible,* "is a melting pot of voodoo, black magic, Satanism, witchcraft and just enough Santeria thrown in to glorify the gods and goddesses of the occult. . . . The exaltation of sorcery and black magic in the film . . . is virtually gratuitous."

Over inky, stormy skies and ominous music, the narrator intones that, according to legend, there was once a king in the mystical land of Prydain who was so evil and cruel that "even the gods feared him." Because no prison could contain him, the king was dispatched—alive—into molten metal, where his "demonic spirit" was transformed into a great, black cauldron. Evil men searched for the hidden pot for centuries, because they knew that the cauldron's owner would acquire the power to reanimate an army of the dead and, with his legions of newly immortal soldiers, conquer the world.

This all seems very far away from a sunny, green clearing where an old man and his young assistant tend their farm. But the old man senses in his bones that something is wrong, something having to do with the Horned King, the land's current monarch and a "black-hearted devil." For the farmer's young helper, Taran, any dramatic change from his menial role would be welcome. "I'm a warrior, not a pig keeper," he declares to the farm animals. Taran's only concern is that the wars will end before he has had an opportunity to fight and to distinguish himself as a great warrior. "War isn't a game," his master cautions. "People get hurt."

Hen Wen, the pig, is more than a farm animal. It can see the future, and may know how to locate the Black Cauldron. The old man tells Taran to take the pig to the hidden cottage on the edge of the forbidden forest, for safekeeping from the Horned King. When the lad boasts that he is not afraid to fight the villain, his master offers another warning, that "untried courage is no match for his evil." Taran assures the old man that he won't fail in his mission.

In his castle, the Horned King is equally determined that Taran will fail. The skull-faced monarch is certain that, in short order, the Black Cauldron's "evil power will course through my veins," and its deathless legions will worship him. "How long have I thirsted to be a god above mortal men," he declares. Taran, in the woods, has his own, slightly less grandiose dream of glory, namely, to become a great warrior. During his reverie, Hen Wen wanders off and is soon plucked from the forest by one of the Horned King's two griffins. Taran tracks the flying dragons to the Horned King's castle, finding it full of thugs, gremlins, and snarling dogs, celebrating in a great room. Their leader materializes supernaturally, in an explosion of lightning and fire, prepared to extort a vision of the Black Cauldron from the defiant pig. Tumbling into the room, Taran convinces Hen Wen to provide the vision to save the animal's life.

An accident enables the boy to free the pig, redeeming his earlier failure, but he is recaptured and placed in a dungeon. Taran's imprisonment provides the opportunity for some introspection, in particular the hollowness of his earlier boasts. Just as this insight dawns, a glowing orb appears in the cell and a young woman pushes up a stone from the floor, climbs up, and introduces herself as Princess Eilonwy. She asks the boy if he is a lord or a warrior.

With no one present to contradict him, Taran could easily claim either title, but he has learned his lesson and introduces himself as an assistant pig keeper. Eilonwy voices her disappointment, but both set off to find a way to escape. Instead, they stumble into the burial chamber of an ancient king, where Taran discovers a gleaming sword. The weapon, he quickly learns, is enchanted. Whenever he faces an enemy in combat, the adversary the castle thugs call "pig boy" is invincible. Taran becomes intoxicated with the power that flows from the glowing blade. His dream of valor is realized, as he leads the princess and a luckless minstrel to freedom.

Glory or no, there is still the matter of Taran's primary responsibility to Hen Wen, the prophetic pig. The trio of escapees knows that if they do not find the Black Cauldron before the Horned King, they will all be killed. As with the ring in Tolkien's trilogy, the embodiment of unbridled power, the cauldron must be destroyed in order to save the world. A series of misadventures with fairies and a whirlpool leads Taran and his companions to the domain of three witches who know the whereabouts of the Black Cauldron. But the only way they will give it to Taran is if he will give the witches his enchanted sword of his own free will. The leader of the witches makes certain the boy knows the cost he is asked to pay to serve the greater good. With it, she reminds him, "you could be the greatest of warriors." Taran is willing to make the sacrifice: "I offer my dearest possession for the Black Cauldron."

The ground shakes and cracks open as the cauldron emerges, spewing fire. Although they now have the evil object, the witch leader informs them that it cannot be destroyed. Its evil powers can be neutralized only if a living being voluntarily climbs into it, an act that would mean certain death. Sacrificing an enchanted sword, a possession, is one thing; giving up your life is quite another. Even here, in a frankly occult tale, Disney writers and animators resort to a resurrection motif. Christians believe that Jesus knew he would have to die in order to "neutralize" the sins of the world. As the three companions and their fairy guide sit around the evening campfire, they are glum. The fairy says that there is nothing for Taran to do but go back to feeding pigs—even though he is still one pig short. He gets no rise from the boy. "Without my sword, I'm nothing," he says, "just an assistant pig keeper." *Sic transit gloria.* It is up to Princess Eilonwy to preach the Disney gospel, even in this godless world. You *are* somebody, she insists. "You must believe in yourself," she tells him. "I believe in you." The support session is interrupted by the Horned King's griffins, which have been trailing the trio in hopes of locating the Black Cauldron.

In a grotesque parody of biblical resurrection, the Horned King takes possession of the Black Cauldron at the castle and begins to call forth the dead of centuries past. A green mist seeps from the container and brings to life skeletons buried throughout the castle, organizing them into fighting ranks. Taran knows he must give his life to stop the king's malign conquest, but before he can, a companion from the forest named Gurgi intervenes. The creature, which has shown cowardice in the past, says that it would be wrong for Taran to die, since he has friends. Gurgi, with no friends, is a better choice, so he throws himself into the cauldron. The conquering legions die (again) in their tracks, and the Horned King is sucked into the Black Cauldron, which sinks through the floor of the castle. Even without his enchanted sword, Taran demonstrates his courage as he helps his friends escape in a boat from the burning, collapsing castle. Soon after they wash ashore, the cauldron surfaces nearby. Taran starts to wade out toward the bobbing pot, when the three witches appear in the sky above. "He's got what he wanted, and still he's not satisfied," their leader says. They want the cauldron back, and offer the boy another trade: the glowing sword, for a warrior. Taran looks longingly at the glowing weapon, hanging in the air before him, and rejects the proposition. "I'm not a warrior, I'm a pig boy. What would I do with a sword?" He offers them an alternative: the cauldron for the life of his friend, Gurgi. At first, the witches say that is impossible, but in a whirlwind the cauldron is gone, leaving in its place what appears to be the creature's body. Is this sequence yet another intentional or unintentional reference to the resurrection? As happens in Disney films, heroic characters who seem to give their lives to save others often turn up alive. So it is with Gurgi, who revives.

Beneath all of *The Black Cauldron*'s hocus-pocus is the story of a young man coming to terms with what he does, and how that defines who he is. At the end of the film, Taran does not turn out to be a long-lost foundling prince. He is a pig keeper at the beginning of the movie and a pig keeper when it ends. His courage and honesty and willingness to sacrifice—like Gurgi's—come from within. Neither God nor stars nor fairy godmothers intervene in his life to transform him, and the one thing that does make him something else—the enchanted sword—he willingly gives away.

Chapter Nineteen

Shorts: Pagans, Jews, and Christians

*B*efore there were Disney animated features there were "shorts"—at first silent and black-and-white—drawn by Walt himself. These evolved into immensely popular color cartoons and, finally, to the full-length movies. Gradually, as the features became a studio staple, production of the cartoons and shorts trailed off, except for seasonal specials. But until they faded from screens, the shorts played a significant role in the Disney canon—and its balance sheet. An early color cartoon, *Flowers and Trees,* which earned an Academy Award in 1932, featured talking trees, prefiguring the controversial willow in *Pocahontas.* For the most part, religion and the spiritual realm were off-limits for the cartoons and "featurettes," as the fifteen- to twenty-five-minute films were sometimes called. An exception is *Skeleton Dance* (1929), a black-and-white cartoon based on Saint-Saens's *Dance Macabre,* which included a portrayal of skeletons rising from their graves. Another exception is *Goddess of Spring* (1937), which retold the Greek myth of the goddess Persephone. "The introduction of Greek mythology into Disney's works was the precursor of his embracing a wide range of anti-biblical themes, including black magic, witchcraft, sorcery and mysticism," wrote Perucci Ferraiuolo in *Disney and the Bible. Goddess of Spring* was not a success "with Bible-believing Christians, who knew who created the earth and who continue to care for it and for what reasons." *Father Noah's Ark,* a 1933 Silly Symphonies release, passed without significant controversy. This version of the Genesis story begins with construction of the vessel nearly complete, eliminating any need to portray a dialogue between God and Noah. However, when the

109

storm rages, Noah, his sons, and his daughters-in-law beseech the Lord, on their knees and waving their arms, to deliver them. (The Noah story is so appealing to animators that Disney has done it twice since, including a segment in *Fantasia 2000*.)

In a 1937 interview with *Time* magazine, Walt Disney insisted—as he did throughout his career—that there was no deeper meaning to his cartoons and shorts. "We tried consciously to put some social meaning into one of our cartoons in the Silly Symphonies series, but it was a tremendous flop," he said, a reference to a telling of the King Midas story called *The Golden Touch* (1935).

If there was no meaning in the cartoons, there was some meanness, whether intended or unintended. Like other studios of the time, Disney produced at least half a dozen cartoons lampooning Africans and African Americans. During the 1930s, Africans were regularly portrayed by various studios as cannibals with big lips and bones through their noses. African Americans were shuffling crows and obsequious stable boys, maids, and mammies. In a more benign portrayal, popular jazz musicians such as Cab Calloway sometimes appeared in Disney cartoons.

If Disney had no compunction about caricaturing Africans and African Americans, there was good reason for the studio to sidestep religion, as the studio's experience in 1933 with *The Three Little Pigs,* from the Silly Symphonies series, demonstrated. The film was a huge success, "acclaimed by the nation," wrote Bob Thomas, in *American Original.* "The wolf was on many American doorsteps, and 'Who's Afraid of the Big Bad Wolf?' became a rallying cry." The song, wrote Kathy Merlock Jackson, in *Walt Disney: A Bio-Bibliography*, "was perfectly timed so that it struck a chord with audiences who responded to the wolf as a symbol of the threat they were facing—the Depression. . . . If the three pigs could outwit the wolf, Americans could beat the Depression." The third pig, the smart one, sang "I have no chance to sing and dance, for work and play don't mix." As Richard Schickel observed in *The Disney Version,* the song's philosophy was straight out of Herbert Hoover, "stressing self-reliance, the old virtues of solid, conservative building and of keeping one's house in order." Despite its content, the new Roosevelt administration, which had just defeated Hoover, made the song its unofficial anthem.

However, *The Three Little Pigs* struck a sour note, at least for Jews. In a critical sequence the wolf disguises himself as an obviously Jewish peddler, with a large hooked nose, bushy black beard, and a Yiddish accent. The American Jewish Congress called the characterization "vile" and "revolting." In response, Roy Disney wrote the organization's director, on behalf of himself and his brother Walt: "We have a great many Jewish business associates and friends and certainly would avoid purposely demeaning the Jews or any other race or nationality. . . . I regret that it is impossible to eliminate this scene from the picture. . . . It seems to us that this characterization is no more than many well-known Jewish comedians portray, themselves, in vaudeville, stage, and screen characterizations." John Culhane, of New York University, recently suggested that the use of the Jewish stereotype in *The Three Little Pigs* was not a slight to Jews but a positive reference to the trust most Americans of the time had in Jewish peddlers. After World War II, the sequence was reedited to make the wolf into a Fuller Brush man, with what sounds like an Irish accent.

This episode is usually the starting point in any discussion of whether Walt Disney was himself an anti-Semite. Opinion on this point remains divided to this day. "Disney appears to have shared, in mild form, some of the anti-Semitism that was common to his generation and place of origin," Richard Schickel wrote in *The Disney Version*. "His studio was notably lacking in Jewish employees." Some claim that his attitudes were formed when he was a child, subject to dinner table diatribes against international Jewish financiers by his father, Elias. Others assert that Walt was resentful toward some New York film distributors he dealt with early in his career, that he was infuriated at Jewish writers and animators who joined the 1941 strike at Disney, and that he held grudges against the Jewish studio owners who were his chief competitors. Walt sent his younger daughter, Sharon, to the Westlake School for Girls in Holmby Hills at a time when the school, for the most part, excluded Jews. His older daughter, Diane, made her debut at the Las Madrinas Ball, decades before any Jewish girls were admitted.

Marc Eliot, in *Walt Disney: Hollywood's Dark Prince,* quotes Walt making an anti-Semitic remark about Robert Morganthau, Franklin Roosevelt's Treasury Secretary, over a billing dispute for a wartime training film the studio produced for the government. "Disappointment and resentment seemed to bring out his latent anti-Semitism," according to Leonard Mosley's biography, *Disney's World,* including using a Yiddish accent to make a point about Jews. "Walt was prone to remarks about Jews, I guess like everyone else," recalled animator Ward Kimball in a 1986 interview with Michael Barrier (posted on his Web site, michaelbarrier.com).

But screenwriter Maurice Rapf, who worked on *Cinderella,* defended Disney. "He knew I was Jewish," he told interviewers in *Tender Comrades,* "but I don't think he was an anti-Semite." Others echoed his brother Roy's letter to the American Jewish Congress, pointing to Walt's many longtime Jewish coworkers and friends—who vigorously disputed the charge—and the business relationships he maintained throughout his life. They also cited the fact that in 1955 he was named Man of the Year by the Beverly Hills chapter of B'nai B'rith. Biographers Katherine and Richard Greene take the same basic anecdotes recounted by other, critical researchers and conclude that the allegations of Walt's anti-Semitism are a myth. "How do myths like Walt's supposed anti-Semitism begin?" the Greenes asked, in an essay for the official Disney Web site.

> Did Walt make offhand comments about the Jewish union members during the painful strike of 1940? Likely. Might some of his executives have harbored anti-Semitic feelings that were wrongly ascribed to Walt himself? Very possibly. Did some of his early cartoons—notably "Three Little Pigs"—contain the kind of unpleasant Jewish caricatures that were common to many cartoon studios at the time? Certainly. Did a few Jewish men who had difficult relationships with Walt speculate that the reason was because they were Jewish? Also yes. Does all this add up to an anti-Semite? Not by any means. In fact, the authors of this essay are Jewish, and from the perspective of a decade of research into Walt Dis-

ney have looked carefully through the record—letters, memos, conversations with reliable sources—for any evidence that Walt may have harbored a dislike of Jews. . . . Even when Sharon dated a young Jewish man, her parents didn't voice any objections.

Absent convincing evidence to the contrary, I do not sense in Walt Disney the kind of instinctive, vitriolic, intellectual anti-Semitism of someone like Henry Ford—whom Walt admired for other reasons. Rather, I think it is more likely a combination of his early-twentieth-century, middle-American prejudice and the hard-knuckled, rough-and-tumble atmosphere of the movie business in New York and Hollywood, where Jews and other immigrants often had the upper hand. If there is a spectrum of anti-Semitism, I tend to be more understanding—if not forgiving—of that manifestation born of pure economic competition.

Johnny Appleseed, a 1948 short based on the life of the legendary John Chapman, provided another opportunity to incorporate biblical faith into a narrative. The young man is first seen at his farm outside Pittsburgh in the early years of the nineteenth century, harvesting apples. As he does, he sings a song, "The Lord Is Good to Me." In it, the farmer thanks God for all the things that have been given to him, like the sun and the rain, which make his apples grow. But Johnny feels a stirring, as he watches the wagon trains of pioneers heading west, past his orchard. He would like to join them, but as a scrawny fellow, he feels he is not hardy enough to go. "That's when a miracle happened," according to the narrator. Johnny's guardian angel appears, in the form of a grizzled frontiersman in buckskin and coonskin cap. The angel tells the young man that he has all it takes to become a pioneer: faith, courage, and a level head. When Johnny says he has no gear, the angel hands him a sack of seeds, a cooking pot that doubles as a hat and, "for pretty darn good readin' there ain't nothin' finer than your book." The book, of course, is a large, black Bible with an embossed cross on the cover (which is also the Disney collectors' souvenir pin from the film). Thus equipped, Johnny sets out for the West, with no knife and no gun. As he plants his first orchard, small woodland creatures scamper around his Bible, and take to him as if he were St. Francis of Assisi. In the decades that followed, the narrator explains, Johnny succeeded because "he was planting his own boundless faith." Forty years later, the guardian angel returns to take his now white-bearded charge to heaven, telling Johnny that his work on earth is finished. They leave his "mortal husk" leaning against a tree, a smile on his face. In addition to his legacy of apples, Johnny leaves faith and love behind. The white clouds in the sky, the narrator says, are apple blossoms from John's heavenly orchard.

The most explicitly "Christian" animated short film made by Disney studios is *The Small One,* produced in 1978. In the film, a boy living in the arid countryside of first-century Judea has an old donkey, Small One, that he loves. As the twenty-five-minute film begins, the boy's voice is heard singing over the credits, to the donkey. The song seems to be about the youngster and the animal, but as the film unfolds it becomes apparent that it is about something much more. Somewhere a friend is waiting for you, he sings, who needs you to make the day better. There is a place for each small one—"God planned it that way." Give, while you are able, to someone lesser than yourself, because each being brings a needed gift.

The boy loves the animal, and Small One returns that affection. The other donkeys in the stable are jealous, since the boy's pet is no longer able to pull its weight when the family goes to gather firewood in the wilderness. The boy tries to cover for Small One, but his father tells him that animal can't work enough to justify what he eats. Since the donkey's strength is gone, the father says, Small One must be taken to the city and sold. The boy is disappointed, but asks that he be permitted to take the donkey to the city to make certain Small One will find a good home. In the stable, he sings another song to the animal to comfort him, promising to find a new owner who will be "someone special." That someone special, the lyrics suggest, is not just a good donkey owner. It is someone who will be a constant companion, providing a friendly face; a gentle presence who will share laughter and tears; someone who will need you and love you, even after it is time to say goodbye. Sound familiar? As if to punctuate the point, divine shafts of moonlight stream down through the stable roof onto the boy and the animal as the song ends.

In the walled city, possibly Jerusalem (or perhaps Sepphoris, near Nazareth), no one seems to want the creature, except for his hide. The merchants and vendors in the city, who look more like medieval Arabs or Ottoman Turks than first-century Judeans, scoff at the boy's offer to sell the donkey. Offended, the boy insists to one prospective buyer that Small One is "gentle and kind. And good enough for a king's stable!" The dispirited boy and his donkey wander the streets, both collapsing into sleep in an alley as night falls. They are awakened as an unnamed man wakens them gently, saying, "I need a gentle donkey, to carry my wife to Bethlehem." Both the boy and the donkey know instantly that this is the right match. Paid a piece of silver for his playmate, the boy bids the donkey farewell, urging him to "Be strong of foot and follow your new master." The last scene in the film depicts a silhouette of Joseph leading Mary on Small One toward Bethlehem. A single star above them brightens, radiating lines that form a large cross. The word "Jesus" is never spoken. "We didn't need to say the name—it's obvious," said Don Bluth, the film's writer and director, noting that the donkey's face brightens when the sale is made. "You feel good about where the donkey is going." As for the lyrics in both songs, Bluth said they are "close to what I believe. It's a theology to which I subscribe."

The Small One was produced during the period of company drift, between the death of Walt Disney in 1967 and the arrival of Michael Eisner in 1984. The film had a relatively short shelf life, appearing in theaters in 1978 with a rerelease of *Pinocchio* and then sporadically on the Disney Channel. Ron Miller, Walt's son-in-law, was in charge of the studio at the time. He said that *The Small One,* based on an original story by Charles Tazewell, was a story with "heart," according to John Canemaker, in his book *Nine Old Men and the Art of Animation.* Bluth, who recalled that he was "working my way up the ladder" at the time at Disney, later went on to do *The Land before Time, An American Tail,* and *The Secret of NIMH* for different studios. He had a tight budget for the Disney short, which he said explained why he wrote the lyrics with a partner and why the boy in *The Small One* looks so much like Mowgli in *The Jungle Book.*

Every December, TV screens are filled with animated Christmas tales for children—from *A Charlie Brown Christmas* and *Frosty the Snowman* to specials featuring everyone from Babar to Barbie. From the beginning, studio executives saw *The Small One*'s "repeat possibilities" for Christmas airing. "This is the type of film that they tend to bring back every year at the holiday season," said Disney's archivist, David Smith. "It's a likely candidate for that." Yet it never happened. *The Small One* has not become part of television's holiday rotation. It was last released on video in 1994 and is now unavailable—except on spirited eBay auctions. Some observers suggest that the film is being held back because the always crowded Christmas market—including newer, nonreligious shorts and holiday specials starring Mickey Mouse—would overshadow such a modest work. Others suggest it might be because the film isn't that good, or because it is sharply out of step with Walt Disney's non-exclusive religious philosophy.

The movie's fate is a mystery to those who helped make *The Small One* and those who still cherish its memory, hoping for the day when the story can again brighten young lives at the holiday season. "It is saturated with what is the holiday season and Christmas spirit," said Bluth, who is now an independent producer. Howard Green, who as a young publicist prepared the press kit for *The Small One*, is another strong booster. "It should be more of a perennial," said Green, now Disney's vice president of studio communications. "It's a good show." Indeed, the little film still has a strong hold on the hearts of many Disney fans, especially Christians. Tim Hodge, who worked as a Disney animator in Orlando from 1992 to 2000, recalled seeing it in theaters while a high school student. Years after seeing *The Small One* for the first time, Hodge purchased several original animation cells from the film, which he was able to afford only because "there wasn't very much demand for this forgotten little cartoon." Hodge, who later worked as a story supervisor and director for VeggieTales animated films in suburban Chicago, said that religious references have been rare in Disney animation. *The Small One* is one of the few instances in which the word "God" is spoken or sung by one of Disney's animated characters. "I remember really liking it," he says. "It was a very sweet story, a little predictable, but gutsy and comforting to me to see a story in a biblical, historic setting."

There are critics who are not so sure that *The Small One*'s obscurity is a great loss, and who consider it to be more of a Don Bluth movie than a Walt Disney movie. The film was considered "saccharine," according to Leonard Maltin, author of *The Disney Films*. "It just didn't catch on with the public," said John Culhane of New York University. "It never got a great emotional reaction among audiences." He himself believes it to be a good story and a moving story. "But it's not a Disney story," he said. "Disney is not about telling anybody who God is, and that God is a Christian or a Jew or Muslim or Hindu or Buddhist. He didn't tell that kind of story—it's exclusive. Walt promoted what he said were values and beliefs common to all mankind. That was what he was interested in. Disney films are very high on values and morals, but not to one particular way to God."

Part Two

The Eisner Years: 1984–2004

Chapter Twenty

Michael and Jeffrey: The Jews

For most of Michael Eisner's life, being Jewish was never "an issue"—an expression he uses several times, in one form or another, in his autobiography, *Work in Progress.* But when it comes to Disney, Eisner's religion has been and still is very much an issue. The same was true for Jeffrey Katzenberg for the decade he spent working with Eisner at the studio. Neither man would discuss the issue of Judaism or personal religious practices for this book, nor would representatives of their respective companies, Disney and DreamWorks SKG. This is entirely understandable. In the present, polarized environment, many in Hollywood choose to keep their religious and spiritual lives—or the lack thereof—to themselves, for reasons of privacy or self-preservation. However, the matter of ethnic identity is another matter entirely, at least for Jewish executives in the entertainment industry or any other business.

Few would acknowledge it publicly, but the coded language of anti-Semitism is always there: *"These people"—these Jews—"will do anything for money."* It simmered beneath the surface during the religious boycott of Disney in the 1990s, and continues to rear its head from time to time. In one infamous reference, which he later claimed was an exaggeration, Eisner provided ammunition for this charge, claiming that the most important goal for the Walt Disney Company was to make money. "We have no obligation to make art," he wrote shareholders. "We have no obligation to make history. We have no obligation to make a statement. But to make money, it is often important to make history, to make art, or to make some significant statement."

As recently as October 2003, *New Republic* editor and ESPN commentator Gregg Easterbrook, writing about the Miramax release *Kill Bill* by director Quentin Tarantino, referred to Eisner and Miramax head Harvey Weinstein as "Jewish executives" who "worship money above all else, by promoting for profit the adulation of violence." Easterbrook, a senior editor, wrote on the magazine's Web site that "Disney's C.E.O., Michael Eisner, is Jewish; the chief of Miramax, Harvey Weinstein, is Jewish. Yes, there are plenty of Christian executives who worship money above all else, promoting for profit the adulation of violence," the preoccupation of *Kill Bill*. But, he wrote, "recent European history alone ought to cause Jewish executives to experience second thoughts about glorifying the killing of the helpless as a fun lifestyle choice." In the uproar that followed, Easterbrook apologized for the remarks, but he still lost his job as a commentator for ESPN, a Disney subsidiary.

In the early days of Hollywood, Walt Disney was one of the few studios—if not the only one—not controlled by immigrants, most of whom were Jews. But in 1984, this bastion of WASP, middle-American values passed to the control of three men: Eisner, Katzenberg, and Frank Wells. Wells, who served as the company's president, wasn't Jewish, but he might just as well have been. Eisner writes that Wells's unofficial title was "vice president of *mishegoss*," a Yiddish word meaning craziness. In the wake of the riots in Los Angeles that followed the verdict in the 1992 Rodney King beating case, Wells dragged Eisner to a Sunday service at the First African Methodist Episcopal Church in south-central Los Angeles. Disney, at Wells's initiative, had started a number of programs to help create jobs and assist small businesses in the depressed area. The Reverend Cecil Murray invited Wells, who was white, and Eisner to appear in the pulpit. Eisner confessed to feeling "a bit awkward," an inhibition that Wells—who immersed himself in the music, swaying and clapping—did not share.

By the mid-1990s, this transfer of power to Eisner, Wells, and Katzenberg, which proved so profitable to stockholders, was seen by many as a betrayal of Walt's notion of traditional family values—all for filthy lucre. Eisner had fashioned the company "into a haven for churning out anti-family and anti-Christian movies for the sake of money, prestige and all-encompassing power," wrote Perucci Perraiuolo in *Disney and the Bible,* at the height of the clash between religious conservatives and the entertainment giant. The book's cover features a drawing of Mickey Mouse reclining in an office chair, smoking a cigar, with his feet on the desk, between piles of money. Next to him a Bible has been dumped into the trashcan. Even Disney's own employees used offensive imagery; some workers referred to the theme parks as "Mousewitz." In the eyes of many evangelicals, "Disney, once a conservative force within the U.S. under the auspices of Walt Disney, had gone over to the 'liberal' camp," wrote Darlene Juschka, in her paper, "The Wonderful Worlds of Disney and Fundamentalism," delivered in Orlando in November 1998 at the annual meeting of the American Academy of Religion. "Disney, once a producer of movies which only upheld a narrow and conservative view of Americanism, an Americanism that was profoundly Protestant Christian, now made movies that clearly located that Americanism in the secular world. Christianity, as such, is no longer part of the Disney paradigm." Yet, in an April 10, 1999, interview with Simon Hattenstone, of the British newspaper the *Guardian,* Eisner said he had never been asked whether it was strange for a Jew to be heading Disney, in light of the charges that Walt was an anti-Semite. However, Hattenstone observed, Eisner seemed "uneasy with the subject" when it was raised. No wonder.

Michael Eisner's forebears were Jewish immigrants from Germany and Bohemia who prospered in the United States. Sigmund Eisner, Michael's great-grandfather, came from the Bohemian village of Horazdovice to the United States in 1881. Beginning as a peddler, he parlayed two sewing machines into a company that manufactured uniforms for the Boy Scouts and for the U.S. Army, including Teddy Roosevelt's Rough Riders. He married Bertha Weiss, from a German immigrant family who were founders of the town of Red Bank, in northern New Jersey. Sigmund shared his largesse with Jewish charities, including $50,000—an enormous amount at the time—to support the nascent Zionist settlers in what was then Palestine, according to Kim Masters, writing in *The Keys to the Kingdom: How Michael Eisner Lost His Grip*. Rabbi Stephen Wise, a leader of the Reform Jewish movement, spoke at the patriarch's funeral in 1925, noting his pride in his Judaism. Local synagogues received bequests from his $12 million estate, as did Christian churches of a number of denominations, including African American denominations. If anything, Michael Eisner's mother's family was even more successful than his father's family. Margaret Dammann's family founded the American Safety Razor Company.

Michael Eisner himself was raised on Park Avenue on the Upper East Side of Manhattan, and spent vacations at his maternal grandparents' estate in Westchester County. His parents moved in German Jewish circles of the Loeb and Lehman families, an old money set chronicled in Stephen Birmingham's book *Our Crowd*. For the most part, the family was insulated from anti-Semitism, although Michael's sister Margot had at least one early brush with prejudice. A competitive ice skater, she practiced at several locations, but not at the New York Skating Club, above Madison Square Garden. "Eventually I learned that Jews were not allowed membership," Michael wrote in his autobiography.

"I grew up in an affluent family, but as a child I never thought much about it," he wrote. "I just assumed that everyone lived the way we did." He attended the mostly Christian Allen-Stevenson School not far from his home, on East 78th Street, where he said no one made much of his religion. Neither he nor his sister attended any religious services growing up. In 1944, before news of the European Holocaust was widely known, the Eisner family hired a German housekeeper. "It wasn't for many years that I realized how unusual and even awkward it was for a Jewish family to have a German maid while the United States was at war and Hitler was exterminating Jews throughout Europe," he wrote. "Eventually we would discover that at least sixteen Eisners, many of them my great-grandfather's siblings, had died in the Czechoslovakian concentration camp of Theresienstadt."

Eisner's religious and moral identity was shaped by his father,

Lester. "While my father was proud to be Jewish, the death of his mother had undermined any faith in organized religion. There was slightly more interest on my mother's side of the family, but we were more cultural Jews than religious Jews." Eisner's relationship with his father was often problematic. "The biggest area of conflict in my own life was trying to meet my father's expectations, both morally and intellectually," Michael wrote in his autobiography. From him, "I learned the ethically straight and narrow path: no shortcuts and no playing the angles." His father had "fierce ethical standards. He maintained a strict code of conduct even when doing so meant hurting his own interests." Lester built an early television set for the family and, at first, the only show the family watched was *Texaco Star Theater,* with the Jewish comedian Milton Berle. Michael's parents had a rule—which the boy often broke—that he had to read for two hours for every hour of television he watched.

In *The Keys to the Kingdom,* Kim Masters quoted an Eisner family friend, Susan Baerwald, describing Eisner's mother, Maggie. "She was Jewish, but not *very* Jewish. German-Jewish—very American and successful." Maggie Eisner also had a strong social conscience. She served as president of the Irvington Institute, a hospital that treated children with rheumatic fever. It was here that young Michael had his first experience of noblesse oblige. Working at the hospital, he said in his autobiography, "opened my eyes to those less fortunate than I was."

From the age of eight through twenty-two, Eisner attended a spartan New England summer camp. "By far the most important formative experience in my life was going to Camp Keewaydin in Salisbury, Vermont." The camp was the nation's second oldest, and his father had gone there as a boy. Other prominent campers included West Virginia Senator Jay Rockefeller and the author John McPhee. "To a remarkable degree, my core values were shaped in the crucible of those camp summers. . . . The highest virtues were helping the other fellow even as you learned the tools of self-reliance." Days frequently ended with the singing of Boy Scout songs in a circle, where campers and counselors "bowed to the Southwest wind Shawondasee." On its current Web site, Camp Keewaydin describes the ritual today, which sounds like a kind of

Quaker or Unitarian youth group activity, with Native American overtones: "A non-sectarian Sunday service called Sunday Circle is held each week, out of doors whenever possible. At Sunday Circle, a member of the camp staff speaks to the boys about such values as friendship, appreciation of nature, sharing, teamwork, and caring for each other." In 1999, Eisner told Simon Hattenstone of the *Guardian* newspaper that "I got more out of this camp than I got out of any school, any book, any lecture." (Eisner's planned book on life lessons from Keewaydin called *Camp* from Warner Books was postponed for a year from its Father's Day, 2004, launch in the midst of Disney's corporate upheaval in March 2004.)

As a prep school student at Lawrenceville School in Princeton, New Jersey, Eisner admitted to "testing the limits of authority." It was here that he had his first serious encounter with anti-Semitism. There, he recalled in his autobiography, "I was made aware for the first time of how being Jewish somehow made me different, an outsider. Until one classmate called me a 'kike,' prompting one of the only fistfights of my life, it had literally never occurred to me that some people didn't like Jews. Now the issue was in the air, and I hated the consequences. I hated being put in a category. I hated the jokes directed at me about Temple and Bar Mitzvahs and Saturday School. Like my father I was proud to be Jewish, but I hated being viewed as different." Without the grades to attend an Ivy League school, Eisner chose to attend Denison College in Ohio, a historically Baptist school with about 1600 students. "My being Jewish wasn't an issue. There were perhaps a half-dozen Jews, and we were considered more an oddity than a threatening social minority."

In 1964, after graduating from Denison, Eisner met Jane Breckenridge at a Christmas party in New York. Her family background was Swedish and Scottish, and she had been brought up Unitarian. Reflecting on when he went to her home in upstate New York to meet his future in-laws, Eisner wrote in his autobiography, "I suspect that neither of her parents had ever really known anyone Jewish before me, but it was never an issue." A longtime Eisner friend speculated to Kim Masters that Maggie Dammann

Eisner was so assimilated that she was probably "thrilled" that Jane wasn't Jewish.

It was not until 1984, at the age of 42, that Eisner said he had his "first important brush with the fact that life isn't always fair." This was no revelation about poverty or illness or death. The precipitating event for the insight was when he was not offered the top job at Paramount Studios, as stipulated by his contract. However, he received instead a hefty compensation package and, within months, he had a new job as head of Disney. His hiring was largely engineered by two men, Roy Disney, Walt's nephew; and his ally, Los Angeles businessman Stanley Gold, who at that time was also chairman of the board of Hebrew Union College, the rabbinical seminary of Reform Judaism. Eisner said that from the first, he recognized that animation, then under the direction of Roy Disney, "represented the heart and soul of Disney." At Disney under Eisner, there was not much in the way of entertainment material dealing with the Jewish experience. An exception was a live action film commissioned for the Disney Channel, called *Friendship in Vienna,* a wartime drama dealing with the relationship between a Jewish family and a Catholic family during the rise of Hitler. Another, more lighthearted example was *Full Court Miracle,* also on the Disney Channel, a Hanukkah comedy-drama about a hapless basketball team at a Jewish day school in Philadelphia that is coached to victory by a down-on-his-luck African American player with NBA dreams.

Nowhere in his autobiography does Michael Eisner make mention of his adult religious practice or his personal philanthropy. On one occasion in the late 1990s, local Disney officials asked the Congregation of Liberal Judaism, a Reform congregation in Orlando, for tickets required to attend High Holidays services for the Eisner family. Temple officials agreed, but the tickets were never picked up. Similarly, Eisner is largely silent on the subject of Israel. Writing about *Aladdin,* he admitted, "I had always been slightly uneasy about a film set in the Middle East, a part of the world that I didn't know and didn't feel comfortable trying to portray." In his chatty letters to shareholders in Disney's annual report, he discussed aspects of his family life, both significant and trivial, but never anything about his spiritual life. He did recall in *Work in Progress* a visit in the mid-1990s to the U.S. Holocaust Museum in Washington, D.C., with his wife. "The experience was at once horrifying and deeply affecting; a vivid, three-dimensional evocation of the genocide of more than 6 million people, among them many of my own European relatives. Especially moving was the room containing thousands of pairs of shoes that had been confiscated from Jews as they were about to be gassed to death. The powerful smell of leather made the experience even more immediate. Jane and I were affected as well by the museum's meticulous recreation of the process by which one town was transformed from a thriving, happy community to a barren one in which nearly all the residents were killed by the Nazis."

Eisner, who was in the midst of an unsuccessful effort to build an American history theme park in Northern Virginia at the time of his visit to the memorial, couldn't resist casting an analytic eye to the facility. He noted with favor the "contrast to the static exhibits at so many museums," including those devoted to early American presidents. The Holocaust Museum used "a truly multi-media approach to history," he wrote. "The museum's creators used many of the dramatic tools and techniques that Walt Disney had pioneered—film, animation, music, voice-over narration—in this case to recreate and evoke the horror of the Holocaust."

If Eisner did not embrace his Judaism, neither did he appear to have been drawn to any other belief systems. The single reference he made to "divine intervention" in his autobiography was when the outdoor premiere of *Pocahontas* in New York's Central Park was not rained out. Neither was he attracted by any New Age beliefs, despite the later charges of his religious critics. That infatuation, common in Hollywood, "passed me by," he wrote; a dinner party with New Age guru and public television star Deepak Chopra left him unimpressed. In a July 2, 2001, article in the *New York Times* that dealt with a public relations blunder made by Time Warner during a cable television dispute with Disney, Eisner told reporter Seth Schiesel, "I almost became religious. It was like a gift."

Thinking he might not survive surgery following a heart attack in July 1994, Eisner told his wife and two of his three sons at his bedside that, if he died, his wife should not buy a new house and that he wanted to be buried above ground. But he recalled saying nothing about a rabbi or a Jewish funeral. Later, he received an emotional, ten-page letter from Larry McMurtry, reflecting on the Texas novelist's own heart surgery. Eisner wrote back with his postbypass thoughts about mortality:

> I am different. My life has a finite sense to it, and there is certainly a hollowness that comes with such realizations. I try not to think about it, but I think about it all the time. . . . When all is said and done, I do feel in the hollow of this new life one strange thing that you do not mention. I feel one positive. I feel one rush that offsets all the feelings you related. I feel one enormous explosion which I haven't felt since my first son was born. I died. And I know what that is. Although I feel the ceiling of death, at the same time I accept death for the first time and even look at it without fear. Death has always been for me the feeling of air turbulence, hitting the shoulder of the highway. . . . Not now. It simply is. I have been there and it was okay.

For much of his tenure as head of the entertainment giant, Eisner was lauded, and not just for the fat years of exponential earnings and rises in the stock price. "Eisner turned out to be more Walt than Walt," Jim Collins and Jerry Porras wrote in *Built to Last: Successful Habits of Visionary Companies.* "Eisner understood and appreciated—indeed, had unabashed enthusiasm for—the Disney values." But in December 2003, Roy Disney resigned his positions as Disney's vice chairman and head of feature animation, with a blast at Michael Eisner's leadership. Together with longtime ally Stanley Gold, Disney called on Eisner to resign from the company (the two also supported Katzenberg's departure in 1994). The feud between Disney and Eisner had been brewing for years, so the action was not especially surprising. Things had gotten so bad by late 2003 that Eisner tried to block Disney from attending a screening of ideas for upcoming animated films, according to a January 12, 2004, article in *Fortune* magazine. What was surprising was the bitterness of Roy's parting statement and, to me, its almost theological language. Among the things the company had lost under Eisner in the past decade, Walt's nephew charged, was its "heritage." Eisner, Roy wrote, had allowed the perception to develop on the part of "all our stakeholders—consumers, investors, employees, distributors and suppliers—that the Company is rapacious, soul-less and always looking for the 'quick buck.'" In a subsequent filing with the Securities and Exchange Commission, Roy Disney cited the company's "cultural decay" under Eisner. The language sounded familiar. "I believe that our mission has always been to be bringers of joy, to be the affirmers of the good in each of us, to be in subtle ways—teachers," he wrote on his Web site, www.savedisney.com.

At a tumultuous stockholders' meeting in Philadelphia on March 3, 2004, Eisner received a 43 percent no-confidence vote. He kept his job as CEO but gave up his position as board chairman.

Jeffrey Katzenberg, a decade younger than Michael Eisner, grew up just six blocks away from his future boss, also on Park Avenue and also the son of privilege. The son of a stockbroker, Katzenberg's family money was newer than Eisner's, and there was much less of it. Jeffrey attended Fieldston, a private Bronx high school, and went to Camp Kennebec in Maine, founded in 1907, which today calls itself "the Harvard of camps." However, at the age of thirteen, Katzenberg was thrown out of the camp for playing poker for M&M candies. A young man in a hurry, he spent one year at New York University until he dropped out to join the administration of Mayor John Lindsay, a liberal Republican. Ultimately, politics gave way to show business, and Katzenberg gravitated to Paramount, where he worked under Eisner. Katzenberg came over to Disney in 1984, where he enjoyed great success, especially in his oversight of animated features such as *The Little Mermaid, Beauty and the Beast, Aladdin,* and *The Lion King.*

Katzenberg left Disney in 1994, after Eisner refused his demand to be promoted to company president following the death of Frank Wells in a helicopter crash. Eisner has given several reasons for his decision, most having to do with what he saw as Katzenberg's immaturity, brashness, and naked, unbridled ambition. In *Work in*

Progress, Eisner recounted an appearance Katzenberg made at an industry gathering in Sun Valley, Idaho, earlier in 1994. "As always, he was aggressive and outspoken, but he also interrupted the other speakers and cracked bad jokes. I felt that he was representing Disney poorly, especially for someone who wanted to be president of the company." However, there may be something more, something in this passage that reflected the social rift between descendants of New York's German Jewish community, most of whom arrived in the United States in the nineteenth century, and those from Eastern Europe who arrived in the twentieth century. German Jews fancied themselves as cultured, prosperous, restrained, and assimilated by the time their Eastern European cousins arrived at the city's docks—often after crossing the ocean in steerage. For some German Jews the poor, uneducated newcomers were an embarrassment. Many of the Eastern Europeans started with nothing and scratched their way into the middle class—and beyond. One intriguing interpretation, while entirely speculative, is that, at its root, this cultural divide contributed to Eisner's disinclination to promote Katzenberg.

In the middle and late 1990s, when Michael Eisner and the Walt Disney Company came into conflict with conservative Christian groups, including the Southern Baptist Convention (see chapter 37), Jeffrey Katzenberg charted an entirely different course. As a partner with film director Steven Spielberg and music producer David Geffen in the new studio DreamWorks SKG, Katzenberg chose as his first major project an animated feature based on the life of Moses, called *The Prince of Egypt.* In numerous newspaper interviews, Katzenberg credited his two DreamWorks partners with giving him the idea for the film, and for suggesting the best way to approach making it. He told Lloyd Grove, writing in the November 29, 1998, *Washington Post,* that he was discussing possible animation projects with his partners when Spielberg suggested he do *The Ten Commandments.* "I thought of the man Moses," Katzenberg told Grove. "When Steven said *The Ten Commandments . . .* I thought of an incredible, incredible story of a remarkable man—an innocent, Everyman, a sense of humbleness and humility, who didn't see himself having the wherewithal, who never thought of himself or felt the strength of being a leader. Chosen, not wanting to be chosen. Who then rises to a level of extraordinary, extraordinary leadership and heroism. And so for me that's an exciting story. He's a hero." Katzenberg told Cindy Pearlman, writing in the December 13, 1998, *Chicago Sun-Times,* that the thing he remembered most about the Moses narrative was that it was "a story any of us could identify with because we're all flawed—especially me. But we all wish that within us is the ability to do something great."

Then what Katzenberg calls "the greatest piece of professional advice that I've gotten from anybody"—as he told the *Washington Post's* Grove and seemingly every other reporter he spoke with—came from his DreamWorks partner David Geffen. "David said, 'Okay, I think it's a great idea and I urge you to make the movie. However, when you were at Disney you'd make a movie like *The Little Mermaid* and you'd stick any old happily-ever-after ending onto that movie and everybody would think, oh, isn't that cute, isn't that nice. . . . But for this story, when you do it, you must be very faithful to the material. You must be accurate. You must get it right. I'm now going to say four words to you. Please make sure you listen to them carefully, Jeffrey: You don't know anything!' "

In an unprecedented effort, Katzenberg reached out to hundreds of religious leaders and scholars from a spectrum of faiths—Jewish, Christian, and Muslim—to make certain that DreamWorks got the story right. Katzenberg's reach stretched from Jewish scholars and rabbis as far away as Jerusalem to cardinals in the Vatican. Hundreds of evangelical and fundamentalist Christian leaders from around the United States were also involved. In years past, film producers brought in religious leaders to screen films, a pro forma exercise, usually just before release—and too late to make any changes. Not this time. Nearly three years before the film's release, DreamWorks began inviting and paying for groups of religious leaders to attend daylong briefings at the company's facilities at Universal Studios in Los Angeles. During the meetings, Katzenberg's assistants used storyboards to outline the movie's plot, displayed sketches of the characters, and showed thirty-five minutes of rough animation. Leaders were asked for a frank critique after these sessions, and they voiced some concerns. Many of the movie's elements were considered, from the grand to the trivial: what the voice of God should sound like, how much of the Exodus story should be covered, whether to show Pharaoh's backside or nubile maidens bathing Moses. One participant thought ending the film with the crossing of the Red Sea eliminated some of the strongest religious experiences, including Moses receiving the Ten Commandments. Katzenberg said the crossing of the Red Sea was a logical dramatic climax to the film. However, about fifty of the religious leaders' suggestions were accepted, according to DreamWorks. But, most importantly, those involved said they got a fair hearing. Jack Shaheen, the author of *Reel Bad Arabs: How Hollywood Vilifies a People,* who had clashed with Katzenberg over *Aladdin,* said the experience with *The Prince of Egypt* was entirely different. Of course, you can't please everyone. Even before the film was released there, some in Egypt called it "a work of Jewish revisionist history that distorts the golden age of Egyptian history" and was an example of "a Jewish-dominated Hollywood . . . yet again showing bias against Arabs and Muslims," according to the April 17, 1999, *Guardian* of London.

"No one has ever done this before," former PBS movie critic Michael Medved told me for an article that appeared in the *Orlando Sentinel* of April 10, 1998. "It's precisely the type of reaching across dividing lines that America desperately needs." Orthodox Rabbi Daniel Lapin, head of a Seattle group called Toward Tradition, agreed. "They really made an exemplary and good faith effort." But he emphasized that he viewed the film "as entertainment, not religious instruction." Conservative Christian leaders were equally appreciative. "They understand that if they're going to appeal to the Judeo-Christian audience and make this movie successful, they must be true to the biblical account," said the Reverend Lou Sheldon, head of the Traditional Values Coalition in Washington, D.C. "The overall thrust of the story is true to the person of Moses, how God called him and how Moses responded." The Reverend Jerry Falwell said that "Spielberg and Katzenberg got this one right because they intended to," predicting that the film would create an interest in the Bible. "Dream-Works has been very open to constructive criticism and has worked very hard to make this a positive contribution to American families," he said. "Where they do use hyperbole it does no damage to the message."

But was Katzenberg's effort simply a marketing gimmick? Ted Baehr, chairman of the Christian Film and Television Commission, worried that there was concern that the involvement of religious leaders might backfire at the box office if people saw the movie as a propaganda vehicle or an effort to court conservative moviegoers. "I don't think there's any danger of that," said Medved, who is Jewish and has written extensively on the cultural politics of Hollywood. "This goes way beyond a marketing ploy. What Jeffrey has done is to demonstrate that respect, inclusiveness, and diversity . . . do not mean selling your soul to the religious Right."

But others were not so sure. "They want to capitalize on religion—because religion is hot—but they don't want to offend," said Todd Gitlin, author of *The Twilight of Common Dreams: Why America Is Wracked by Culture Wars.* In an interview following the film's release, Gitlin noted that some of the same evangelical and fundamentalist Christians DreamWorks consulted had at about that time been vociferous in criticizing the content of Disney films and Disney-owned ABC-TV shows, books, and personnel policies.

The Prince of Egypt's producer, Penny Finkelman Cox, said the consultations did nothing to compromise the filmmaking process. "There was no reason not to accommodate them," she told the *Los Angeles Times* in 1998, and her response made sense to Christian leaders. "Whenever someone wants to deal with issues that are of extreme importance to a faith community, it just makes good sense to try to get the input of that community in order to not needlessly offend them," said the Reverend Richard Land, head of the Southern Baptist Convention's Ethics and Religious Liberty Commission, which was at that time spearheading his denomination's boycott of Disney. "Clearly," he said, "there is an enormous market out there for entertainment that affirms the basic values of the faith community, and that is wholesome viewing for the whole family."

As it turned out, the release of *The Prince of Egypt*—which told the story of the first Passover—in December 1998 was almost coincident with the Jewish holiday of Hanukkah. But rabbis in the Orlando area at least, where Disney World is located, were not concerned about any confusion, pointing out that Hanukkah is a minor holiday that has been inflated in the United States simply because it occurs at the same time of the year as Christmas. "I don't think it's a bad thing at all," said Rabbi Alan Londy, then in the pulpit of Temple Israel in Orlando. "The primary story of the Jewish people is the leaving of Egypt. Anything that educates the pop culture about that is a good thing." Congregations heeded one of the studio's slogans: "Let my people go—to see this movie." During Hanukkah, the Congregation of Liberal Judaism, a Reform temple in Orlando, joined other area synagogues and the Jewish Community Center of Greater Orlando to rent a theater for a group showing of *The Prince of Egypt*. Rabbi Steven Engel, the congregation's spiritual leader, said Passover and Hanukkah have similar themes. "There is a message of congruity between the two," he said, "and that is the message of religious freedom." Rabbi Sholom Dubov of Congregation Ahavas Yisrael, an Orthodox congregation in Maitland, Florida, lauded DreamWorks for creating the animated feature. "It's a great thing," he said. "It's very bold for them to take a story such as this and make use of modern techniques to tell it." Rabbi Merrill Shapiro of Congregation Beth Am in Longwood agreed that the movie was unlikely to overshadow Hanukkah, although "it wouldn't be such a bad thing if it happened."

The Christmas season often is associated with three wise men from the East bringing gifts for Jesus. In 1998, the three Jewish moguls who run DreamWorks hoped their Hollywood creation also would be prized by Christians. The relationships that Katzenberg and DreamWorks forged with evangelical leaders paid off. Ancillary marketing included gospel versions of the soundtrack on CD. The Reverend Howard Edington of Orlando's First Presbyterian Church was one of the religious leaders who attended an early screening in Hollywood, a session that also included Campus Crusade for Christ founders Bill and Vonette Bright. A month before the release, Edington flew to Miami to meet with Katzenberg and others involved in making the film. As a result of his trips, Edington preached five successive sermons on the subject of Moses and *The Prince of Egypt*, calling it an "astounding accomplishment" and "a wonderful movie" that he urged all church members to see. First Presbyterian also rented a theater for a showing of the film, in hopes of making it a commercial success. "I'm pushing this movie," Edington acknowledged, "but this is worth pushing because of the potential it can have on what Hollywood produces. . . . Our society needs the ripple effect created by a wonderfully positive movie." Robert Knight, then cultural affairs director for the conservative Family Research Council, said he had been invited from Washington, D.C., to Los Angeles to preview and react to the film, which he liked. Knight told the *Washington Post* that Katzenberg's political outreach operation was "first-class."

Several newspapers dubbed the feature *"The Zion King,"* a pun on the Disney smash hit *The Lion King,* suggesting the relationship between the Pharaoh Rameses II and Moses was an analog to that of Eisner and Katzenberg—which Katzenberg laughed off. What he refused to laugh off, or respond to, were questions about his own faith. By contrast with Eisner, Katzenberg maintains a higher Jewish profile in Southern California. He is a member of Temple Emanuel in Beverly Hills, where his children attended religious school and had their b'nai mitzvahs. He told one reporter that his rabbi helped him get over his anger following his departure from Disney. (On the other hand, he worked through the High Holidays to complete *Aladdin,* according to the January 4, 1999, *Jerusalem Report.*) In Los Angeles, Katzenberg's name appears on lists of donors to Jewish and Israeli causes. He served as cochairman of a $10,000-a-person fundraising event for Aish HaTorah, an Orthodox group building a facility in predominantly Arab East Jerusalem, and is a backer of the Museum of Tolerance, a Holocaust exhibit. In 1999, the American Jewish Committee honored him for his humanitarian and charitable contributions.

But Katzenberg was adamant when questioned about what role his own Judaism played in his decision to make *The Prince of Egypt* with Geffen and Spielberg. "Being Jewish isn't why we made this movie," he told the *Jerusalem Report* in the same 1999 article. Also typical were his responses to questions from Jeff Simon, film critic for the *Buffalo News,* in an interview that appeared on December 13, 1998. Simon started off the telephone interview with what he acknowledged was a tough question. "The old Hollywood studio heads seemed, by general consensus, to be a little bit afraid of their own Judaism," Simon said. "They kept their religion out of their movies by and large. Not you. And despite the universality, certainly not here. Could you talk a little about the change?"

Katzenberg wouldn't bite. "I only know how to answer these kinds of questions one way, and that is honestly, and I can tell you that really wasn't a factor in wanting to tell the story. . . . For me, I wanted to tell the story of a man. That's what captivated me—not my heritage, not my personal connections." Simon tried to ask the same question about Jewish influence another way, but Katzenberg held firm. "I can't answer for other people. I really have to be honest with you. I have no perspective on that. I think there's this notion outside of Hollywood that those in Hollywood are very reserved or guarded or lacking in the importance of faith in their life. I don't see that to be the case. I don't think empirical information would prove that to be the case. I just don't feel that way."

The *Orlando Sentinel*'s Jay Boyar had a similar experience with the DreamWorks executive. "Katzenberg did something unusual," the movie critic recalled. "He offered himself up for an interview, as if he were one of the film's creators. But then he refused to take any personal responsibility for the origin and shape of the spiritual content. To me this makes no sense."

Chapter Twenty-One

The Little Mermaid (1989):
Upward Mobility

As the beloved movie that launched a hundred thousand lunch boxes, that gave its title character's name to uncounted now-teenaged girls, and that began the modern merger of the animated feature and the Broadway musical, *The Little Mermaid* is a film any writer approaches with caution. As if all that is not daunting enough, the production was a resounding critical and commercial success, beginning the Michael Eisner/Jeffrey Katzenberg animation era for Disney. It also marked the emergence of more active, assertive young women at the center of the studio's narrative. To be sure, the change embodied by *The Little Mermaid* is, at best, incremental. "Ariel resembles most of Disney's other heroines, in that she represents royalty, lives in a male-dominated world, and ultimately finds fulfillment through marriage to a prince," according to Janet Wasko, in *Understanding Disney*. The critical difference is *how* the character finds that fulfillment.

The Little Mermaid is the start of a saga about intermarriage. On the surface—and below—it is about a girl with fins and a boy with legs who fall in love. Ariel, youngest daughter of King Triton, ruler of the sea, is enamored with all things human. She prowls shipwrecks and salvages artifacts from the ocean floor, sometimes daring to spy on passing, nineteenth-century sailing ships. These activities enrage her father, who fears that her explorations among the sea-dwellers' natural enemies will leave her "snared by some fish-eater's hook." Humans are barbarians, he thunders, dismissing the species wholesale. Ariel—whose name appears in at least five books of the Old Testament—snaps that they are not barbarians, that she is sixteen years old and no longer a child, and that she can

138

make her own decisions. As long as she lives under Triton's ocean, the king says, the teenager will obey his rules, and she will never return to the surface. This is an argument meant to resonate with fathers and daughters on the other side of the screen—and it does.

Ariel has been collecting her finds in a cavern, which is almost a shrine to civilization above the water line. On one wall, as Dan Brown points out in his blockbuster novel *The Da Vinci Code*, is George de la Tour's *The Penitent Magdalene*, a portrait of Mary Magdalene cast out. The mermaid says that she cannot see how a world that makes such wonderful things could be bad, a common but flawed understanding of materialism and its relation to culture. What a society makes is no indicator of its goodness. Ariel sings, longingly, that she wants to be part of the human world, to be with people, to watch them dance, to walk in the sun, and to read books. In such a land, she believes, parents will not reprimand their daughters—a line that must have provoked thousands of hoots and pokes in the ribs.

The light of fireworks above the water draws Ariel back to the surface, this time to observe a shipboard birthday celebration for Eric, a handsome prince with no parents. As the multiracial crew sings and dances, a councilor reminds Eric that the people of his kingdom are ready for him to settle down. The prince does not object, but he insists that he believes in love at first sight, and will know when he finds the right girl. A storm comes up suddenly, and a bolt of lightning sets the ship afire. Out of control, the vessel breaks up on the rocks not far from shore. The crew jumps over-board, but in the confusion Eric sees that his sheepdog has been left behind on the burning deck. He returns to rescue his pet, an act of bravery Ariel witnesses. So Eric is handsome, young, royal, sin-gle, an animal lover—and a hero. Naturally, the little mermaid is a goner, flippers or no. The prince's successful effort to save his dog exhausts him, and he sinks below the surface, giving Ariel an opportunity to rescue him and to bring him to the beach. He regains consciousness enough to see her face and to hear her sing to him. Now he is a goner too.

Ariel's new infatuation soon becomes apparent to her sisters, and then to her father. All assume that she has settled on a merman, one of her own kind, and they are happy for her. But when Sebastian the crab—who sings memorably of how idyllic life is under the sea—reveals Prince Eric's identity, King Triton explodes. Humans are all the same, he says, "spineless, savage, harpooning, fish-eaters—incapable of any feeling." Ariel says that she only tried to save a drowning man. Her father replies that she should have let him die, which would have left "one less human to worry about." At this point in the story, Eleanor Byrne and Martin McQuillan wrote in *Deconstructing Disney,* the outcome is instantly telegraphed: "Triton will inevitably learn his lesson, recant his ill-founded prejudice and not only come to accept his daughter's love for Prince Eric but also use his magic powers to give Ariel legs so that she might become human too." Not for about forty minutes, however. The mermaid lets slip that this discussion comes too late, that she is in love with the boy, prompting her father to use his magic trident to destroy every human artifact in her cave. This is a tirade that speaks to the inexplicable fascination that girls and young women sometimes have for boys and young men from different races, religions, nations, and cultures—not to mention the forbidden attraction of classic "bad boys." It is a durable and appealing construct, as Disney learned in 1984 with its hit live-action version of this story, *Splash,* its first PG-13 film, released under the Touchstone label.

Into the story comes Ursula the Sea Witch, the most grotesque characterization that Disney writers and animators have created for a female villain up to now. To begin with, she is fat and old, rarely a good combination for a woman in these stories. And she doesn't talk; she brays. The official Disney explanation is that she is based on the Norma Desmond character in the classic film *Sunset Boulevard.* In fact, she was modeled on the modern drag queen Divine, according to the film's directing animator, Reuben Acquino, cited in *From Mouse to Mermaid.* The hints she drops early in *The Little Mermaid* suggest a previous experience in King Triton's court not unlike that of Lucifer in heaven. For some reason, never explained in the movie, Ursula was banished or exiled from the castle. From her own dark realm, and with the help of two eel spies, the witch observes Ariel's growing love for Eric and her corresponding conflict with Triton. In this, she spots an opportunity to add to her "garden," which is composed of sea creatures who failed to keep their bargain with Ursula and, for this transgression, were turned into forlorn kelp. The eels lure Ariel with the promise of bringing her to "someone who can make your dreams come true." Ursula offers Ariel a deal. For three days, Ariel will have legs, but in exchange she will have to give the witch her voice. If the mermaid can get the prince to give her a kiss of true love before sunset on the third day, Ariel can stay on land and wed. However, if she fails, the mermaid must join Ursula's garden. Ariel is smart enough to grasp that, even if she succeeds, she will fail. Becoming human could mean that she never sees her father or sisters again. Right, Ursula says, "life is full of tough choices." This has often been the fate of those who marry outside of their faith or culture. Still, Ariel agrees, and she is deposited onto the shore.

On the strand nearby, Prince Eric is wondering if he will ever find the beautiful girl with the beautiful voice who saved his life. With help of his dog, he does indeed find Ariel, who seems to be mute. Ariel moves to the young man's seaside castle, and appears to be heading to the altar, until Ursula transforms herself into a beautiful young woman with the little mermaid's own sweet voice. Ursula's plan is to use the captive Ariel as leverage to regain her power over Triton. Things are made right between the mermaid and the prince, and the true lovers are reunited, but the sun sets before they can kiss. Ursula attempts to claim her winnings, and a titanic struggle ensues. King Triton, finally acknowledging the legitimacy of his daughter's love for the human, sacrifices his power to spare his daughter. Prince Eric, however, destroys the witch, and both the sea dwellers and the human beings attend the wedding of Ariel and Eric.

"I have an exercise that I do with kids all the time after they see *The Little Mermaid*," said Rabbi Daniel M. Wolpe of the Southwest Orlando Jewish Congregation, a fan and student of Disney. "I ask them what the movie has to say about intermarriage. Usually, they all give the 'American' view—it doesn't matter what makes you different as long as you love each other. Then I point out that, intentionally or not, the movie actually gives a more Jewish answer—Ariel converts. There is an understanding that differences of culture, faith, and traditions can create barriers to a successful relationship. And since Prince Eric cannot 'convert' to mermaidism, she converts."

As anyone (like me) with experience with intermarriage can testify, the wedding ceremony is only the first of the challenges the couple will face. In the case of the little mermaid and her prince, a straight-to-video sequel fleshes out what this kind of relationship means, even under the best of circumstances. In *The Little Mermaid II: The Return to the Sea*, the couple has a child, named Melody. For her own safety, they tell their daughter nothing about her mother's mermaid heritage. Yet something pulls the twelve-year-old Melody toward the sea, so much that she sometimes pretends she has fins. When she learns the truth about her watery background, the girl resents her mother for keeping it from her. Ariel tries to explain to the rebellious preteen that her parents hid her background only to protect the girl, which they now realize was a mistake. In contrast to Rabbi Wolpe's view, the sequel ends with an agreement that the girl will try to live in two worlds, since "it doesn't matter if you have fins or feet." It is not always possible to split the difference—or ignore the differences. If only life were that simple.

Academic skeptics notwithstanding, *The Little Mermaid* does speak to more than the issue of intermarriage. It represents the beginning of a seismic shift in Disney's animated features, under Eisner and Katzenberg, in the way young women are portrayed. In contrast to her predecessors, Ariel acts rather than being acted on. She makes decisions and takes risks. Yes, she is a spoiled royal and her success is defined by her marriage to a prince. But Ariel needs to be seen in what will be an evolutionary context, that is, in light of the characters that will follow her to the screen in the next two decades: *Beauty and the Beast*'s Belle, Pocahontas, Mulan, and Lilo. In this, Disney is an indicator—if a trailing one—of the changing role of women in the West.

Chapter Twenty-Two

Beauty and the Beast (1991): Feminism, Transformation, and Redemption

Oddly, for a studio that has done as much as any other in Hollywood to equate beauty with goodness, Disney makes the opposite argument in *Beauty and the Beast*—at least conditionally. The movie wraps this proposition in an instructive tale of a short-sighted, inhospitable host. (Most, if not all, religious traditions urge hospitality toward strangers. According to Jewish tradition, Sodom's sin was not the sexual act it came to represent; rather, it was the inhospitable treatment its people gave to the city's visitors. Jesus urged the welcoming of strangers, and there is the advice in Hebrews 13:2, that strangers should be treated hospitably, since "by doing that some have entertained angels without knowing it.")

Beauty and the Beast's opening narration explains that there was once a young, French prince who had everything he could want (except, apparently, parents), yet he was still spoiled, selfish, and unkind. On a bitterly cold winter's night, an old beggar woman comes to his castle, offering a rose in exchange for shelter. The young man, portrayed in an illustration as a sixteenth-century nobleman wearing a crown topped by a small cross, turns her away. His reason for this ungenerous and inhospitable act is simply that he is repulsed by her appearance. Giving him one more chance, the crone warns the prince that he should not be deceived by appearances, that true beauty comes from within. Rejected again for her ugliness, the woman is transformed into a stunning enchantress. She will not accept the prince's apology, because she sees that there is no love in his heart. Instead, the woman pronounces a curse on the man. She changes him into a frightening, burly, furry beast and casts a spell on the prince's castle and all that reside there. The Beast is devastated, and hides his monstrous form in the castle, a magic hand mirror providing his only glimpse at the outside world. According to the spell, the beggar's rose will bloom until the prince's twenty-first birthday. If before that day he can learn to love another, and win another's love before the flower's last petal falls, the curse will be lifted. Failure means he will remain a beast forever. No one knows better than the prince how difficult it will be to find someone so extraordinary that she will be able to overlook—much less love—such a frightening visage. Naturally, he becomes despondent.

In the nearby village there is just such an extraordinary and beautiful young woman, named Belle, who is literally centuries ahead of her time. She is a reader, and a fast one at that, with a weakness for fairy tales filled with sword fights, magic spells, and disguised princes. When not caring for her inventor-father—again, there is no mother in this family—Belle longs for something beyond her predictable, provincial life. She has no interest in a match with the handsome but empty-headed Gaston, the village's best hunter, mainly because of his "positively primeval" view of women's place in domestic life. "It's not right for a woman to read," he proclaims. "Soon she starts getting ideas, thinking." The only reason Gaston wants to marry Belle is because she is the most beautiful girl in the village, nothing more. He is so certain that she will agree that he sets up a wedding ceremony, complete with priest, outside her door before she even agrees to marry him. When she refuses, Gaston is both dumbstruck and humiliated. In this and other respects, "*Beauty and the Beast* is a men's movement response to feminist nagging," according to Matt Roth, writing in the March 1996 issue of the film journal *Jump Cut*.

As a character, Gaston is an anomaly in a number of ways, a transgressive figure. A sunny, virile young man and an excellent huntsman, he is also a villain, which goes against the Disney grain. (Female antagonists in early Disney features, beginning with the evil queen in Snow White, have been dark beauties.) And despite Gaston's determined pursuit of Belle and his attraction to the village girls, some critics see a subtext of stereotypical gay narcissism in his portrayal. "He is the epitome of camp," Roth wrote. "He is only truly interested in male gazes, and blossoms in the midst of his all-male lodge, where he sings a show-stopper celebrating his own masculinity." Andreas Deja, an animator on the film who is openly gay, said he patterned Gaston on "preening West Hollywood muscle clones" he would see at the gym, according to *Disney: The Mouse Betrayed,* by Peter Schweizer and Rochelle Schweizer.

Belle's eccentric and easily befuddled father, Maurice, innocently stumbles into the Beast's castle, enraging the creature. Demonstrating that he has learned little from the experience that has cursed his life, beyond self-interest, the Beast throws the old man into the dungeon. After all, it is not the love of a white-haired man that can break the spell. Belle rushes to the castle, where only the girl's offer to exchange herself for her father's freedom mollifies the Beast—whose appearance repels her. The castle's servants, transformed into talking furniture and kitchenware by the spell, recognize that the girl probably represents their master's last chance to return things (and them) back to normal. As explosive and savage as he has become, the Beast also acknowledges the situation, but he despairs of his prospects: "She'll never see me as anything but a monster." The Beast is able to change at least the tone of their relationship by risking his life to save the girl from a savage attack by wolves during an escape attempt. Belle nurses him back to health out of gratitude and, after several false starts, he begins an intellectual seduction. It is a frankly self-interested process, although in the midst of it, the Beast does seem to change. "I've never felt this way about anyone," he says, before throwing open his library to her. As the creature evolves, Belle's feelings toward him change as well. She wonders, in a song, why she hasn't noticed his transformation from being "mean, coarse, and unrefined" to someone "sweet, almost kind and dear." The Beast observes that she no longer recoils from his appearance. Of course, Belle has not lost her sight or sense, and admits that he is no Prince Charming.

For all her good feelings toward the Beast, Belle misses her father terribly. The Beast magnanimously releases her from her promise to remain with him forever and sends her off. With the last few petals of the enchanted rose about to drop, this sacrifice has tremendous significance, with eternal consequences. "I love her," he explains. Back in the village, Belle learns that the spurned Gaston has had her father locked up and will not free him unless she agrees to marry him. She refuses this bargain, and Gaston blames the Beast, leading a mob of townsfolk to the castle to kill him. The villagers sing, "We don't like what we don't understand, in fact it scares us." (CBS anchorman Dan Rather, in a column written for the March 22, 1992, *Los Angeles Times* saw *Beauty and the Beast* as an AIDS allegory. Think of the Beast's spell as a metaphor for the disease "with the same arbitrary and harshly abbreviated limitations on time, and you feel the Beast's loneliness and desperation a little more deeply. He's just a guy trying as hard as he can to find a little meaning—a little love, a little beauty—while he's still got a little life left.")

The battle between the two rivals is unequal, as the Beast at first refuses to unleash his fury. In the ensuing struggle, Gaston stabs the Beast in the back, apparently killing him, but the hunter falls to his death from a high parapet. Belle weeps over the Beast's body, and as the last rose petal falls, she utters the magic words: "I love you." Multicolored beams of light shoot down from the sky, lifting the Beast's inert body, resurrecting him and returning him to human form. Only when she looks into the prince's blue eyes (a mirror to his inner beauty?) is Belle convinced that the two beings are one and the same. *Beauty and the Beast*'s subversion of the traditional aesthetic goes only so far. At the film's conclusion, the Beast does turn into a typical Prince Charming—an auburn-haired hunk resembling the model Fabio—the castle and its servants are restored, the music plays, and the grand ball commences.

In addition to its view of aesthetics, *Beauty and the Beast* contains some other narrative evolutions for Disney animated features, reflecting a growing sophistication. Dead and dying animals, shot by Gaston, appear *on*-screen in this feature. The villain Gaston appears to perish at the end of the film. A very different kind of sexuality also makes an appearance in this movie, although in passing. Gaston's empty-headed, young female admirers are portrayed with large breasts and low-cut dresses (in contrast to Belle's more modest neckline). A street vendor in the village pays a bit too much attention to the ample décolletage of a pretty, middle-aged customer, prompting a conk on the head with a rolling pin from his homely wife. Behind the curtain in the Beast's castle, the candelabra seems to be frolicking with the feather duster, a dalliance that continues when both are turned back into servant and maid. This is a long way from the stork bringing baby Dumbo to the circus.

"This tale helps to forward the image of unloved and unhappy white men who need kindness and affection, rather than criticism and reform, in order to become their 'true' selves again," wrote Susan Jeffords in *From Mouse to Mermaid*. "*Beauty and the Beast* is more than just a 'don't judge a book by its cover' morality play that characterized so many of it predecessors. For Belle is, for all intents and purposes, a Disney Feminist. And Gaston is a Male Chauvinist Pig, the kind that would turn the women of any prime-time talk show audience into beasts themselves. . . . The Beast is The New Man, the one who can transform himself from the hardened, muscle-bound, domineering man of the '80s into the considerate, loving, and self-sacrificing man of the '90s."

For children and adolescents, parents might want to use *Beauty and the Beast* to begin a serious discussion about the way appearance affects the way we see people. As a complement, or maybe as an antidote, I'd also have them watch DreamWorks's *Shrek*. In this great "anti-Disney film," the heroine gives up her conventional beauty for love, becoming a green-skinned "beast"—with no regrets. Children can be incredibly cruel to peers, based on physical appearance. This is particularly true when these instincts are reinforced every day by media and popular culture and—worst of all—advertising that exalts aesthetic perfection, something unattainable for most. Having a beast turn into a handsome prince is an easy sell. But what about schoolmates who are not thin, or blond, or who don't have skin like unblemished porcelain? How should they be treated? If not angels, might not they become valued friends, or even dates? The next time a son or daughter makes a disparaging remark about another's looks, it might be helpful to ask how Belle might find the beauty in someone like that.

Chapter Twenty-Three

Aladdin (1992): Encountering Islam

For many Muslims in the United States and around the world, a single, offensive line of dialogue in *Aladdin* quickly obscured the hit movie's moral messages. The singer, in the film's opening song, which has an exotic, Eastern melody, says he comes from a distant land "where they cut off your ear if they don't like your face; it's barbaric, but, hey, it's home." Clearly, this is the mysterious, Oriental "other," and such a blanket characterization of a region and a culture smacks of ignorant ethnocentrism. There were early warning signs over the line. Howard Ashman, one of the songwriters, was "not unaware of the racist implication of the lyrics," and submitted an alternative lyric, which was later used in video and DVD release, according to Henry A. Giroux in *The Mouse That Roared*. John Culhane of New York University, who wrote a book about the film, *Aladdin: The Making of an Animated Film,* said he also objected to the line when he screened an early cut, and was surprised when it was not taken out. "I never thought that would stay in the film," he told Michael Precker of the *Dallas Morning News* on July 12, 1993. "If *Aladdin* makes one child slink out of the theater because he doesn't feel as good about himself as the other kids, then they've forgotten what Walt Disney was all about." During production, Jeffrey Katzenberg was concerned that a sequence involving a campy bit with the genie might be offensive to gays, according to Disney executive Thomas Schumacher, who is openly gay. "Jeffrey asked if those [scenes] offended me—which might surprise people, because apparently we weren't worried about offending Arabs," he told the authors of *Disney: The Mouse Betrayed.*

Disney reacted to the ensuing controversy as most corporations do: first by dismissing the criticism until the complaints gained sufficient traction, and then backing down as little as possible. A studio spokesman rejected the initial complaints as nit-picking. But when the storm of protest from Arab American and Muslim American groups did not subside, and gained support in the media, Disney apologized. "In no way would we ever do something that would be insensitive to anyone," Dick Cook, then Disney's vice president for distribution, told Precker in a subsequent *Dallas Morning News* article (October 22, 1994). "So, on reflection, we changed it." The line in the video version (and subsequent theatrical releases, but not on the music CD) of the feature became: "It's flat and immense, and the heat is intense; it's barbaric, but, hey, it's home." For the *New York Times,* the change was "progress, but still unacceptable," the paper wrote in a July 14, 1993, editorial. "To characterize an entire region with this sort of tongue-in-cheek bigotry, especially in a movie aimed at children, borders on barbaric." In any event, the fray demonstrated that the era of the acceptance of offhand stereotypes that stretched back decades was finally over.

Lost, to some degree, in the controversy over that single line are a number of broader complaints, beginning with the first character to speak in the movie, a peddler. With an enlarged turban and an equally bulbous nose, the merchant has a fast-talking, wheedling manner that would be recognizably offensive if the character were Jewish. Similarly, most of the villains in *Aladdin* have large noses, dark complexions, facial hair, and speak with accents. Smooth-faced Aladdin has Caucasian features and talks like a tanned resident of Southern California. Princess Jasmine—his love interest—has large, almond eyes, but is otherwise Western. The market and streets of the mythical city of Agrabah seem replete with every Oriental cliché, including sword swallowers, fire-eaters, hot-coal walkers, and snake charmers. Many of the female characters are dressed out of the Western harem fantasy. That is, small, transparent veils on the lower part of their faces and brief tops that bare their midriffs.

More important than the offensive lyric, wrote Jack Shaheen, professor of mass communications at Southern Illinois University, "the mispronunciation of Arab names in the film, the racial coding of accents, and the use of nonsensical scrawl as a substitute for an actual written Arabic language were not removed," according to *The Mouse That Roared.* A number of times in *Aladdin,* characters use the Arabic word for God—*Allah*—as an exclamation: "By Allah," "Allah forbid," "Praise Allah." Yet it is unlikely that writers and producers would feel so free to have Disney characters use the word "God" in this way. In a similar vein, trespassers in a forbidden treasure cave are referred to as "infidels." Would the term "nonbelievers" ever appear in a script? In a December 1992 column in the *Los Angeles Times,* Shaheen had a suggestion for Disney. The company, he wrote, might take a more respectful page from the script of *Aladdin's Lamp,* a 1907 silent film. Characters in that movie say, "Allah gives us the morning" and "Allah gives us the lovely day."

One of the most controversial aspects of Islam's *Sharia* law appears a number of times in the movie. Both Aladdin and, later, Jasmine are threatened with having their hands cut off when they are accused of stealing food. "I'll have your hands for a trophy," a palace guard tells the boy, before he escapes and gives the bread he took to several starving children. While it may be historically accurate—although some Islamic authorities say this is a misunderstanding of *Sharia*—it is fair to wonder whether this is the one example of Muslim jurisprudence that should be highlighted for young viewers in the West. It is likely that these children (and their parents), most with no knowledge of Muslim or Arab history or culture, notice none of this. For them, *Aladdin* is simply a tour de force for the manic humor of Robin Williams, who voiced the character of the Genie. It also refines the winning formula for animated features, in which the visuals and the story work for children, with more sophisticated jokes tossed in for adults. The moral messages are standard Disney issue—a reprise of *Lady and the Tramp.* Aladdin, the poor, orphaned "street rat," realizes that he should not continue masquerading as a prince, thanks to the Genie, in order to marry the sultan's daughter. "I have to stop pretending I'm something I'm not," he says. And girls like Jasmine should not be subjected to arranged marriages, or to contests. "I'm not a prize to be won," she insists.

"It's a marvelous picture," Donald Bustany, president of the Los Angeles chapter of the Arab-American Anti-Discrimination Committee, told the *Dallas Morning News*. "But with all the good intentions, it's still a racist picture." Salam Al-Marayati, director of the Muslim Public Affairs Council in Los Angeles, agreed. "I don't want my child to grow up with any self-hating sentiments," he told McClatchy News Service on May 22, 1993. "All the Arab characters he sees [in the film] are violent or very nasty."

In addition to making the dialogue cut in the *Aladdin* video, Disney attempted to make further amends in straight-to-video sequels, toning down some of the physical characteristics of the Arabs. And when Aladdin is charged with theft this time, even from the sultan's treasury, he is told that the penalty for that crime is life in a dungeon. But there is still room for improvement. As Aladdin and Jasmine prepare to climb the steps for their wedding, church bells are heard, and there is no Muslim imam in sight to officiate at the ceremony. Comic images that pass through the video include a modern, religious Jew, the biblical Moses, and a pig.

The *Aladdin* controversy proved to be round 1 of Disney's clash with Islam and the Arab world. Round 2 reminded the company that globalism has a potential downside. In the late summer of 1999, the government of Israel announced plans to open an exhibit at Epcot's Millennium Village at Walt Disney World. Criticism of the exhibit began in the Middle East and soon spread to the United States. The 2,400-square-foot display was part of a temporary World Showcase pavilion, involving twenty-three countries, and was devoted to the city of Jerusalem. Supported by a $1.8 million grant from Israel's foreign ministry, the multimedia exhibit included a ride called "Journey to Jerusalem." Arab American and Muslim American groups, together with officials from Arab governments, voiced concern that the exhibit would psychologically bolster Israel's claim to an undivided Jerusalem—including Arab East Jerusalem—as the capital of the Jewish State. Negotiations over the city's status were then underway between the Israelis and the Palestinians. The General Secretariat of the Arab League issued a letter of reprimand, raising the possibility of a boycott of

Disney products because of "negative portrayals of Arabs" in films such as *Aladdin*. As the furor grew, Walt Disney World officials met quietly with Arab leaders in Washington, D.C., on September 15, 1999. The group, which included ambassadors of the United Arab Emirates and Morocco, watched a video of the exhibit and gave Disney a memo outlining their concerns. In response, Israeli government officials said they would make no changes in the exhibition. Eitan Bentsur, director general of Israel's foreign ministry, called on Disney Chairman Michael Eisner not to "surrender to the political pressure," according to Richard Verrier in the September 17, 1999, *Orlando Sentinel*.

A behind-the-scenes settlement provided that there would be no references to Jerusalem as Israel's capital in the exhibition, although it was never clear that any such notations had been planned. For its part, the Israeli foreign ministry said that it was pleased, since the recognition of the city's status was implicit. "It's regrettable that we were brought into a debate from the beginning on which we have no position or any power to resolve," said Bill Warren, a spokesman for Walt Disney World. "We would very much like to get back to the business of providing quality entertainment, and that's our intent." On September 24, twenty Arab foreign ministers met in New York City to discuss a possible Disney boycott because of the exhibit, but decided against such action, although several American Muslim organizations said they were still considering a boycott. Esmat Abdel-Meguid, general secretary of the Arab League, which convened the New York meeting, credited Eisner for deescalating the situation. The Disney chairman, Abdel-Meguid said, "was a man who's looking for peace, and his response was positive." Influential Arab businessmen such as Saudi billionaire Alwaleed Bin Talal Bin Abdulaziz, a major stockholder in struggling Euro Disney, also counseled against any boycott, interceding with Arab leaders, including Yassir Arafat, according to an interview with Richard Verrier, in the January 26, 2004, *Orlando Sentinel*. "Alwaleed said that once Eisner assured him that 'Disney has no religion,'" the Saudi businessman swung into action.

The politics of the Middle East are also sometimes the politics of Hollywood. It is curious that Jeffrey Katzenberg should be more concerned with possible slights to gays in *Aladdin* than to Arabs, Arab Americans, and Muslims in the film. Or perhaps not, given Katzenberg's vigorous and public support for Israel, and for right-wing religious groups there such as Aish HaTorah. By contrast, Michael Eisner's worldview—as head of a publicly traded multinational corporation—has to be less parochial, and so he was in his handling of the Epcot controversy. And, despite the major financial bequest by his great-grandfather Sigmund Eisner to early Zionist settlers in what was then Palestine, Michael Eisner's support for Israel is unknown.

A larger, and perhaps more interesting question to ask is: What would the outcome of the *Aladdin* controversy have been if it had taken place *after* the terrorism horror of September 11, 2001? All of the stereotypes included in the movie were revived—with a literal vengeance—in the weeks and months that followed the tragedy. To President George W. Bush's credit, the chief executive repeated that Islam was not America's enemy, nor was the Arab world. Notwithstanding, I think it will be many years before American children will be able to watch *Aladdin* without connecting the characters with our image of Arab terrorists.

Chapter Twenty-Four

The Lion King (1994): Karma on the Savannah

The last in a string of monster hits for Disney animators, *The Lion King* cautiously offers an alternative cosmos, edging away from the Judeo-Christian universe that characterized the company's full-length features since *Snow White*. Rob Minkoff, the film's director, said that the film attempted "a level of spirituality, something slightly metaphysical," according to the June 12, 1994, *New York Daily News*. In another departure for the studio, its message was presented with a genuinely African sensibility, complete with songs and chants in native languages and African American actors speaking major roles. The opening sunrise sequence on the African plain begins with a song that is infused with the continent's rhythms and energy, "Circle of Life." Creatures great and small, predators and prey, gather at Pride Rock to acknowledge the birth of an heir to Mufasa, the Lion King. The lyrics explain the concept of the "Great Circle of Life," which draws on the Hindu tradition that earthly existence is part of a never-ending cycle—although there is no specific reference to reincarnation. In the rousing, gospel-style rendition of the song, the animals sing that, from the day they are born, they begin moving through this cycle and that, through "faith and love," they find their proper place. Without question, this is not Christianity's tradition and promise of resurrection.

Yet there is a ceremony that appears to replicate infant baptism. The lion cub Simba is anointed by Rafiki, a baboon seer—first with juice and then with dust from the earth—the wise old monkey moving his thumb across the animal's forehead, much like a Catholic or Anglican priest does with an infant. Held up before the animal throngs, a shaft of light shines down on Simba through the clouds, confirming a heavenly blessing. As the cub grows, he learns more about how life in his world operates. Existence is finite, even for kings, Mufasa instructs Simba. A monarch's time to rule "rises and falls, like the sun." And his power is limited, the father explains, because "there is more to being king than getting your way all the time." Life in the wild exists in a delicate balance, and all creatures must be respected. With antelope leaping by the father and son during this tutorial, Simba asks a logical question: Why respect these beasts, if they are destined to become food for the pride? Because, Mufasa says, "when we die, our bodies become the grass, and the antelopes eat the grass, and so we are all connected in the Great Circle of Life."

Mufasa warns Simba that their realm does not extend to the "shadowy places," where their natural enemies, the hyenas, hold sway. Zazu, the king's parrot councilor, adds his own observation, that the hyenas are "slobbering, mangy poachers." But Scar, Mufasa's sly, black-maned younger brother, is able to tempt the gullible Simba into making a trip to the forbidden area, accompanied by his female playmate, Nala. Along the way, the cubs learn from Zazu that they are betrothed (arranged marriages are *always* disparaged in Disney features), a practice Simba says he will abolish when he becomes king. "I can't marry Nala," he says, "she's my friend" (and likely his half sister). This leads Simba into a rousing song called "I Just Can't Wait to Be King," arguably Freudian, which slides over the implicit reality that the cub cannot become ruler until his father dies. Giving the watchful Zazu the slip, Simba and Nala find their way to the elephants' graveyard, where they encounter the hyenas. Some critics of *The Lion King,* in what I believe is a stretch, charged that the pack is suggestive of an urban gang, in part because the characters are voiced by African American (Whoopi Goldberg) and Hispanic (Cheech Marin) actors. "It's clear that Simba is on the wrong side of the tracks, in a bad neighborhood, surrounded by 'the projects'—he's caught in the inner city," wrote Matt Roth, in *Jump Cut.*

At first the two cubs flee, but when Nala slips and falls behind, Simba bravely returns to defend her. However, it is Mufasa who returns to save them both. Simba's disobedience provides what psychologists and educators call a "teachable moment." The cub is chastened, knowing that he has done wrong. As his father begins to speak, Simba looks to the ground and observes that his tiny paw is dwarfed by his father's large print. Mufasa says he is disappointed with his son, more than he is angry. Simba says he only wants to be brave, like his father; the king replies that he is only brave when he has to be. "Being brave doesn't mean you go looking for trouble," Mufasa says. This line of instruction leads Simba to ask if father and son will always be together. Rather than giving the cub—and the young children watching—a straight answer to a very large question, the father asks his son to look up into the vast, night sky. The great Lion Kings of the past, Mufasa explains, "look down at us from those stars. . . . So whenever you feel alone, just remember that those kings will be there to guide you—and so will I."

There is great danger to the natural order of succession coming from within the royal family. Scar, Mufasa's brother, displaced in line by Simba, is planning what he calls the coup of the century, with the help of the hyenas. The king's brother promises the wild dogs a steady stream of meat, thus, in Roth's view, "creating the Welfare State." The pack, apparently anarchists, first think that getting rid of Mufasa will mean no more royal rule, no more kings. Scar quickly disabuses them of that notion. Baring his teeth and his ambition, Scar again lures Simba into harm's way, this time to a steep, dry gorge, where the hyenas set off a massive stampede of wildebeests. Mufasa is then summoned by his younger brother to save the cub, but through Scar's treachery, the king is trampled to death after saving his son. Simba believes his actions have led to his father's death, and he accepts his uncle's suggestion to flee. Scar then orders the hyenas to kill the cub, and only Simba's flight into a cactus bramble (a nod to B'rer Rabbit's briar patch?) enables him to escape death. Scar delivers a disingenuous funeral oration for Mufasa, assumes the crown, and installs the hyenas as enforcers and Praetorian guards. His regime reeks of totalitarian images and colors: the goose-stepping ranks of hyenas; the outline of a gold fascist eagle; and a red silhouette of Soviet Communism's hammer and sickle. (Some critics also see Scar, effete and without a mate, as a negative gay stereotype. He was drawn by a gay animator, Andreas Deja, who did both Gaston in *Beauty and the Beast* and Jafar in *Aladdin*. Sean Griffin, in *Tinker Belles and Evil Queens: The Walt Disney Company from the Inside Out*, asks if others see the "gay-tinged villainy" by "watching how Jafar arches his eyebrows in disdain, or in the sneer that curls Scar's mouth as he endures the heterosexual patriarchy in which he finds himself.")

Annalee Ward, in *Mouse Morality*, detected aspects of a more traditional Judeo-Christian framework at this point in the movie. Simba falls from grace and effectively expels himself from paradise, leaving Satan (or the serpent) on the throne. He wanders in the wilderness, nearly dying in a dry, cracked wasteland, until he is saved from vultures by a fast-talking meerkat named Timon, and his friend, a slow-witted warthog named Pumbaa. Some have complained that Timon and Pumbaa, both male, appear to be a couple, and as such represent another of the film's gay clichés. Or, they may just be good friends. In any event, the two companions take Simba to a lush, Edenic land and introduce him to their interpretation of the concept of karma, a deterministic philosophy shared by Hinduism and Buddhism. As Timon explains the concept, "Bad things happen, and you can't do anything about it." So, the meerkat advises, live by this African variation, "Hakuna Matata," which he says means, since you can't do anything about life's vagaries, there is no point in worrying about them. It is, Timon and Pumbaa sing, a "problem-free philosophy," with no rules or responsibilities.

As time passes, Simba grows into a carefree young adult with his friends, much like Shakespeare's Prince Hal in *Henry IV, Part 1* and Mowgli in *The Jungle Book*. However, there is plenty of trouble in Scar's realm: There is no food or water in the Pride Lands, and the lionesses won't hunt. Well-fed on insects, Timon, Pumbaa, and Simba are free to muse on the nature of the night firmament. Timon, "the smart one," believes that the stars are fireflies that got stuck in a big, dark place. Pumbaa, "the dumb one," thinks they are "balls of gas, burning billions of miles away"—the correct answer. The discussion draws Simba back to thoughts of his father. The stars, he tells his friends, are "great kings of the past."

Hunger drives young Nala from home to hunt in the area. Only Simba's intervention saves Timon and Pumbaa from being devoured by his childhood companion—mirroring the story of Androcles and the Lion. Nala is shocked to discover that Simba is alive and, as required of all animals in Disney's previous animated features, she takes the mating initiative. But she also insists that he return home and save the land from Scar and the hyenas. Half-heartedly, Simba tries to explain to her Hakuna Matata. The female will have none of this self-indulgence, however. If Simba avoids his responsibility to the pride, she argues, everyone will starve, and not just the lions.

Rafiki has had a vision of Simba, alive, and the conjurer makes his way to where the young lion is grappling with his future. Simba wants advice, so Rafiki naturally assumes Buddhism's double lotus position, the *gama honza*. The lion is told to look at his reflection in a stream, since Mufasa lives within Simba. Then Mufasa himself materializes in the clouds, first in a black-and-white image, but gradually shifting to a glowing, gold form. In an ethereal, echoing voice, the old lion urges his son to look inside himself, and to remember who he is. "You are more than what you have become," he intones (as only the actor who portrays him, James Earl Jones, can intone). "Take your place in the Great Circle of Life. You are my son, the one true king." As Simba hurries home with grim determination, he learns that, while change is good, it may not be easy. His home is desolate, but, as he asks himself, "If I don't fight for it, who will?" However, before Simba can rally the pack and challenge Scar for leadership, he must publicly acknowledge his part in the responsibility for his father's death, which he does. In his climactic battle with Scar, amid a fire started by lightning, Simba prevails, but—per Disney protocol—he does not kill his uncle himself. After a final act of treachery by Scar, that task falls to his betrayed allies, the hyenas. The true kingdom is restored, blessed by a providential, cleansing rain. More time passes and the film's opening is reprised, as Simba and Nala present their own new cub to their subjects.

The Lion King represented a critical juncture for Disney's animated features, according to Donald E. Fadner's paper, "Disney Gets Religion," delivered at the 1998 meeting of the American Academy of Religion in Orlando. The film articulates what Fadner called "an alternative religious vision." Starting with *The Lion King,* "the greater-than-human dimension of the stories has been much more explicitly 'religious,' i.e., focused on objects of reverence that, while inspiring and supporting the development of the characters, do not intervene directly with magical solutions to their dilemmas. This forces the characters to find within themselves the necessary spiritual resources to solve their problems."

Africans watching *The Lion King* may view the movie through a different historical prism than Westerners. Traditional African leaders once ruled their unspoiled—if not entirely peaceful—continent. In the nineteenth century, European colonialists took the land from them and arbitrarily divided it, often with little regard for ethnic outlines, simply to suit their political and economic needs. Then, in the last decades of the twentieth century, the continent was reclaimed by Africans—in some cases by force. For these viewers, Simba's restoration may resonate in a special way, although they are themselves still living with the divisive consequences of colonial-era borders. The same year *The Lion King* was released, Nelson Mandela, an African leader himself of royal lineage, was elected president of South Africa in that nation's first free, multiracial election.

The Lion King demonstrated that, after all the decades of caricature and stereotype, it was indeed possible for Disney—under the invigorated and increasingly confident leadership of Eisner and Katzenberg—to reach beyond the Western experience and the Judeo-Christian construct. With the critical help of the studio's writers, producers, and animators—and African American artists—they could encounter a different culture and successfully adapt it to the Disney tradition. A good story, memorable songs, and engaging animation combined for enduring entertainment and, most importantly for the company, a billion-dollar cash machine.

Chapter Twenty-Five

Pocahontas (1995): Animating Animism

*E*ven before the film's title appears on the screen, over a scene of early-seventeenth-century London, *Pocahontas*'s terms of engagement are sketched out in a song that draws on religion. English settlers have been recruited to sail across the ocean to an unknown land for "glory, God, and gold, and the Virginia Company." The New World, the yeomen have been promised by their commercial employers, is "like heaven." But there are also demons lurking in this paradise. All on board know that one of the dangers, an impediment to the guarantees of easy riches, is the Indians. But with the party is Captain John Smith, the renowned and impossibly handsome soldier. Their leader is Governor John Ratcliffe, a pompous poseur with a swishy valet and a pampered bulldog, working on what he admits is his last chance to succeed in the court of King James I. Ratcliffe, a hypocrite, speaks inspiringly of the freedom and prosperity that awaits the company, while in private he dismisses the crew as "witless peasants" whose only value is "to dig up my gold."

On the other side of the Atlantic, the film's moral deck is being stacked even higher. Unaware of what is about to befall them, Native Americans are living a blissful, bucolic life—in total harmony with nature. They are fit, handsome, and beautiful, with no sign of disease or malnutrition. Their livelihood comes from planting corn, hunting abundant game, and fishing the rivers and streams. Young people play a game that appears to resemble lacrosse, or sit around a campfire while a shaman conjures up spiritual images from the smoke. Not all of life is peaceful—warriors return home from battling marauding tribes, reporting victory.

Pocahontas, daughter of Chief Powhatan, is troubled about a puzzling dream she has been having, involving a spinning arrow, and she resists her father's plans for her to marry the band's bravest warrior, Kocoum. For guidance in these matters, she paddles her canoe to see Grandmother Willow, a gnarled, ancient tree that comes to life to provide wisdom to Pocahontas. All around, the tree says, are spirits. "They live in the earth, the water, the sky. If you listen, they will guide you."

What guides the approaching English is nothing so ethereal. It's greed, and of a particular nasty, despoiling variety. Ratcliffe imagines "an entire new world, chock full of gold, waiting for me." The governor tells John Smith that it will be his job to handle the Indians: "I'm counting on you to make sure those filthy heathens don't disrupt our mission." Stepping ashore, Ratcliffe plants the Union Jack and claims the land and its riches for James I, calling their settlement Jamestown. He wastes no time directing the men to unload the ship, start work on the fort and, most of all, to start digging, reminding them what Spanish conquistadors such as Cortés and Pizarro found when they arrived in the Western hemisphere. "For years they've been ravaging the New World of its most precious resources," the governor says, pausing for effect. "Now, it's *our* turn." He drops a dagger point into a parchment map of the Americas, where Virginia is marked with a pile of gold coins. There follows a song and production number called "Mine, Mine, Mine," which can only be described as a hymn to avarice. Ratcliffe urges his men to dig up Virginia, and they happily agree, beginning a wanton destruction of the land and the forest.

The Indians are perplexed as to how to respond to the invaders. At a council meeting in a great lodge, the shaman calls up a vision from the campfire smoke. "They prowl the earth like ravenous wolves, consuming everything in their path," he says. Some suggest an attack. Near the shoreline, Pocahontas is drawn to the white men, and to one white man in particular, John Smith. She trails him as he scouts the land and, when they finally meet near a waterfall, she is suddenly able to communicate with him because she follows Grandmother Willow's advice to "listen with your heart." Their meeting seems blessed, as tiny leaves and glowing bits first swirl around their touching hands, and then around their bodies. "That these two exceptionally good-looking characters are both the heroes and the subjects of the film's romance indicates a moral vision that equates good looks with good character, as well as suggesting that people are right for each other when they are equally attractive," according to Annalee Ward in *Mouse Morality*.

The couple agrees that their names sound equally strange to each other. But Smith has no doubt about the superiority of Western civilization. In a friendly yet patronizing way, he explains that the settlers will teach the Indians how to make the most of their land, like building decent houses. "We've improved the lives of savages all over the world," he says with pride. Pocahontas bridles at the word "savage," with Smith arguing that it is not pejorative, just another way of saying "uncivilized." In fact, the young woman says, savage means "not like you." She segues into the film's hit single, "Colors of the Wind," a plea for human understanding, diversity, and reverence for the earth and nature. The first verse takes direct aim at the Europeans: "You think you own whatever land you land on, The earth is just a dead thing you can claim." *Pocahontas,* said Thomas Schumacher, senior vice president of Disney Feature Animation, "is a story that is fundamentally about racism and intolerance, and we hope that people will gain a greater understanding of themselves and the world around them. It's also about having respect for each other's culture," according to the article "Redesigning Pocahontas" by Gary Edgerton and Kathy Merlock Jackson, in *Journal of Popular Film and Television.*

Finding no gold in the ground, Ratcliffe becomes convinced that the Indians must have it, and the only way to get it is to march on the village and kill all the inhabitants. In order to do that, the governor must first dehumanize the enemy—a familiar practice still in use today around the world. Smith, enlightened by his encounter with Pocahontas, argues for another course, only to be dismissed as a traitor to his race. Anyone who so much as looks at an Indian without immediately killing him will be tried for treason and hanged, Ratcliffe says, for those still unconvinced. A party of warriors searching for Pocahontas stumbles into a skirmish with the settlers, a clash that leaves Kocoum dead and infuriates the Indians. They capture Smith and schedule his execution the following day. Powhatan tells Pocahontas that his daughter's disobedience has caused Kocoum's death.

The Jamestown settlers march out to attack the Indians, to save Smith and get the gold they are convinced is there. For their part, the Indians—now reinforced by their allies—prepare to meet the invaders. As the two groups approach their confrontation, they sing themselves into a fury, describing their enemies with precisely the same words—savages, demons, devils, vermin. But by this time in *Pocahontas,* even a child can see that this is a false, belated symmetry. There is no moral equivalence in this battle. The Europeans are portrayed as agents of unalloyed evil. Moreover, we know how the larger story will end: North American Indians will eventually die or be driven onto desolate reservations scattered across the continent. Plagued by broken treaties, doomed rebellions, disease, starvation, poverty, suicide, and alcoholism, their only hope will be finding oil under their land—or building casinos on it. In the end, immediate carnage is avoided, although an errant shot by Ratcliffe wounds Smith and sends him back to England to recover, separating him from Pocahontas. This explains why this Disney feature does not end with the male and female leads living happily ever after (leaving open the possibility for a sequel).

Conservative Christians, uneasy about what they saw as the Walt Disney Company's cultural drift in the mid-1990s, found plenty to criticize when *Pocahontas* was released: New Age beliefs, pantheism, nature worship, multiculturalism, and an extremely jaundiced view of America's earliest settlers. Kerby Anderson, head of a Christian think tank called Probe Ministries, said the movie was "a politically correct fairy tale passed off as history," replacing the truth with "a subtle but insidious version of New Age Animism." The critics claimed that the Jamestown settlers' religious faith and Pocahontas's baptism and conversion to Christianity—memorialized in a mural in the U.S. Capitol rotunda—were unfairly excluded in the Disney version. The settlers' first act after landing, setting up a wooden cross and offering a prayer, is absent from the film, noted syndicated columnist Don Feder in a column siding with the critics. There is no portrayal of the Reverend Robert Hunt leading the company in daily prayer. "The first Christian convert in Virginia, Pocahontas, is transformed into a pagan priestess who gets advice from trees and weaves white magic," Feder wrote in the *Boston Herald* of June 21, 1995. *Movieguide* magazine, published by the Christian Film and Television Commission, called the release "ultimately pantheistic" and said, "Many moral Americans will complain that *Pocahontas* is too New Age as it spreads its ecological spiritualism." The Reverend Lou Sheldon, head of the Washington, D.C.-based Traditional Values Coalition, agreed. "What you have is the secularization of a very, very significant event in the founding of America, which was the christening of Pocahontas into the Christian faith," Sheldon said in the *Orlando Sentinel* of July 16, 1995.

Disney officials, including Chairman Michael Eisner, replied that Pocahontas's conversion took place after the action depicted in the movie. But in the straight-to-video sequel, *Pocahontas II: Journey to a New World,* which covers her relationship with John Rolfe, her future husband, and her trip to London, no mention is made of her conversion or her life as a Christian. The company did have other defenders. Robert Schuller, pastor of the Crystal Cathedral in Garden Grove, California, and host of the "Hour of Power" television program, defended Disney's portrayal. If Pocahontas's conversion had been included in the film, Schuller said, critics might raise the legitimate historical issue of whether the act was voluntary. Some historians say the conversion took place while the girl was held captive in Jamestown. Because entertainment is a secular business, Schuller said, Disney filmmakers are wise to avoid "oppressing their market with sectarian religious teachings," while "being faithful to the classic values that come from Western civilization."

Why is the absence of Pocahontas's conversion to Christianity such a sore point with religious conservatives? Donald E. Fadner suggested one explanation in his paper "Disney Gets Religion," delivered at the American Academy of Religion meeting in Orlando in November 1998: "It takes a historical icon that has been used in the past to legitimate their view of America—Pocahontas's conversion representing native recognition of the superiority of Christianity," and with it the justification of European conquest "to build a great nation, under God—and turns it against them." The film, Fadner concludes, "is a mythic tale that calls, among other things, for a movement into a post-Christian era of *religious democracy,* where the diverse ways in which the human spirit can express its deepest longings and creative potentials will be celebrated and protected."

Misgivings were not confined to religious conservatives. There were also critics among Native Americans and historians and activists who claimed that the story had been hopelessly distorted to fit the film's narrative. Some objected to Pocahontas's portrayal as a willing collaborationist. Others cited the transformation of a preteen—in historical accounts—to a nubile babe in off-the-shoulder buckskin, with pouty, collagen lips. "Jeffrey Katzenberg told me to make her the finest creature the human race has to offer," supervising animator Glen Keane told *Entertainment Weekly* in its June 23, 1995, issue. (One model for Pocahontas was the teenage daughter of Russell Means, the Indian rights activist who voiced the role of Powhatan.) After Native American protests, a particularly offensive lyric, in which an English character denounces Native Americans, saying, "Their whole disgusting race is like a curse," was changed in the video to "Here's what you get when races are diverse."

American Indian actors were forced to defend their participation in the film, which includes their speaking and singing in historically accurate language. Means called *Pocahontas* "the single finest work done on American Indians by Hollywood," according to Janet Wasko's *Understanding Disney*. "Because it's Disney, millions of children forever are going to see this in their most formative years, and it's going to affect how they see my people and our culture all the way through their lives." Means released an open letter to coincide with the film's opening. Disney, he wrote, has "admitted that the real reason the European males came over here in the first place was to rob, rape, and pillage the land and kill to gain respect from the other sacred colors of the human race."

Conservatives complained about the characterization of Rat-cliffe. The governor, a historical figure, "carries the racism and greed of the movie," supervising animator Duncan Majoribanks said in the film's press kit. He is a "fascist," said the animator who drew him, according to Ward's *Mouse Morality.* "Obese and obnoxious, he is the antithesis of what Powhatan stands for." "His lifestyle epitomizes the vulgarity of the colonists when compared to the lifestyle of the Native Americans." But Disney animators rejected charges that the hated governor was overdrawn. "If we want to be absolutely historically accurate," the film's story head Tom Sito told the authors of *Disney: The Mouse Betrayed,* "you know what happened to the real Sir John Ratcliffe? When the Indians captured him, he was nailed to a tree and skinned alive. That would have been a choice Disney moment. Maybe a good song sequence."

It is possible that there is an element of unintended payback in *Pocahontas*'s malign portrayal of Virginia's founders. The state's modern residents—who take their colonial past *very* seriously—played a major role in one of the Walt Disney Company's greatest debacles, the failure of "Disney's America," a 150-acre, history-based theme park planned for the hunt country of Prince William County, Virginia. But just ten months after plans for the contro-versial project were announced, in September 1994, company offi-cials bowed to local protests—some of which attributed to Michael Eisner personality traits similar to the rapacious Governor Rat-cliffe—and cancelled "Disney's America." *Pocahontas,* released the following year (but in production for years*),* may have been Michael Eisner's departing, cinematic valentine to Virginia.

Chapter Twenty-Six

The Hunchback of Notre Dame (1996): The House of the Lord

*S*et in and around a famed cathedral, *The Hunchback of Notre Dame* was the first Disney feature to put traditional religious faith—in this case, pre-Reformation Catholicism—at the center of the narrative. And it would be difficult to find a more thoroughly Christian film, one which stands the devoutly anticlerical novelist Victor Hugo, the author of the book on which it is based, on his head. At every critical stage of the Disney version, it is the church—in the person of the cathedral's archdeacon—that interposes, or attempts to interpose, itself between the villain and his evil intentions. Belief in a loving, forgiving God anchors the story, along with implied condemnation of abortion, euthanasia, and racism, and of moral resistance to genocide. The words "God" and "Lord" are spoken and sung more frequently in this movie than in all previous animated Disney features combined, and there are crosses everywhere.

Previously, wrote Eleanor Byrne and Martin McQuillan in *Deconstructing Disney,* the studio "approached the name of God with an almost Hebraic zeal (that it should never be stated) yet here it is invoked in a manner both pious and puritan." Songs faithfully incorporate or adapt Catholic prayers and chants adapted from Latin. The key plot alteration from the novel to the animated feature is the profession and motivation of the villain, Claude Frollo. In Hugo's version, Frollo was a priest and a hypocritical church official, archdeacon of the Cathedral of Notre Dame. On the screen, he is a judge and governmental official—a largely secular figure—with a genocidal preoccupation with Gypsies as agents of moral decay. Admittedly, this largely positive interpretation of religion is not without exception.

Disney executives would have no part of Hugo's intent to criticize the church and its leaders for their failure to defend the poor and the powerless. They feared it would be "too controversial," according to Will Finn, head of the film's story team, cited in *Disney: The Mouse Betrayed* by Peter and Rochelle Schweizer. "So we had to secularize Frollo," he said. At the same time, the animators did their best to subvert this order from above. "We did everything visually to indicate that he was supposed to be a priest," Finn said. They succeeded in this representation of Frollo, according to Ward. "In almost all respects except the title, he is presented as a religious leader. The association of the church with this kind of evil leadership implies a church that is ineffective if not full of vice— the very thing Hugo was criticizing in the original novel. Religion . . . appears as an impotent, irrelevant caricature. . . . By relegating the church, and more specifically God, to irrelevancy, Disney refuses to admit a serious role for religion."

Unquestionably, there is throughout the film a strong current attacking religious and moral hypocrisy, which some have seen as an attack on the Christian Right. "It's about the complexity of a religious figure who is torn between good and evil, chastity and lust," said Finn. "The cathedral evokes the spirit of the Christian God, though it does so in a way that counteracts the judgments of some who claim to speak for that God," wrote Donald E. Fadner, in his paper "Disney Gets Religion." While Frollo's stated goal as judge is to purge the world of vice and sin, according to the opening song, he "saw corruption everywhere except within."

The film's action begins years earlier when, as head of the city's department of justice, Frollo is persecuting a small band of Gypsies, whom he refers to as "vermin," who are trying to slip into Paris. He pursues one of them, a young woman carrying a small bundle as she flees through the snow toward Notre Dame, in hopes of sanctuary. But, from his saddle, the magistrate struggles with her over the bundle, leading to her death on the church steps. His prize, he learns to his disgust, is not stolen goods but a misshapen infant—in his eyes a monster and a demon. Just as he is about to throw the baby down a well, to certain death, the cathedral's archdeacon emerges and stops him. Killing the woman on the steps has put Frollo's soul in mortal danger, the priest says. As penance, he must spare the baby and provide for his upbringing. Frollo accepts, saying, "Our Lord works in mysterious ways," at the same time musing that the child may be of use to him one day.

Named Quasimodo and raised in the cathedral, the boy becomes the church's bell ringer, his only friends three wisecracking gargoyles. He is physically grotesque but good-natured and sensitive, an underdog "symbolically viewed as being an angel in a devil's body," according to the film's production notes. The young man is "trapped between heaven above" and "the gritty streets of urban Paris viewed as hell." As the raucous Festival of Fools approaches in the square below, Quasimodo longs to join the world outside. Frollo, joining his ward for a meal and instruction in the bell tower, forbids it. The judge's version of the alphabet, which Quasimodo repeats, reflects Frollo's view of the world: Abomination, Blasphemy, Contrition, Damnation, and Eternal Damnation. The boy's other lesson is to be reminded that he is deformed and ugly—a monster—an outcast who would be scorned and jeered by people if he ever ventured out. Yet the lure of the festival, where common people "mock the prig and shock the priest," and Quasimodo's frustration with being excluded for being different, are too much for him to resist.

At first euphoric, the foray ends in disaster, and crushing humiliation for the boy. He is rescued by a voluptuous and fiery Gypsy dancer, Esmeralda, in the process defying the infuriated Frollo before the crowd. For this act of rebellion, she is forced to flee into the cathedral for sanctuary, where the archdeacon welcomes her. She asks the cleric why there is such disdain for people who are different—Gypsies or hunchbacks. "You can't right all the wrongs of the world by yourself," he says. Gesturing heavenward, the archdeacon says, "Perhaps there's someone here who can." She walks the length of the church—in the opposite direction of more prosperous worshipers who are praying for material and earthly rewards. As she looks up at the magnificent, stained glass windows, Esmeralda sings a song, "God Help the Outcasts," which is essentially a populist prayer. Gazing at a statue of Mary and Baby Jesus, she asks for pity for outcasts like herself and her people, wondering if Jesus was once an outcast himself. "She looks up to a curiously un-Catholic Madonna (if there were to be a puritan statue of the Virgin Mary this would be it)," according to Byrne and McQuillan in *Deconstructing Disney*. Instead of wealth, or fame, or love, the Gypsy prays for mercy for the poor and the downtrodden, which are also the children of God.

"Can you hear the gospel in that song?" asked the Reverend Michael Catlett in his 1997 sermon. "For years we've listened to 'His Eye Is on the Sparrow' and heard within those words and music the assurance that God cares for us, no matter how insignificant we may feel. In some ways, isn't that what 'God Help the Outcasts' is about? God loves and cares for marginalized people, and we have a responsibility to love and care for one another, too. Many folks in churches and crusades have heard 'His Eye Is on the Sparrow,' but countless millions have watched the video and took their children to the Disney movie in which Esmeralda sang of the love of God that knows no bounds, the grace of God that is extended to all people. Isn't that gospel, too?"

Frollo is tortured by his lust for Esmeralda, an unrequited passion that curdles into obsessive hatred. In the song "Hellfire," the judge prays to be delivered from his sin, prostrating himself before a roaring fire, with a cross above it. (Some observers, such as Jim Davis, religion writer for the *South Florida Sun-Sentinel*, note that it is an empty cross and not a traditional Catholic crucifix.) Blessed Mary, he sings, "you know I am much purer that the common, vulgar, weak, licentious crowd." This and other songs are sufficiently full of damnation and warnings about temptation that their theology would be at home in many fundamentalist pulpits today—that is, if Frollo's torment were not so reminiscent of televangelists such as Jim Bakker and Jimmy Swaggart, whose ministries were brought down by sexual scandal. "The Disney people probably had their religious critics in mind when creating this scene, suggesting that it is they, rather than Disney, that are obsessed with sexuality, seeing it everywhere they look, censuring others in the hope of overcoming their attraction to what they condemn," wrote Donald E. Fadner, in "Disney Gets Religion." Frollo's pursuit of the dancing girl, who has been aided in her repeated escapes by Quasimodo, becomes more destructive. Other Gypsies will not betray her for money. A miller on the city's outskirts who admits to giving shelter to the outcasts is nearly burned to death with his family (unprecedented violence for Disney animation). "The question of 'ethnic cleansing' is as much a background to the film as the computer-animated cathedral," according to *Deconstructing Disney*. Similarly, these scenes provide inescapable parallels with the Holocaust that nearly wiped out the Jews and Gypsies of Europe during World War II. "Frollo's hatred of the gypsies also associates him with Hitler," the authors wrote. In wartime France, peasants in the countryside sometimes were more exemplary in protecting Jewish fugitives from the Nazis than were the citizens of Paris.

Captured by Frollo, Esmeralda refuses his final offer to submit to him and is about to be burned at the stake as a witch. Again, the cathedral's archdeacon tries to come to her aid, but soldiers block the cleric. It is Quasimodo who snatches her from the flames and returns her to the sanctuary of the cathedral. Frollo disregards the protection of the church and, again brushing aside a protesting archdeacon, pursues Quasimodo and Esmeralda to the bell tower for a final confrontation. As he is about to kill the couple, Frollo shouts a vaguely biblical curse, "And he shall smite the wicked and plunge them into the fiery pit!" Just then, the judge falls to his own death, in an act of divine intervention. The next day, Esmeralda introduces Quasimodo to the cheering—and accepting—crowd outside, as the bell ringer is approached and then embraced by a young girl. And a little child shall lead them.

Hunchback's timing was significant, if coincidental, opening less than ten days after the company came under fire from the Southern Baptist Convention, the nation's largest Protestant denomination, which was threatening a boycott. "One might argue that it is now possible for Disney to make religion visible because it is only now necessary for Disney to make it visible," wrote Byrne and McQuillan. Whether by design, as the *Deconstructing Disney* authors suggested, or by dumb luck, as others maintained, the initial response to *The Hunchback of Notre Dame* was favorable. "We would certainly applaud any effort by Disney to reaffirm its long-standing, pro-family values, pro-traditional values, family-friendly atmosphere," said the Reverend Richard Land, president of the denomination's Christian Life Commission. Land, who was assigned to monitor Disney's policies, told the *Orlando Sentinel* on June 21, 1996, that "Southern Baptists are going to respond favorably whenever there is an accurate and sympathetic portrayal of Christian values in an entertainment medium." Other family values activists reacted positively to the film. The Reverend Lou Sheldon, head of the Washington, D.C.-based Traditional Values Coalition, said that two months before *Hunchback*'s opening, a Disney vice president predicted—correctly—that he would be pleased with the film's view of religion. "I am thrilled at what I hear about *Hunchback,* that Disney is seeking to honor Christianity and its role in Western civilization," Sheldon said. "I only pray that it will accomplish much good in the minds and hearts of its viewers." Robert Knight, then director of cultural studies for the Washington, D.C.-based Family Research Council, suggested that the company might want to spin that interpretation to its benefit. "If Disney is as smart at marketing as it gets credit for, then inclusion of positive religious elements would be a natural marketing strategy even if the Disney management does not comprehend the importance of those elements," he said.

There were some words of caution, as well. Ted Baehr, chairman of the Atlanta-based Christian Film and Television Commission and editor of the magazine *Movieguide,* warned against misinterpreting the film's content as a response to family values critics, because production of *Hunchback* began in the summer of 1993—well before the protests against Disney gained momentum. Baehr, who has extensive contacts within the film industry, said he expected more pro-family films from Disney as a result of the protests, although company officials "will never admit it." Paul Hetrick, vice president of Colorado Springs-based Focus on the Family, agreed. "They certainly wouldn't tell us if we were a factor." The positive portrayal of faith simply may be an "occasional sop in the direction of religionists to keep everyone happy. That's not going to wash."

Disney officials would not comment on the motivation for *Hunchback*'s religious content, beyond general comments on the subject included in the film's press kit. "The movie speaks for itself," said Disney vice president John Dreyer. "People take away from movies and literature and art a great deal of what they bring to it," he told Gayle White of the *Atlanta Journal Constitution.* However, in the press kit, Don Hahn, the film's producer, who is known for his Christian beliefs and who once addressed the convention of the National Religious Broadcasters, pointed out that there is "no fairy godmother, no spell to be broken" in *Hunchback.* Later, appearing on ABC-TV's "Good Morning America," Hahn was asked what the film's message was. "There are many people in our society that are different from us, for a variety of reasons," he replied. "Don't discard those people, because they all have great worth. There's a great nobility of the human spirit that we should celebrate. And that's what this movie's about."

Still, some remained unconvinced. "This is not a film that is going to be reassuring to the religious community," said Michael Medved, then co-host of PBS's *Sneak Previews,* downplaying the significance of the religious songs and sequences. Medved, the author of *Hollywood versus America* and, although Jewish, a favorite of Christian conservatives, was critical of what he said were the film's anti-Catholic undertones, and that it was so dark overall. Medved's point about bleakness is a fair one. For all of its positive portrayal of faith—and despite a questionable "G" rating—*Hunchback* is a serious film and sometimes frightening, and is no more a movie for young children than Hugo's novel is a fairy tale.

There is an underlying reason why conservative evangelicals and fundamentalists, then gearing up to high dudgeon in their crusade against Disney, did not embrace *The Hunchback of Notre Dame*. Many of them, I believe (but cannot prove), were reluctant because they saw the movie as a *Catholic* rather than a *Christian* film—something that did not happen with Mel Gibson's *The Passion of the Christ.* While modern Southern Baptists will make common political cause with Catholics on issues such as abortion, cloning, and stem cell research, this is often a marriage of convenience. Theologically, these are still strange bedfellows, as anyone

Chapter Twenty-Seven

Hercules (1997): Superman, Samson, and Delilah

*M*aking light of a religion—much less reducing it to a musical comedy—is a lot easier when there are few adherents around to object, as in the Greek religion at the center of *Hercules*. The central stories of many modern faiths might also seem ridiculous and unworthy of credulity if presented in such a fashion. Yet even in the context of a pagan pantheon, Disney is able to demonstrate in *Hercules* that there are aspects both universal and distinctive in every belief system. Taking this approach was a significant departure for the studio, according to Ron Clements, who, with John Musker, wrote and directed the movie. It was the first time a Disney animated feature was based on classical myth rather than on a fairy tale or folktale, he said in a short documentary included with the *Hercules* video.

The religious syncretism begins with the opening song, "The Gospel Truth," which runs through the film. It is sung by a Greek chorus that has been transformed into a choir of African American women—the first positive portrayal of African American women in an animated Disney feature. Clements said that this musical amalgam was a good fit for the movie because *Hercules* is "about hope, and it's about dreams." The first time through, the song outlines an alternative, Greek version of the earth's creation to that found in Genesis, punctuating each section of the account with the line, "That's the gospel truth." Later in the movie, in other songs, are the lines "Say amen" and "Bless my soul." Some Christian critics were offended by the musical appropriation, arguing against interweaving religious and pagan tradition.

Zeus, presiding over the heavenly Olympus, is celebrating the birth of his son Hercules. As in *Sleeping Beauty,* a late, ill-tempered guest arrives at the festivities. Hades—a literal hot head, with a burning coiffure—is freshly arrived from his domain below, which he describes as "dark, gloomy, and full of dead people." Arguably a precursor to Lucifer, Hades was expelled from Olympus and longs for return and rule. Baby Hercules is the primary impediment to Hades' goal. The Fates tell the Lord of the Dead that the only way he can triumph over Zeus is if Hercules' immortality can be neutralized so he can then be killed. Although Hades' demonic minions bungle the task, the baby is abandoned along a road, where he is discovered by an older couple. "For so many years we prayed to the gods to bless us with a child," the wife says to the husband. "Perhaps they've answered our prayers." (In the myth, it is she who bears Hercules to Zeus.) The husband agrees, and the couple raise the infant as their own. "Hercules grows up the only adopted son of a farming couple with Midwest accents," according to Eleanor Byrne and Martin McQuillan in *Deconstructing Disney.* "Here the familiar motif of innocent farm-boy who longs for adventure is invoked (we might think of Luke Skywalker and Clark Kent, to name only two of America's most enduring myths about its own innocence)."

Young Hercules is awkward with his superhuman strength, and yearns to be like other, normal children. Ostracized and treated like a freak, he feels out of place. "I would go anywhere to feel like I belong," he sings. His adoptive parents reveal his origins, and they suggest he go to the Temple of Zeus to find answers. The boy, like many adopted children, tells his parents he is grateful for all they have done for him, but he feels a need to know more about his first family. At the temple, Hercules says, "Almighty Zeus, please hear me and answer my prayer. Who am I, and where do I belong?" Change the name of the deity, and the supplication is identical to prayers offered today around the world. What follows, of course, is quite different: fire, lightning, and a huge, stone statue of Zeus that comes to life. Hercules flees in terror, before his father can regain his attention. The boy asks the adoptee's obvious question, "Didn't you want me?"

For Hercules to return to Olympus, he must become a hero

before he can become a god. In the film's press kit, director John Musker called Hercules "the common man's hero." Tom Schumacher, Disney's vice president for feature animation, said in the production notes that the film is "about the idea of strength, of who you are, and what character is. It also deals with the notion of what celebrity is." Hercules goes into training and, as he matures, he begins attracting attention in the city of Thebes for his feats. Like most sons, Hercules yearns to be a hero in his father's eyes. He brings accounts of his early successes, rescues, battles—his own action figure—to the temple, in hopes of qualifying as a hero. "Being famous is not the same as being a true hero," Zeus tells him. When Hercules asks what more he must do, the father replies, as Disney sages are wont to do, to "look inside your heart."

Hercules has attracted attention elsewhere. Hades, learning that Hercules was not killed as an infant, as he had been told, sets out to finish the job, so he can "change the cosmos." In order to do so, he enlists the beautiful Megara, who has had fatally bad taste in men. She has sold her soul to Hades to save the life of a previous boyfriend who, by way of thanks, "ran off with some babe," the dark lord reminds her. Megara makes her way into Hercules' theme park and outmaneuvers his groupies. Like Delilah with Samson, she attempts to woo the young strongman. Megara has second thoughts about what she is doing, but Hades is able to convince Hercules to give up his power for twenty-four hours—long enough for his army of Titans to conquer Olympus—in order to save the girl from the underworld. "There's a whole cosmos out there waiting for me," Hades says, launching his attack. As his monsters destroy Zeus's temple on Mount Olympus, Hades shouts, "I'm home!" just as Lucifer might.

Although without his superpowers, Hercules is persuaded by his goat-legged trainer and by Megara to battle the Titans. The woman redeems her earlier betrayal by saving Hercules' life, but she is critically injured as a result. Since Hades had promised Hercules that Megara would not be harmed, their bargain is broken, and Hercules' powers return, enabling him to come to Zeus's rescue. His father proclaims him a true hero, because, his mother explains, gesturing to Megara, "you were willing to give your life to rescue this young woman." Zeus says, "For a true hero is not measured by the size of his strength, but by the strength of his heart." Hercules becomes a god, and is welcomed home to Olympus. However, that means he will have to give up his true love. So he asks Zeus to allow him to return to earth with Megara, and his request is granted.

Hercules can be summed up in one sentence: A child is born divine, lives on earth through young adulthood, inspires the love of a fallen woman, dies, lives again, and returns to earth. Sound familiar? When combined with the use of the gospel Greek chorus, the elements of the tale may seem uncomfortably close to the story of Jesus. As Joseph Campbell has noted, no one has a copyright on religious metaphor or classic storytelling. With animosity growing among conservative evangelicals and fundamentalists against Disney, it is unlikely that this movie was conceived as an intentional affront. At the same time, if the company had been in any way intimidated by the controversy, it could have killed the film or postponed its release. *Hercules* did not add fuel to the controversy largely because by 1997 many conservative Christians and fundamentalists had given up on Disney's animated features.

Chapter Twenty-Eight

Mulan (1998): Woman of Valor

Women warriors and leaders, like the title character in *Mulan,* appear throughout the biblical tradition. Judith cut off the head of the Assyrian general Holofernes, Jael drove a tent peg through the head of the Canaanite commander Sisera, and Rahab gave shelter to the Israelite spy Caleb. Deborah, in the book of Judges, was a prophet as well as a military and political leader. Elsewhere in Judges, "a certain woman" threw a millstone from a tower, critically injuring the evil Abimelech. Queen Esther saved the Jews in Persian exile from extermination, resulting in the festival of Purim. Hannah defied the Syrian Greeks in the Hanukkah story, sacrificing her seven sons to resistance. Of course, none of these women had to resort to cross-dressing, as Mulan does, to achieve distinction. *Yentl* came much later.

China, where *Mulan* is set, has had a different experience with women leaders. The two empresses that led the Middle Kingdom, Wu Zedian and Cixi, both found the route to power through the bedchamber, and are reviled by the Chinese people. In postrevolutionary China, much the same is true of the wife of Chairman Mao, Chiang Qing, whose bid for power as part of the Gang of Four was crushed. Through most of the nation's pre-Communist history, including the period of this feature, the status of Chinese women was a function of their value as wives. This is the case with Mulan, the outspoken daughter and only child of a prosperous, happy, provincial household. In contrast to most of Disney's animated protagonists, she has a mother, father, and a grandmother—all of whom are still alive at the end of the movie. As the girl prepares for a crucial meeting with the matchmaker, trying to remember the qualities most desired in a wife, her father retreats to a small, family temple in a pagoda. In a representation of Confucianism that is simplified but generally respectful, he kneels and prays to his ancestors that Mulan will impress the matchmaker and thus uphold the clan's honor. When his daughter stops to see him, already late to her appointment, he decides he needs more worship. Mulan's mother, waiting impatiently at the town's bathhouse, has the same reaction. "I should have prayed to the ancestors for luck," she says to her own mother, who is waiting with her. "How lucky can they be?" the grandmother asks, perhaps injecting a glib, Western take on ancestor worship. "They're dead."

Mulan rides up to the bathhouse, sitting on her horse like an experienced rider, and is immediately thrown into preparation for the meeting. As attendants do last-minute touch-ups to get her ready for the matchmaker, they sing that a good marriage will "bring honor to us all." What men want in a wife, in addition to a bearer of sons, is a hard worker with a calm demeanor, a porcelain doll with an attractive hairdo and a tiny waist. For such a woman, they sing, "men will gladly go to war." Much as she wants to bring honor to her family, this is not Mulan's identity or her destiny. The meeting with the matchmaker is a debacle, blasting any chance for marriage, so she slinks back, shamefacedly, to the family compound. Later, the girl looks at her reflection, and wonders why she must conceal who she really is from her family. She sings that she will never be a perfect bride or a perfect daughter. Mulan's father comforts her, saying that the blossom that blooms late is the most beautiful of all.

China is facing a much larger problem, one that will soon affect Mulan and her family. Barbarian invaders identified as "Huns" storm the kingdom's northern border, the Great Wall. In Beijing, the white-bearded emperor discusses strategy with his army commander. The general suggests a line of defense around the palace, but the benevolent emperor orders the troops out into the countryside, "to protect my people." To do so, a general conscription is ordered, despite the commander's insistence that the professional forces are sufficient. "A single grain of rice can tip this scale," the emperor says. "One man may be the difference between victory and defeat."

But the price of defending the common good is common sacrifice, a Chinese tradition. Each family throughout the realm is required to supply one soldier. Although a middle-aged veteran, both honored and partially disabled, but without a son, Mulan's father accepts the scroll with the emperor's summons. The girl sees that her father is in no condition to go to war, and protests to the recruiter, who has no time to listen to her pleas. A woman should hold her tongue in a man's presence, the haughty official snaps. In a civilization that prizes filial piety, Mulan has no better luck arguing with her father that honor is not worth dying for. "It's an honor to protect my country and my family," he shouts, slamming down his teacup. "I will die doing what is right." The father knows his place, and his daughter should know hers as well. Frustrated, Mulan turns to prayer, lighting incense and kneeling before a large, stone tablet in the pagoda. Whatever the response, she is next seen cutting her hair, binding her breasts, taking her father's sword and padded armor, and riding off into the night with the family's conscription notice.

If Mulan were searching for celestial guidance at the temple, she wasn't listening very carefully. Her actions disturbed the natural order and also disrupted the cosmos. A wind snuffs out the incense and, from the engraved stone stelae, a white-bearded spirit carrying a staff swirls out. He summons a small dragon spirit, who in turn conjures up the family's other ancestors, all of whom are scandalized by Mulan's actions. One accuses her of being a crossdresser, while another warns that "traditional values will disintegrate." The small dragon, called Mushu and voiced by a jive-talking Eddie Murphy, accidentally breaks a stone dragon and pursues Mulan in order to cover his error. He complains about being sent on such a task, "all because Miss Man decides to take her little drag show on the road."

"There is a very clear underlying message about honesty and truth and how your greatest empowerment comes from being your own true self," said Thomas Schumacher, vice president of Disney's animation unit, in the film's production notes. At the same time, Schumacher acknowledged that Mulan's effort to save her father's life is based on "a profound lie." This is a fundamental flaw for Annalee Ward in *Mouse Morality*. "The underlying message is not that a person should be honest; rather, it is that one should be creative in one's communication, including lying whenever it's necessary to achieve one's goals. That may be widely accepted in the United States, but it is not a pro-social message." Yet Ward lauds Disney for breaking stereotypes by presenting traditional Chinese values infused with a Western interpretation.

When Mushu catches up with Mulan, she is outside of the military encampment, despairing of being able to pass as a young man. "It's going to take a miracle to get me into the army," she says. Although this is China, hundreds of years in the past, the word "miracle" sends Mushu into a full-blown riff as a blazing hot African American preacher. "Did I hear someone ask for a miracle?" he shouts in the familiar call-and-response cadence. "Salvation is at hand," the dragon tells Mulan, as organ music swells. What is at hand is Mushu's advice on how the girl should act to pass herself off as a man—advice that works. The camp's leader, Captain Shang, a handsome son of the Chinese army commander, approaches the raw recruits in a way much like drill instructors have done throughout history—calling them girls, the ultimate insult to their masculinity. During the training that follows, all of the citizen soldiers progress, but Mulan excels, because she uses her head.

Summoned to aid the regular army and block the invaders in a snowy pass, Shang and the troops discover a burned-out village and thousands of slain Chinese soldiers, including the captain's father. Shang drives his sword into the snow, sets his father's helmet on it and kneels before the makeshift shrine. But there is little time to mourn if they are to defend the emperor. They quickly stumble into an ambush and seem doomed, until Mulan disobeys Shang's orders and sets off an avalanche that decimates the barbarian hordes. The girl also rescues her wounded captain and is herself severely wounded, which leads a doctor to discover her secret. Saved by a woman—no greater dishonor! Why did she do it, they ask her? "Maybe what I really wanted was to prove I could do things right," Mulan explains. For her heroism, Shang spares her from execution—the law's penalty for a woman who dresses as a man—but she is expelled from the company, and shunned.

Mulan is not finished coming to China's rescue. The barbarian leader and many of his followers did not perish in the landslide. They infiltrate Beijing's victory parade for Captain Shang, and have planned their uprising for the heart of the imperial compound, the Forbidden City. No one will pay attention to Mulan's frantic warnings and, just as the emperor proclaims "Heaven smiles down on the Middle Kingdom," the attack begins. Again, the brave and quick-thinking girl acts when the male soldiers are flummoxed, getting her army buddies to reverse roles and dress as women to distract the barbarian guards, enabling Mulan and Shang to defeat the barbarian leader and save the emperor. In gratitude, the girl is honored before a cheering crowd, presented with the barbarian leader's sword and a royal medallion—"so the world will know what you have done for China"—and offered a position on the imperial council, which she declines. Instead, she heads for home.

The emperor suggests to Captain Shang that he shouldn't let Mulan get away. "The flower that blooms in adversity is the most rare and beautiful of all," he says. When the captain doesn't catch his drift, the emperor makes it simple: "You don't meet a girl like that every dynasty." Home again, Mulan presents the sword and medallion to her father, to honor their family. But, instead, he embraces the girl and says, "The greatest gift and honor is having you for a daughter." And guess who soon arrives for dinner? Captain Shang, with love in his eyes and honorable intentions, is nearly smothered by Mulan's mother and grandmother in their anticipation of a possible marriage.

Although not a megahit in the United States at the level of *The Lion King*, *Mulan* did well at the box office and was also popular in China. A look at the closing credits suggests why. Numerous Asian names are included in the list of voice actors, writers, editors, and animators. The film may have missed some fine points of Confucianism, such as the subtle difference between veneration of ancestors and worship of them as deities. Still, this was a serious attempt to present a belief system outside the Judeo-Christian tradition: Joan of Arc with a happy ending. Byrne and McQuillan see something more sinister at work. "*Mulan* is Disney's attempt to 'open' the vast potential of the Chinese market," they wrote in

Deconstructing Disney. "A film made in the 1990s which reprises a myth of Chinese national origins, simultaneously invoking the People's Liberation Army defense of China's border, in a more or less unequivocal way, has an explicit agenda."

What might Disney's agenda be? Nothing less than a full-scale assault on the Chinese market—movies, television programming, merchandise, music CDs, and theme parks. In the nineteenth century, the cry of Western business interests eager to sell their wares in the Middle Kingdom was "Oil for the lamps of China." James B. Duke, a U.S. robber baron, helped build his American Tobacco Company trust on the Chinese market, inserting photos of scantily clad Western women in each package of cigarettes. Disney stumbled briefly in its China offensive in 1997, when Disney's Miramax subsidiary released the live action film *Kundun,* directed by Martin Scorsese. That movie, which harshly portrayed China's role in Tibet, was a commercial failure—always a cardinal sin at Disney. More critically to Disney's global goals, the film also offended the Chinese Communist leadership in Beijing, jeopardizing a multibillion-dollar entertainment market. A senior official in the Chinese film ministry, Kong Min, said *Kundun* represented "an interference in China's internal affairs," according to a March 27, 1998, article in London's *Independent* newspaper.

As so often in the company's history, Disney animators came galloping to the rescue, with *Mulan.* Following the film's release and its favorable reception in China, Disney signed a deal with Beijing to construct a theme park in Hong Kong, to open in 2005–2006. There have been repeated rumors of additional Disney theme parks in Shanghai and Beijing. Also signed was a deal with Chinese television, "under which Mickey Mouse cartoons will appear daily, in kids' prime time, on China's biggest television channel," according to Jonathan Weber, writing in the February 2002 issue of *Wired* magazine. The potential audience for such a channel is 225 million households, a prize already coveted by Disney's rival, Rupert Murdoch and his News Corporation. *Mulan* carried the standard for Disney commerce, and carried the day.

Chapter Twenty-Nine

Tarzan (1999): Taming the Savage

*O*ne way to avoid any hint of racism in *Tarzan,* which is based on the novels of the 1920s and 1930s by Edgar Rice Burroughs, was to tell a story set in Africa without any Africans. Every character in the movie is a European or an animal. The sounds of African drums and rhythms are heard on the soundtrack even before the movie's title appears on screen, but no drummers are ever seen. Why no Africans? Conveniently, according to Phil Collins's opening song, the film's setting is "a paradise untouched by man," a world where the peaceful, simple life is "blessed with love." Neither are there any explicit references to any sort of religion in the film. Yet the first words of Collins's song put *Tarzan* squarely in the Disney gospel tradition: "Put your faith in what you most believe in."

A late-nineteenth-century sailing ship is ablaze just off the African coast as the movie begins. From the deck, a man lowers a lifeboat with an anxious woman and a baby and then jumps overboard to row them to shore. They build a home from salvaged wood from the wreck in a tall tree not far from the beach, and settle in. Nearby, in the misty highlands, a family of silverback gorillas, led by Kerchak, is also nurturing a young one. But their offspring wanders off into the jungle. There it is killed (again, offscreen) by a big cat, which leaves the gorilla parents desolate. Not long after, the still grieving mother ape, Kala, hears the sound of a cry and goes to investigate. In the humans' tree house, amid bloody paw prints and signs of an attack, she finds an infant boy. Kala sniffs the child and inspects it, noting the affinity—both are primates with opposable thumbs. Just then, the fierce jungle cat—the same one that killed her baby—springs down from the rafters, intent on finishing its human meal. The mother ape battles the big cat, a cheetah or leopard named Sabor, and flees into the jungle with the baby.

However, the reconstituted arrangement of child and parents is neither neat nor symmetrical. Kerchak, while appearing sympathetic to the mother's sense of loss, has not sired this young one. And this baby will not replace the one they lost, he says gently. Kala knows this, but, she says, the creature needs her. The baby must be returned, he says, even if that means that the jungle will claim the child; that is nature's way. Kala insists, and Kerchak reluctantly agrees, making clear that while the child—called Tarzan—may stay with the apes, that will not make him the silverback's son. As the child grows (mysteriously acquiring a loincloth), Kerchak's resistance to Tarzan filters down. Tarzan's young contemporaries shun him because he is different, referring to him as a "hairless wonder." The boy's exuberance, and his desire to do anything to fit in with his brothers and sisters, leads to an elephant stampede that nearly wipes out the gorilla family. Kerchak dresses down Tarzan, saying the human will never be one of them. The older ape's concern is not simply about parentage and species prejudice; as leader, he is responsible for the safety of his extended family.

Tarzan knows he is not like his brothers and sisters, and this eats at him. He slinks off to a stream and ponders his appearance, at one point coating his skin with mud in order to make him appear more simian. Kala attempts to comfort him and to minimize what separates the boy from the gorillas. Their hearts, she tells him, are exactly the same. Tarzan makes a pledge similar to those made by countless minority members and outcasts throughout history. He will earn Kerchak's respect and acceptance by becoming the best ape ever. And the effort appears to be heading for success, although with some modification. Something within Tarzan (his humanity?) manifests itself, leading him to make and use a spear with a stone point to gather fruit. He also intuits the skill to make a shelter from the tropical rain for family members, to swing from vines, and "to surf" large tree limbs. As this action unfolds, another Phil Collins song extols "faith and understanding" as the way to journey from boy to man: "Son of Man, look to the sky, lift your spirit." Tarzan's transition is sealed when he comes to Kerchak's aid and—using the spear point—kills the same cat responsible for the death of his parents and of Kala's baby. The ape man lays the corpse of Sabor at Kerchak's feet, and backs away in fealty.

In a sequence that appears to be an homage to *Bambi*—if not a direct steal—the sound of a shot is heard in the distance, a flight of frightened dark birds marking the location. Man is in the forest— the rain forest, this time—and again it signals trouble. Tarzan investigates, and finds a dotty English anthropologist and his attractive daughter, Jane, with a pompous hunter and guide named Clayton. All are in search of the highland gorillas, although members of the party see the primates very differently. For Clayton, they are savage brutes that would as soon rip your head off as look at you. Jane and her father see the apes as members of a family, to be studied. Tarzan rescues Jane from a screeching pack of baboons while his ape siblings and young elephant friend are off smashing the humans' campsite. (In a very sly joke, the elephant exclaims, "The horror!" when he first sees the humans' encampment, using a famous line from Joseph Conrad's seminal African novel *Heart of Darkness*, and used again by Marlon Brando's character in the film *Apocalypse Now*, which was based on *Heart of Darkness*.)

Kerchak, who instinctively recognizes the danger inherent in these interspecies encounters, assembles his family for a warning: The humans should be avoided at all costs. Tarzan objects to the blanket prohibition, based on his brief time with his species, and insists that the humans mean the apes no harm. Kerchak says he is not willing to risk their safety, even if Tarzan is. The ape man asks if the silverback is just threatened by anyone different from him— a charge with an obvious double meaning. It is too late to stop Tarzan, who goes to the encampment, where Jane and her father give the eager student a crash course in Western civilization. In return, Tarzan leads the humans to the gorillas' nesting place, provoking a fight with Kerchak, who accuses the ape man of betraying his family. Kala takes her confused son to the abandoned tree house where his parents died, where Tarzan sees himself in a family photo. Whichever path he chooses, Kala tells the young man, she wants him to be happy. She will always be his mother, Tarzan replies.

The painful decision for Tarzan is to don his biological father's Western clothes and to accompany Jane on the steamship back to England, where he hopes to meet Darwin, Kipling, and Queen Victoria. But the hunter Clayton has other plans—to capture the apes and sell them to zoos. He locks Tarzan, Jane, and her father in the ship's hold and, with a group of ne'er-do-wells, returns to the jungle with dozens of cages. Surprised, the apes have no hope of resisting, until Tarzan escapes the ship and comes to the rescue, as Phil Collins reprises, "Put your faith in what you most believe in." Clayton shoots Kerchak, but, in a fight with Tarzan, the hunter then unintentionally hangs himself. For an animated feature, the brief sight of the lower portion of Clayton's lifeless body, dangling above the jungle floor, breaks more new ground for explicitly dispatching a Disney villain. Kerchak, himself dying, forgives Tarzan for his betrayal, charges him to look after the ape clan and, with his last breath, he calls the ape man his son.

In *Tarzan,* Disney's storytellers hedge their bets some in portraying this latest encounter between man and nature. Both sides contain elements of good and bad. Kerchak acts rationally throughout the film. He accepts Tarzan into his family against his better judgment, to help heal Kala's loss, and he disciplines the human when Tarzan puts the clan in jeopardy. The big cat is a predator, and takes advantage of vulnerable prey, as it should in the wild. For their part, the humans raised in civilization—with free will—are also both good and evil. Jane and her father are innocents. Clayton and his henchmen are villains. But because the humans are not sufficiently evolved to accept the apes as equals, the encounter between the two cannot, and does not, end happily.

Chapter Thirty

The Emperor's New Groove (2000): Eminent Domain

*L*ike King Ahab of ancient Israel, the monarch in *The Emperor's New Groove* covets the choice land of one of his subjects. But unlike his biblical precursor, Emperor Kuzco is not bound by the law of his fanciful Peruvian realm to offer to buy the mountaintop village. So there is no reason to plot murder to get it, as Ahab's wife Jezebel did in order to acquire Naboth's vineyard. Instead, Kuzco merely summons to his Inca palace one of the land's peasant owners, Pacha, to inform him of the imminent seizure. What Kuzco really wants to know is where the sun hits the peak, so he can figure out where to locate the swimming pool for his new summer palace, which he plans to call Kuzco-topia. Pacha, a large, simple llama herder, is shocked by the news that his family's home for six generations will soon be destroyed and they will be evicted. His village already supplies crops to the palace, which he thinks is a sufficient contribution to the empire. When he protests the seizure and asks Kuzco where the people of the village will go, the petulant teenaged emperor says he doesn't know and doesn't care. He is the ultimate developer-villain, with hubris added.

No one would mistake the boy for a just ruler, thanks to the unctuous voice characterization of the actor David Spade. Kuzco—another title character with no parents in sight—has been raised as a pampered, absolute monarch, his every whim catered to, when not anticipated. Naturally, this power has corrupted him. He is completely self-centered and self-absorbed, believing himself to be the king of the world and, in the words of the opening song, "the alpha, the omega." For example, an old man with a cane has the misfortune to be behind the emperor when Kuzco is backing up, throwing off his "groove." For this offense, the old man is immediately tossed out a high palace window (but not to his death). None of the prospective brides presented to the young man is suitable, and he is insulting in rejecting them. The emperor is so preoccupied that, behind his back, an advisor and sorceress named Yzma has been ruling the empire. She is another of Disney's aged, female grotesques, "scary beyond all reason," as several characters note. When a petitioner complains that his family has no food, Yzma rejects his plea. "You really should have thought of that before you became peasants," she snaps.

On the eve of his eighteenth birthday, Kuzco fires Yzma, explaining that he feels he is ready to govern. The advisor and her hunk boyfriend, Kronk, plot to get rid of the emperor and hang onto power. A magic potion, designed to poison Kuzco at dinner, turns him instead into a talking llama. Yzma orders Kronk to take the emperor outside the city and finish him off, as the huntsman was ordered to do to Snow White. But, although muscle-bound and slow-witted, Kronk has a conscience. In classic cartoon fashion, a small angel appears on one of his shoulders and a devil on the other, an effort to demonstrate how Kronk's mind works, according to the movie's DVD commentary. The angel urges Kronk to act rather than to allow the llama, in a sack, to drop off a high waterfall in the palace. "Don't listen to that guy," the devil says. "He's trying to lead you down the path of righteousness. I'm going to lead you down the path that rocks." Kronk admits to being confused by the conflicting advice and, while he is making up his mind, the sack with the emperor bounces onto the back of Pacha's cart, unknown to the herder as he trundles toward home.

After greeting his young children and visibly pregnant wife (a first for a Disney animated feature), Pacha discovers the talking llama, which he first assumes to be a demon. Kuzco wants to return to the palace and force Yzma to turn him back into the emperor, but the herder warns that the route is dangerous if you don't know the way. And Pacha will not help unless the summer palace is moved elsewhere, a proposal that goes nowhere. "I don't make deals with peasants," the llama says, still clueless about how little power he wields in his present incarnation. Kuzco, ever haughty, determines to set out alone for the palace, through the mountains and jungle. In short order the llama is fleeing for his life from a pack of jaguars, and his life is saved by the good-natured Pacha. This experience does little to transform Kuzco, who will not back down on plans to build the summer palace. Pacha is dumbfounded that anyone could be so heartless. "How can you be this way?" he asks. "All you care about is building your summer home and filling it with stuff for you?" Despite his anger, the herder is selfless; unbidden, he places his only blanket over the llama, shivering in his sleep. In the morning, Kuzco finally relents on the summer resort plans, and the two shake on their agreement.

At the palace, Yzma is delivering a self-serving and completely disingenuous eulogy at Kuzco's royal funeral, a rerun from Scar's oration in *The Lion King*. The young emperor will live on in our hearts, she says, losing little time in replacing one personality cult with another. An hour's walk distant, the herder and the llama approach a rickety, wooden bridge, high above a gorge. Pacha crashes through and, dangling, calls for Kuzco's help. But the llama tells him he lied to his new friend, that he had no intention of keeping their bargain. This is what the DVD commentary characterizes as a "moment of defeated expectations." The emperor reveals that all along he had planned to imprison the herder for life once he was restored to his throne. Now he will just let Pacha fall to his death. "Why did I risk my life for a selfish brat like you?" the herder wonders. "I was always taught that there was some good in everyone. But you proved me wrong." In retrospect, Pacha says he should have let the llama die, which would have solved all his problems. Twisting the knife, Kuzco says, "That makes you ugly *and* stupid." The tone and substance of the discourse shifts suddenly when the llama also plunges through the bridge, now dangling opposite Pacha. Their subsequent battle destroys the bridge, and sends them both hurtling into the gorge and the crocodile-infested stream far below. Only by working together—linked back-to-back, they climb up a split in the rock—are they able to save one another. Revising his opinion of Kuzco, Pacha says, "There is some good in you after all." The herder amazes the emperor by saying that, because of his handshake promise, he intends to lead Kuzco the llama on the four-day detour to the palace. Despite his assertion that he is not a complete chump and will not carry the animal, the peasant is soon seen carrying the animal, duped by Kuzco's bogus claim of low blood sugar.

Yzma, insecure on the throne, is outraged when Kronk admits that he never killed the emperor. So they begin a search of the kingdom to locate Pacha and Kuzco, bumping into them at a roadside inn. The llama misinterprets Pacha's efforts to save him as a ruse for betrayal, again, projecting his own venality on the herder. His friendship, Kuzco concludes, was only a ruse. It was, he says, "all an act, and I almost fell for it." The two flee Yzma and Kronk in different directions, but reunite in Pacha's field, where he is tending the other llamas. "Maybe I wasn't as nice as I should have been," Kuzco acknowledges. Together, they return to the palace, and Yzma's lab, to find the antidote that will turn the llama back into the emperor. But Yzma will not give up without a fight. She raises her skirt, causing Kuzco and Pacha to recoil. However, she is just reaching for a lethal-looking dagger strapped to her thigh. The herder and the llama relax—it's evidently a less frightening prospect to face than her sexuality. She tosses the dagger to Kronk and orders him to finish them off, yet he is again paralyzed by his conscience, in the form of the angel and the devil on his shoulders. Impatient, Yzma calls him a big, dumb monkey and, more hurtfully, criticizes his baking. This is too much, even for the little devil, who urges Kronk to get rid of Yzma instead. The angel suggests, on the other hand, "From above, the wicked shall receive their just reward." Ever the literalist, Kronk interprets this to mean the heavy iron chandelier hanging above Yzma's head. He cuts the rope holding it up, but the woman miraculously survives. A frantic chase sequence ensues as Yzma takes the wrong potion and is accidentally transformed into a kitten—a double pun on the name of the voice actor who plays her, Eartha Kitt, and her 1960s film role as Catwoman. At a critical point in their madcap effort to seize the right antidote that will return either Yzma or Kuzco—but not both—to human form, Kuzco forgoes an opportunity to seize the vial in order to save his long-suffering friend Pacha from a fatal fall. This unselfish choice is validated when

Pacha and the llama then repeat their earlier back-walking stunt, together recovering the vial. Kuzco is restored to the throne. A deeper transformation involves the emperor, who apologizes to the old man with the cane who survived being tossed out of the window at the beginning of the movie. At the close, Kuzco has built a modest home near Pacha's, and the two friends enjoy sliding down a natural waterfall.

Since 1937, with *Snow White,* Disney's animated features have taken gigantic strides in the way they portray characters of other colors and cultures. This development has paralleled an increasingly assertive role for young women. The one convention the studio has had the most difficulty giving up—even in the Eisner-Katzenberg era—is its antagonism toward older women characters, in particular ugly and/or overweight villains who use younger men as henchmen. In recent films, this antipathy continues with a disturbing, sexual element. Misogyny is a loaded term, and probably used too often. But it is difficult for Disney to avoid the charge in a film like this, the stylishness and verve of Eartha Kitt notwithstanding.

Chapter Thirty-One

Atlantis (2001): Adventure Capitalism

A Disney animated feature is not the place to expect a hard-edged critique of U.S. foreign policy and of Western cultural imperialism, but that is surely one way to understand *Atlantis*. For all the swashbuckling, wisecracking, ethnically balanced characters, and New Age fantasy—and all the time it takes to make its point—this is a movie about white America's dark side. There is a brave, determined idealist—a young, white man personifying what is best about this nation—at the center of the narrative. Yet beneath the surface, like a hungry, malevolent shark, lurks a tale of an inexorable drive to seize a gentle people's cheap energy, backed by the muscle of military might. Set in 1914 in Washington, D.C., and in an imaginary metropolis on the ocean floor, *Atlantis* carries with it a message with inescapable, modern reverberations.

Milo Thatch works in the boiler room of the Smithsonian Institution, which doubles as the museum's department of cartography and linguistics. An orphan (once again, no parents) who was raised by his explorer grandfather and trained as a language expert, he is now a young man, obsessed with locating the mythical city of Atlantis described by the Greek philosopher Plato. The movie's prologue establishes that the civilization did exist on the ocean's surface, as Plato claimed, but that it was plunged to the depths by a tidal wave involving an unearthly energy source. Quirky and innocent, Milo is convinced that he can locate the ruined city and, in the process, vindicate the memory of his grandfather, who was discredited for his own efforts to locate Atlantis. The people of the city, Milo believes, had developed electricity, powered flight, and advanced medicine; they had harnessed an energy source more powerful than coal or steam.

But the lords of the Smithsonian, graybeards and fussbudgets all, are equally convinced that Milo is headed down the same blind alley that destroyed the grandfather's career. One director tells the young man that he has a lot of potential and should not throw it away "chasing fairy tales" like his grandfather. Their august institution supports expeditions "based on fact, not folklore." When they put off Milo's latest plea to search for Atlantis, he resigns and returns, disheartened, to his apartment and his cat. Waiting for him in the dark is a femme fatale in a sexy black dress with a shoulder strap that keeps slipping. The German-accented woman, named Helga, tells Milo she has a proposition for him, and soon they are driving through the dark, rainy night, finally pulling through the gates of an estate.

An eccentric millionaire—his eccentricity denoted by the fact that he practices yoga while conducting a conversation—introduces himself as Preston Whitmore, a friend and admirer of Milo's grandfather. Whitmore wants to know how committed the young man is to finding Atlantis. When Milo says he would go alone in a rowboat, the older man tells him that won't be necessary. With the help of an ancient, illuminated text Milo's grandfather left with Whitmore for safekeeping and a well-equipped submarine, an expedition has been arranged. Years earlier, the millionaire explains, when buffoons at the museum dragged down the grandfather "and made a laughingstock of him," Whitmore promised to keep faith with his quest and with his grandson. By making good on that pledge, he says, looking up at a portrait of Milo's grandfather, "I'm going to the afterlife with a clear conscience, by thunder!" Whitmore tells the young man that, by participating in the expedition to Atlantis, he will be building on the foundation left him by his grandfather, whose favorite saying was "Our lives are remembered by the gifts we leave our children."

The core crew of the huge submarine is a diversity dream team: a muscular and brilliant doctor, half African American and half Native American; a Latina woman mechanic; an Italian demolitions expert; and two feisty seniors, a male cook and a female telephone operator. However, a large corps of men dressed in World War I-style uniforms—shallow, WWI-era helmets, Sam Browne belts, and jodhpurs—also march onto the vessel. The expedition's commander, Lyle Tiberius Rourke, who is also in uniform, addresses his subordinates by their rank when he gives orders, although it is not clear whether the troops are on active duty or simply veterans who kept their uniforms. They seem to be forerunners of today's private, corporate, "executive security" firms. As they march on board, Milo says to Rourke and Whitmore—who is not going along—that his grandfather believed that you could never put a price on the pursuit of knowledge. The cost of this expedition, which is clearly considerable, is "small change compared to the value of what we are going to learn on this trip." Rourke replies, with irony that will become apparent only later, that the expedition "should be enriching for all of us," as Whitmore shoots him a knowing glance behind Milo's back.

Deep beneath the ocean, near Iceland, Milo prepares the crew for what they may soon encounter. Showing them a projector slide of a sea creature, which he believes guards the entrance to Atlantis, he quotes Job 41:19 and its description of Leviathan: "Out of his mouth go burning lights; sparks of fire shoot out." As they near the site, they see wrecks from throughout history, all failed efforts at the same quest. Suddenly their submarine is attacked and destroyed by a mechanical sea monster—a virtual copy of the one described in Job. Throughout the battle, Rourke remains the unflappable military man, directing the surviving crewmembers to abandon ship in escape vehicles. They wash up in a cave-like air pocket on the ocean floor that forms the entrance to Atlantis, and hold a memorial service for their recently fallen comrades. A candle is lit and set inside an upturned pith helmet, which drifts out into the water, but no religious words are said, no religious icon shown.

The surviving expedition members begin their trek along an ancient highway, soon encountering a monumental rock sculpture that Milo estimates had taken a thousand years to carve. It is blocking the road, so it must be destroyed, to no one's objection. Watching this brief sequence, it is hard not to think of the great Buddhas in Afghanistan that were destroyed by the Taliban regime in 2001, despite protests from around the world. By night, around the camp-fire, Milo reveals much about himself. He sees the expedition as an opportunity for discovery, teamwork, and adventure, and wonders whether it is the same for the others, or whether they are just in it for the money. While they do want money, frequently it is to fund a personal dream. The Latina mechanic wants to build another machine shop for the family. The Italian demolition expert—it is difficult for anyone familiar with U.S. history of the period not to associate him with an immigrant anarchist—wants to rebuild his family's flower shop, which was blown up by what he calls a "sign from God." There is also some of the standard Disney misogyny. Milo is warned that old Mrs. Packard, the telephone operator, sleeps in the nude and sleepwalks, so the young man is issued a mask to cover his eyes.

After a series of adventures, and a nighttime attack by Atlanteans, expedition members reach the city and find, to their apparent consternation, residents living in what amounts to a bio-sphere. "We are explorers from the surface," Rourke says, not missing a beat. "We come in peace." Helga Sinclair, the femme fatale who is now second in command, tells Rourke that there were not supposed to be any people here. This changes everything, she tells him, cryptically. This changes nothing, he retorts. Atlantis's ruler, King Kashekim, speaking in his people's ancient language, chastises his attractive, long-haired daughter—who is dressed in a bikini top and a sarong bottom—that she should not have let the interlopers live. The daughter, Princess Kida, replies that the out-siders might be able to help them. Rourke chimes in, in English, saying they are honored to be welcomed to the city. They are not welcome, says the ruler. He knows what they want, and they will not find it in Atlantis. "We are peaceful explorers," Rourke repeats blithely, "men of science." Then why are you carrying pistols? the king asks. "Our weapons allow us to remove obstacles we may encounter," Rourke replies equally smoothly. Some obstacles can-not be removed by a mere show of force, the Atlantean ruler says, ordering the Americans to leave immediately. Rourke asks to remain overnight, and his request is granted. This conversation could easily have been an exchange between indigenous people and Spanish conquistadors in Mexico, American settlers on the Great Plains, or European explorers in Africa. And it is the first truly ominous note in *Atlantis*.

Milo is urged to talk to Kida and to find out what he can about the city. How did the city get to the bottom of the sea, he wants to know, as she leads him on a tour. "It is said that the gods became jealous of Atlantis," Kida explains. "They sent a great cataclysm and banished us here." The city is an amalgam of the futuristic and the primitive, including massive carved heads similar to those found on Easter Island in the Pacific. A bright, blue light—like a star—floats above the city, providing light and, Milo thinks, power. As the tour progresses, there is an intercut shot of crates of rifles being opened and passed out. Kida sheds her sarong to reveal a bikini bottom, and she leads Milo on an underwater swim, surfacing in a chamber. There he learns from a mural the secret of Atlantis's energy source—a magic crystal.

But when the pair returns and surfaces, they find themselves surrounded by members of the expedition—now all armed. Milo curses himself for being an idiot. "This is just another treasure hunt for you," he says. Rourke explains that he would have told the young man about the expedition's goal earlier, "but it was strictly on a need-to-know basis. . . . I had to be sure you were one of us. Welcome to the club, son." This is a club that Milo says he has no interest in joining, declaring that he is no mercenary. "I prefer the term 'adventure capitalist,'" Rourke says with a smile, a play on the "venture capitalists" that fueled the 1990s technology and Internet boom. Here, at last, it becomes clear that Rourke is a steely villain, and not just a gruff, no-nonsense expedition leader. The characterization is particularly transgressive. Rourke is voiced by—and drawn to look like a brawny version of—the popular television star James Garner. As the lead actor in series such as *Maverick* and *The Rockford Files,* and in a series of endearing commercials for Kodak, Garner always played likeable characters. Although children watching this movie are probably unaware of this background, their parents and grandparents cannot be. Transforming Garner into the villainous Rourke might be a disturbing choice for some viewers and, as his redeeming qualities quickly fall away, the characterization doesn't get any better.

Rourke points out that, despite his misgivings, Milo is entirely complicit in this situation, since the young man "led us right to the treasure chest." The military leader has no idea what he is tampering with by trying to grab the crystal, Milo says. "It's big, it's shiny and it's going to make us all rich," Rourke replies. But the crystal is neither a diamond nor a battery, Milo says, it is a life force, the only thing that is keeping the people of Atlantis alive. If the adventurers take it away, the people of the city will die. The only thing *that* fact will change, Rourke says, is to enhance the value of the stone. Academics, he snorts, "you never want to get your hands dirty." Getting to the heart of the matter—and, by implication, of the Smithsonian—Rourke says, "If you gave back every stolen artifact from a museum, you'd be left with an empty building. We're just providing a service to the archaeological community." What the Western world wants from any "New World"—even if its civilization is thousands of years old—is always the same: riches, energy, and artifacts. The startling fact is that these inescapable conclusions, and these words, are not coming from some political tract but from animated characters in a Disney feature.

Why is this happening? "It may seem incongruous that such an anticapitalist and, arguably, such an anti-Western message comes from a multibillion dollar, multinational company like Disney," said Clay Steinman, professor of film and media studies at Macalester College and coauthor of *Consuming Environments: Television and Commercial Culture.* "But it isn't, because making whites the villains allows the company to keep making narratives centered on white heroes, with a nod to a global, multicultural audience. The white hero is surrounded by sympathetic stereotypes from different backgrounds. In the end, Disney, like any large corporation, is first of all about making money. Whatever its other sources, the ideology of the pictures is shaped by that goal."

Without disputing Rourke's indictment of Western archaeologists, Milo tells him he is not interested in being a part of this effort. In effect, the young man is changing sides, arguably betraying his own people, out of principle. Or perhaps out of his emerging love for Kida—or both. Rourke dismisses him as "an idealist, just like your grandfather." The king refuses to tell the mercenary leader where the crystal is, earning him a beating and then an interrogation at Rourke's pistol point. "I really hate it when negotiations go sour," the commander says, as if this is a civilized proceeding. "Once again, diplomacy has failed us." The callousness provokes some restiveness in ranks of mercenaries, at least among the more enlightened. The African American medic objects to the heavy-handed treatment. "Put a bandage on that bleeding heart," Rourke snaps. "It doesn't suit a mercenary."

Rourke, threatening Kida, forces Milo to read the missing journal page, which leads the mercenaries to a chamber below the palace, where the crystal revolves above a pool of water, surrounded by large, stone masks of Atlantis's dead kings. For the commander, this is the jackpot he has come for, and he is ready to wrap it up. But for Kida, it is much more, both a deity and the embodiment of her dead mother. She falls to her knees, prostrate in prayer. Then she walks across the surface of the water, until she is directly below the glowing stone, and then she rises toward it. There are bursts of energy, the great stone masks of the ancient Atlantean kings drop, and Kida descends, glowing, now embodying the crystal. The scene is both convoluted and confusing, which may be intentional.

Despite the spectacle, Rourke tells expedition members to crate the crystal and the young woman. Milo makes another effort to dissuade the expedition members he has befriended. "You're wiping out an entire civilization," he says, just for money. Rourke tells him to get off his soapbox. "You read your Darwin," he says. "It's called natural selection. We're just helping it along." To punctuate his remarks, Rourke decks Milo with one punch, fully intending to leave him behind with the dying civilization. "You discovered Atlantis," he says. "Now you're part of the exhibit." But some of the more humane members of the expedition are beginning to waver, voicing doubts about what they are doing. "You can't be serious," Rourke says, disgusted. "We're this close to our biggest payday ever, and you pick now of all times to grow a conscience?" They stuck with their leader on previous adventures that included robbing graves and plundering tombs, they agree, but no one was ever hurt. Rourke accepts their desertion, saying that P. T. Barnum was right ("There's a sucker born every minute"), and he soon blows up the single bridge connecting Atlantis to the highway out. Milo reproaches himself again for leading the expedition to the ancient city and causing its destruction.

The dying King Kashekim explains the power of the crystal: "It thrives on the collective emotions of all who came before. In return, it provides power, longevity, and protection. Yet it is not a perfect deity; it developed a consciousness of its own." Ultimately, the power of the crystal overwhelmed the people of Atlantis and led to the city's downfall and submersion, the king explains. Good or bad, if the crystal leaves the city, all will die. Milo resolves to do whatever he can to undo his damage. In what is—thankfully—his last recitation of guilt, the young man again capsulizes his offenses. Eerily, the sentence he speaks could have been spoken by the Native American guide who took Cortés, the Spanish conquistador, to the city of the Aztecs in the sixteenth century. "I led a band of plundering vandals to the greatest archaeological find in recorded history, thus enabling the kidnapping and/or murder of the royal family," he says. Worse, Milo raises the specter of the amoral arms merchant, and of Kaiser Wilhelm of Germany—in the eyes of some, the Saddam Hussein of his day. In effect, on the eve of World War I, he has delivered "the most powerful force known to man into the hands of a mercenary nutcase who's probably going to sell it to the Kaiser!"

Although he has no chance of success, Milo rallies his loyal expedition mates and Kida's Atlantean followers to power up individual flight fighters—like something out of *Star Wars*—to pursue Rourke and retrieve the crystal. It is not the smart thing to do, he concedes, but it is the right thing. He vows to rescue the princess and save Atlantis, or die trying. The scene of the final conflict is the cavernous base of a dormant volcano, whose hollow lava tube leads to the surface and—with some explosive assistance—escape. Preparing to rise in a large balloon, Rourke is gloating: "I love it when I win." The air battle unfolds between the expedition's biplanes and the Atlanteans' futuristic fighters. In the instant before the shooting begins, Milo folds his hands, as if in prayer. Rourke is no coward, but he remains steadfastly craven. When the balloon begins to lose altitude, he tosses his partner, Helga, out of the gondola to her death, as if she were nothing more than ballast. Trying to kill Milo, Rourke touches the crystal and dies a horrible death. "Thank heaven," Milo exclaims.

The explosive charges cause the volcano to erupt, sending a catastrophic wave of lava back toward Atlantis. But by then, the crystal is restored and Princess Kida is released to her previous living form. Before the molten earth can engulf the city, Titans rise up to activate a protective shield.

What were Disney writers and animators thinking when they conceived *Atlantis*? What was their goal? What message did they want to convey? It is hard to believe that Michael Eisner, a notorious micromanager, planned the film as a devastating, unrelenting attack on capitalism and American imperialism. Yet it is impossible to read the movie, at least the last third of the film, any other way. In the end, Milo abandons America for Atlantis. With *Atlantis*, Walt Disney—scourge of left-wing unionism and communism in Hollywood—must be spinning in his grave.

Chapter Thirty-Two

Lilo and Stitch (2002): Send in the Clone

*W*hile the cloning of sentient beings for profit does not immediately suggest itself as the ideal premise for a children's film, *Lilo and Stitch* manages to make it work. The larger theme of the feature is Disney's contention that it is unconditional love—rather than a two-parent household—which most accurately defines a family unit. Woven through this sweet (but not saccharine) story is a reverence for life: What seems to be a monstrous, unlovable creature should not be sent away, done away with, or abandoned. This concept of family, *Ohana* in the native language of Hawaii, where most of the film is set, is that "nobody gets left behind—or forgotten."

In outer space, leaders of the United Galactic Federation are meeting on the planet Turo, to consider charges that an industrial scientist has been conducting illegal genetic experiments for Galaxy Defense Industries. The scientist, Jumba, speaking with a Russian accent, pleads not guilty to acting in such an irresponsible and unethical fashion. Prosecutors rebut by displaying, in a glass case, a small, snarling blue creature with a mouth full of pointed teeth and outsized ears. Nonplussed, the scientist—who is quintessentially mad—explains with pride that the creature is bulletproof, fireproof, and can think faster than a supercomputer. It can see in the dark and move objects three thousand times its size, and its only instinct is to obliterate everything it touches.

So it *is* a monster, says the alien leader, the Grand Councilwoman. Well, perhaps just a little one, the scientist concedes with a hint of pride. That is enough for the military commander, Captain Guntu. The creature, named "Experiment 626," is "an affront to nature," he declares. "It must be destroyed." Calm yourself, the Councilwoman says. Perhaps the creature can be reasoned with, she suggests, and asks the being to give some sign that it understands the proceedings, since its existence is at stake. "Show us that there is something inside you that is good," she says. The creature considers the request, clears its throat, then lets fly with a stream of unintelligible but apparently very naughty expletives. Compounding the offense, 626 then laughs at the effect on the aliens, like a potty-mouthed toddler. This is too much, even for its creator, who denies teaching it to talk like that. The alien leader has heard enough. "Place that idiot scientist under arrest," she orders. ("I prefer to be called an evil genius," he replies defensively.) The creature, she rules, is an "abomination. It is the pure product of a deranged mind. It has no place among us. Take it away." Unabashed by the sentence, 626 responds by using its tongue to slobber over the inside of its glass case.

En route to a prison ship for exile on a desert asteroid, 626 manages to escape its constraints and flee into hyperspace in a small ship. Galactic Federation trackers—who resemble Piglet and Tigger from *Winnie the Pooh*—report to the leaders on the craft's destination. It is headed for "Area 51"—a play on the New Mexico wilderness where space aliens are said to have landed in the mid-twentieth century—and an obscure planet that is mostly covered with water. That could solve the problem, someone observes, since the creature's molecular density is so great it won't be able to survive in water. When the trackers interrupt to say the craft is headed for a small island, it appears Earth is doomed. "We'll have to gas it," says the leader. Not so fast, says a galactic environmental official. The planet is home to a protected species—the endangered mosquito. Other options, such as invading the island, would only cause panic, the environmental official says. The mad scientist and the environmental official are dispatched to Earth to capture 626.

Just off one of the Hawaiian Islands, a pudgy little girl named Lilo is swimming and feeding a sandwich to her fish friends. She comes ashore, pausing on the beach to snap a picture of a fat, white tourist. Lilo is late to her traditional dancing lesson—all the other native Hawaiians she encounters are fit and beautiful—and the ensuing session does not go well. Lilo attacks and bites a girl in her class who calls her crazy for believing that her fish friend controls the weather. The fight, we soon see, is symptomatic of a number of larger problems the girl is having—beginning with depression. A book on her bedroom shelf is entitled *Practical Voodoo*, which she attempts to use to get back at the girls from school. Her parents have been killed in an accident, and her older sister, Nani, is all the family she has left. Lilo's primary consolation is to listen to Elvis records, especially "Heartbreak Hotel." The house, a traditional structure on stilts, is a mess, and a social worker is coming. "We're a broken family, aren't we?" Lilo asks her sister, with whom she often clashes. Both siblings scream in frustration into pillows. "I like you better as a sister than as a mom," the little girl says, as they reconcile.

The creature's spacecraft enters Earth's atmosphere with a fiery trail, which Lilo sees through her bedroom window and mistakes for a falling star, the occasion for a wish. She recreates—after a fashion—a similar scene in *Pinocchio*. Lilo kneels by her bed, but this time she *prays*. "It's me again," she says, clearly addressing God, rather than any fairy. "I need someone to be my friend; someone who won't run away. Maybe send me an angel. The nicest angel you have." This sacred scene contrasts with 626's landing, which is more reminiscent of the infant Superman's from Krypton. The creature emerges from a smoking crater, apparently swearing a blue streak in his own language. He does not appear to be an angel, or the answer to Lilo's prayer. A passing truck smashes 626, and Hawaiian drivers take his remains to the local animal shelter. There the creature has enough sense to transform himself into something that looks like a dog. Nani, in hopes of finding a friend for her little sister, takes Lilo to the shelter the next morning. The creature again demonstrates intelligence by throwing himself at Lilo in what she takes as a spontaneous expression of love. Against the advice of Nani and the shelter attendant, Lilo insists on adopting the creature, which she decides is the angel she prayed for. She names him "Stitch."

The mad scientist, now in Hawaii in pursuit of the fugitive creation, observes Lilo and Stitch leaving the shelter and predicts disaster. His creature is programmed for destruction and mayhem, Jumba tells his alien sidekick, and so is powerless to do anything else. Stitch displays those impulses at Lilo's house, wrecking much of what he sees. But Lilo, who knows what it is like to be alone and unlovable, will not give up on her ill-tempered pet. So, nature or nurture? Lilo draws a sketch of Stitch in the form of a graph, explaining to him that his "badness level is unusually high for someone your size." When she talks to him, is she also talking about herself? For all this affection and forbearance, Stitch wreaks more havoc, costing Nani her nightclub job and thus further jeopardizing her guardianship of Lilo. The older sister guesses—correctly—that Stitch is no dog, but some mutated creature. Nani demands that they return Stitch to the shelter, where death undoubtedly awaits, but Lilo refuses. "He was an orphan and we adopted him!" she yells, invoking the concept of *Ohana,* as explained by their father. The term, Lilo repeats, means family, and family means nobody gets left behind—or forgotten. Nani argues that Stitch hasn't been there long enough to qualify for *Ohana.* Lilo says, neither have I. Nani concedes the argument, saying she hates it when her sister uses *Ohana* against her.

Saved by Lilo, Stitch repays the favor by ripping up the girl's bedroom, and is calmed only when a flower *lei* falls onto his neck. "You wreck everything you touch," she tells her pet, but not in anger. "Why not try to *make* something for a change?" Is this something Lilo is repeating from what an understanding teacher has said to her? Stitch takes her literally, constructing a realistic-looking model of San Francisco—which he immediately destroys in a scene out of an old Japanese monster movie. Again observing from a distance, the scientist Jumba comments that the girl is wasting her time, that the creature cannot ignore its programming—it has no free will. Stitch, he says, was designed to be a monster, but now it has nothing to destroy. "I never gave him a greater purpose," he sighs. "What must it be like to have nothing, not even memories to visit in the middle of the night?"

Sleepless, Stitch goes through Lilo's bookshelf, until he discovers an illustrated copy of *The Ugly Duckling.* The pictures strike such a chord with the creature that he wakes Lilo and he asks for an explanation. She tells him that, at the end, the duckling is "happy because he knows where he belongs." Lilo decides that Stitch looks like an Elvis fan, so she introduces him to the King, starting with "Suspicious Minds." The girl turns her pet into a convincing Elvis impersonator, but the transformation only succeeds in sabotaging Nani's job hunt. David, Nani's would-be boyfriend, lifts their spirits by suggesting they all go surfing. Stitch watches with envy, and Nani and David fuss over Lilo. He is so eager to belong that, despite the danger of water, he joins them on a surfboard. Several adventures follow, as Jumba and his sidekick try again to capture Stitch—without success. Gloom descends again when the social worker appears to inform Nani that he will have to take Lilo from her.

That night, in the girl's bedroom, the sadness is contagious. Stitch is sad too. Lilo shows him a family photo and then explains how her parents died in an accident. She asks him about his parents, and he says he has none. The girl says she hears him cry at night. "I know that's why you wreck things and push me," she says, speaking from her own experience. "Our family's little now and we don't have many toys, but if you want, you could be part of it. You could be our baby and we'd raise you to be good." Stitch looks at the page from *The Ugly Duckling* and heads for the bedroom window. Lilo tells Stitch about *Ohana,* as the creature pauses in the window. "But if you want to leave, you can," she says. "I'll remember you, though. I remember everyone that leaves." Stitch does leave, taking the book into the forest in hopes of being found by his family. Waiting forlornly in a clearing, he is discovered by Jumba. If you are waiting for a family, the scientist says, "you don't have one. I made you. You were built to destroy. You can never belong. Let me take you apart."

Nani has to tell Lilo of the social worker's decision; the girl will have to leave. "Sometimes you try your hardest, but things don't work out the way you want them to," she says to her little sister. "Sometimes things have to change and maybe sometimes they're for the better." The next morning, David has good news for Nani— he has found her a job. But before she can race back to the house to stop the social worker, disaster strikes. Stitch races back to the house, pursued by Jumba, now determined to kill him rather than capture him. Lilo has had enough of the exasperating blue pet. "You ruined everything!" she shouts. But Stitch has learned the girl's lesson. *Ohana,* he says, and Lilo is forced to come to his aid. Lilo does help, to no avail; the house is destroyed, just as the social worker pulls up to take the girl away.

Several frantic escapes and chases ensue, as officials from the Galactic Federation arrive on the scene to reclaim their prisoner. Accused of being foul and flawed, Stitch replies with a newfound self-esteem that he is cute and fluffy. Characters suddenly change sides, with one exclaiming, "Hope for a miracle, that's all we can do." When the smoke finally clears, the Grand Councilwoman asks Stitch who he is. Standing with Lilo and Nani, he says, "This is my family. I found it all on my own. It's little, and it's broken, but still good. Yeah, still good." The alien leader decides to let Stitch remain on Earth. The closing credits are snapshots and postcards of the reconstituted family, full of love and fun.

Lilo and Stitch artfully weaves together disparate strands of Left and Right. There are swipes at the evil defense industry, willing to do anything for money. An officious environmental protection agent averts planetary genocide. And the notion that the nuclear family of mother, father, and children is the only successful model is undermined. Yet the movie also implicitly questions human cloning and abortion. Even *Ohana* echoes President George W. Bush's education law, the No Child Left Behind act. What I admire most about *Lilo and Stitch* is that, finally, Disney puts a short, chubby, sometimes exasperating little girl at the center of one of its animated features. And it works. It *is* possible.

Chapter Thirty-Three

Treasure Planet (2002): Mining the Father Lode

Treasure Planet, the greatest financial disaster in the history of modern Disney animation, was the third and one of the last attempts by the studio—after *Tarzan* and *Atlantis*—to lure boys back to theaters by putting a young man at the center of the narrative. But, as sometimes happens in the movie business, *Treasure Planet*'s monumentally dismal balance sheet obscured a solid story, with important and timely moral lessons for adolescents and teens. The tale, based on Robert Louis Stevenson's *Treasure Island*, is set on a planet called Montessor, an odd mixture of Elizabethan England and some futuristic, space-traveling galaxy that includes human-like beings with animal and insect-like features. At the outset of the movie, a little boy named Jim Hawkins is enamored of stories about the pirate Captain Nathaniel Flint, who years before is reputed to have hidden the loot of a thousand raids on a legendary planet. Jim is a sweet, loving child who shares his bedtime reading with his mother, Sarah, upstairs at the rickety inn she and her sailor spouse run, the Admiral Benbo.

However, in the twelve-year jump in time since the opening sequence, much has changed for Jim and Sarah. (Certain Disney truths endure: the prospects for an intact, nuclear family surviving an animated feature from beginning to end and living happily ever after remain slim.) Their father and husband has abandoned them, returning to a life aboard ship, and shattering the family. Jim, although bright, has turned into a sullen, resentful teenager, not doing well in school and getting into minor scrapes with the law. His mother complains to a sympathetic but geeky customer at the inn named Delbert Doppler that the boy has not been the same since his father left, proclaiming that she is at the end of her rope. Jim spends his time joyriding in a homemade, solar-powered, rocket sail-and-surf board. After one particularly dangerous stunt, he is pulled over by two flying traffic cops and returned home. The officers warn Sarah that, because her son has violated his parole, they are confiscating his vehicle and that if he gets into trouble again he is headed for Juvenile Hall. Clearly, the cops say, Jim is a loser and a dead-ender.

For many households in contemporary cities and suburbs, whether they have two parents or one parent, this scenario is no fantasy. Alienated teens can be extremely frustrating. Sarah pleads with Jim not to throw away his future. What future? he asks bitterly, heading for the harbor to mope and recall happier childhood times. Out of the sky comes a strange vehicle, crash-landing nearby. Jim helps rescue the dying occupant, Billy Bones, whose main concerns are his small, wooden chest and the cyborg—a humanoid robot—he is certain is in pursuit. Inside the chest, the teenager finds a mysterious, metal sphere that he manages to hang onto when pirates arrive and ransack the inn. Jim, Sarah, and Delbert barely escape, but the pirates leave the Benbo a smoking ruin.

At Delbert's home, Jim works the small sphere like a Rubik's puzzle until it springs open to reveal a holographic map that both the scientist and the teenager believe shows the location of Captain Flint's treasure planet. Delbert, a wealthy dilettante with canine features, proposes to finance and outfit a voyage to recover the loot. More than anything, Jim wants to go along on the adventure. For him, it is an opportunity to make a comeback, a fresh start to his life. However, Sarah is reluctant to let him go, for a variety of reasons. "I know that I keep messing things up," Jim tells her. "I know that I let you down, but this is my chance to make things up to you, set things right." More than anything, Jim sees this as an opportunity to redeem himself, and Delbert thinks it might be a good idea—something akin to an Outward Bound experience. "There are much worse remedies than a few character-building months in space," the astronomer says. Sarah, who has raised a child alone and run an inn for many years, is not as starry-eyed as her friend. The woman knows that there is danger involved in a voyage like this, and she does not want to lose her son. You won't, Jim assures her. "I'll make you proud."

At the spaceport, Delbert and Jim make their way to their ship, the RLS Legacy—a name that will have considerable meaning for the teenager as the story unfolds. They meet their captain, a crisp, self-possessed female feline with a British accent, named Amelia. The motley creatures of the crew appear to have been recruited from the *Star Wars* cantina. Jim is put in the charge of the ship's cook, a sinister-looking cyborg named Long John Silver. Like Captain Hook, he has a metal replacement for one hand, as well as an electronic leg. Silver takes an immediate and sternly paternal interest in Jim, ordering him to complete kitchen tasks and to swab the decks. "Heaven help you if I come back and it's not done," Silver admonishes. Later, Silver saves Jim from a nasty encounter with a sinister, spider-like crewmember. When the older man asks the boy if his father ever taught him to pick his fights carefully, Jim is silent. "Father not the teaching sort?" Silver asks. No, Jim replies, "more the taking off and never coming back sort." The cook says he is sorry, only to be assured by the teenager that it is no big deal. "I'm doing just fine," he says, although it is clear from everything we know that he is not fine. As Jim works, a plaintive song is sung called "I'm Still Here," about being caught between boyhood and manhood, and about the feeling of being abandoned. Over the lyrics, Jim recalls a scene from his childhood, when he sought approval from his father, but got only passing attention. "How can you learn what's never shown?" he sings. "Can you help me be a man?" Exhausted by his chores, the boy falls asleep in a chair, and Silver tenderly covers him with a blanket.

Around the ship in the days that follow, Jim allows himself to begin to admire Silver and, at the same time—through hard work and a good spirit—to gain his respect. Delbert's prediction seems accurate. Understandably, the teenager's feelings are tentative: Is this a man worthy of his trust? Jim dreams of seeing his sailor father leaving the family for his ship for the last time; his mother sobs, and the small boy vainly chases the man. Jim's doubts about Silver subside, and as they do the teenager gains confidence and is transformed. When a collapsing star sets off a storm that threatens to wreck the ship and all hands are sent aloft into the masts, Jim saves Silver's life. This act of heroism earns congratulations from Captain Amelia, but the accolade is short-lived. The boy is unjustly accused of responsibility for the death of the first mate, for not securing his lifeline. In fact, the spider has killed the ship's second-in-command by cutting his lifeline, but the blame falls on Jim's incompetence. Silver tries to come to his defense, but the boy's fragile confidence is obliterated. He is convinced he has messed up. "For two seconds, I thought I could do something right." Silver puts his arm around Jim, and tries to buck him up, using florid nautical metaphors. You have the makings of greatness, the cook tells him, "but you've got to take the helm and chart your own course and stick to it—no matter the squalls. And when the time comes, you get the chance to test the cut of your sails and show what you're made of. Well, I hope I'm there, catching some of the light coming off you that day." This moves Jim to tears, and Silver comforts him again. The boy smiles, and drifts off to sleep.

Long John Silver is as conflicted as Jim Hawkins, and he knows it. A pirate and probably a cold-blooded killer, the cyborg has recruited the dissolute crew of the Legacy for a purpose—to steal the treasure when then they find it. Silver acknowledges to his little creature sidekick, Morph, that he is "getting in deep here" in his relationship with Jim. The next thing he knows, his pirate mates on the crew will think he has gone soft, which would fatally undermine his leadership of the plot. Sure enough, his musing is overheard by the spider, which tries to turn Silver's introspective words against him when the conspirators meet below decks, accusing him of having a soft spot for the boy. Unknown to the others, Jim has fallen into a nearby fruit barrel and overhears the discussion. The pirate leader defends himself by assuring the others that he would not risk the treasure for some "nose-wiping little whelp." He insists that he has not gone soft, and that he only "cozied up to that kid to keep him off our scent."

The mutiny erupts, with Jim leaping from the barrel and siding with Captain Amelia and Delbert. In the course of the battle, Silver has the opportunity to shoot the boy—but he cannot. Suddenly, Treasure Planet is in sight, and all hands head for the surface, albeit in different vehicles and different directions. The murderous pirates surround Amelia, Delbert, and Jim in the redoubt of a manic robot marooned on the planet years before by Captain Flint. Silver demands a parley with Jim, apologizing for what he said about the boy and claiming that he did not mean it. If he hadn't convinced his mates that he hadn't gone soft, Silver says, the pirates would have gutted them both. The cyborg has a new proposal for Jim, that they join forces and make common cause against their respective allies. "If we play our cards right," Silver says, "we can both walk away from this rich as kings." In exchange for Jim's map, the pirate leader offers to make the boy an equal partner in the treasure.

The time for trusting defective father figures is past for newly assertive Jim Hawkins. He rejects Silver's duplicitous deal, throwing back at him his earlier talk of Jim's potential for greatness and "the light off his sails." Silver is equally disgusted, observing that his life lessons have been wasted on the boy. "You still don't know how to pick your fights," he says. If the map is not returned by dawn, the pirates will blast the little band of holdouts. Another, more practical reason that Jim cannot turn over the map is that he no longer has it; it is hidden on the Legacy, which is hovering above the planet's surface. With Delbert caring for the injured Captain Amelia, it is up to Jim to recover the map. Aboard the ship, another battle ensues. Jim kills the spider, after learning that the first mate's death came at the claws of the arachnid and not as a result of the boy's failure. Although on the opposite side of this fight, Silver admits to grudging admiration for his student. "Just like me," the pirate tells him, "you hate to lose."

Jim is forced at sword point to turn over the map, and the reunited crew finds Captain Flint's treasure. However, the trove is booby-trapped, set to destroy those who seek it, as well as the entire planet. As chaos ensues, Jim and Silver battle once again. "I like you, lad, but I've come too far to let you stand between me and me treasure," the old pirate says. Yet when he has the opportunity to finish off the boy, Silver can't do it. His better self—the cyborg's spark of humanity—won't allow him to. With the planet about to explode, Jim returns the favor: He risks his life to save his friends and the Legacy, by calling on the same hot-dogging, surfing skills that got the teen into trouble at the film's beginning. Now it is Long John Silver's turn to display parental pride. "Didn't I say the boy had greatness in him?" he asks Delbert and Amelia, before embracing the boy. Jim is something special, Silver tells him. "You're going to rattle the stars." Finally, the teenager has the approval of a father figure.

With some gold that Silver has salvaged from Treasure Planet— and gives to the boy—Jim's mother is able to rebuild the Admiral Benbo Inn. Captain Amelia, now married to Delbert, recommends Jim to become a cadet at the Space Academy. At the party celebrating the inn's reopening, Jim arrives in uniform and shakes hands with the two traffic cops who arrested him. The boy is redeemed, although his mother is still without a partner. Oddly, the triumphant song that plays over the closing credits, "Always Know Where You Are," recaps the lessons Jim has learned, but then introduces a note of reverence and spirituality wholly absent from the movie itself. "Now I'm strong and I won't kneel, except to thank who's watching over me."

Traditionally in Disney's animated features, mothers are the ones longed for by the central characters. In *Treasure Planet,* filmmakers examine the toll exacted by absent fathers, especially on their adolescent sons. For me, the point is made far more persuasively than in any lecture from a government bureaucrat or, worse, from a right-wing, talk radio scold. Dads have a big responsibility, as Jim Hawkins shows. But I wonder if a modern boy in Jim's position, a child whose father has left the family, might actually benefit from watching this movie. While *Treasure Planet* does have a happy ending, I suspect that watching the animated feature might not do much to assuage such a grievous injury. Watching a movie does not equal therapy, nor will it substitute. Parental discretion advised—by me.

Chapter Thirty-Four

Return to Neverland (2002): Faith, Trust, and Pixie Dust II

*I*n a time when children are forced by modern commercial media to grow up too soon, and parents fight what is often a losing battle to preserve innocence and stave off cynicism, *Return to Neverland* argues that the struggle can be won. This victory can be achieved in the face of a much greater threat than television, movies, and pop music—in this case, the monstrous reality of a world war. Departing from its recent sequel strategy, Disney made *Return to Neverland* decades after the original *Peter Pan,* and for big screen release. In the process, the values have been updated to accommodate major changes in modern culture and attitudes, even though the story takes place near the middle of the twentieth century.

It is World War II, and London is suffering under the Nazi blitz. Wendy Darling, Peter Pan's good friend, has grown up, married, and has two children. Her husband is called up for military duty, and as he leaves, he asks his adolescent daughter Jane to help her mother and younger brother. For all that has happened to Wendy since her childhood adventures, she has never forgotten Peter or stopped believing in him. From her balcony, she can still find "the second star to the right." But for young Jane, the ugliness of reality is inescapable, forcing her to discard many childish things. Alone, and wearing a helmet, she picks her way home through bomb-ravaged neighborhoods, taking cover during an air raid. Later, she watches as emergency vehicles and crews race to try to save survivors and recover bodies from the rubble, before she joins her mother and brother in a shelter.

Wendy tries to distract her children from the horror of the war outside with tales of Peter Pan. Jane, despite her youth, already

215

seems beyond such fantasies, preferring to monitor radio broad-
casts. Still, her mother's stories are intoxicating. As Wendy tells of
the time Peter made off with Captain Hook's ship and treasure,
even Jane is drawn in. Hook will never win, the mother concludes,
as long as there is "faith, trust, and pixie dust." These three elements—a concise restatement of the Disney gospel—are too much
for her daughter. Jane snaps, "Poppycock!" There is no more time
for fun and games, she says, for filling their heads with silly stories. In this she sounds more like her curmudgeon grandfather in
the earlier feature. The children of London will soon be evacuated
to the countryside for safety, and when that happens, Wendy wants
Jane to look after her brother Daniel. That means telling stories
about Peter Pan, the mother says. The little boy will need them, as
will Jane. They must have faith, trust, and pixie dust, Wendy
insists. Hardened by what she has seen and heard, Jane says that
they are "just words from your stories. They don't mean anything."
Young Daniel is still a believer: Peter Pan says that faith, trust, and
pixie dust will make you fly. Not content that her own illusions
have been crushed, Jane attempts to destroy her brother's. "Story
time is *over,*" she tells him. "Look, it's a war. Peter Pan isn't real,
and people don't fly." Daniel protests that people *do* fly. Grow up,
she tells him, and give up this childish nonsense. The boy, shaken,
says his sister is lying to him. Wendy is outraged that Jane could
treat her brother this way. "You think you're very grown up, but
you have a great deal to learn."

Jane would like to believe, as she looks out her window. In the
next balcony, Wendy has Daniel in her arms, pointing at Peter's
star. The girl cries, singing through her tears that she is not a child,
that she can take care of herself and that she mustn't let the others
see her weep. She is fine, she sings, but she is also too tired to listen and too old to believe her mother's stories. Jane would like to
believe, but she cannot see what the others see. All she can see is
the reality of her war-ravaged city, so she closes her window.

Company is coming. A pirate ship makes its way through the
clouds, dodging the planes of the RAF and the antiaircraft flak,
heading for Wendy's house. It is Captain Hook, arriving to kidnap
Wendy—for whom he mistakes Jane—to use as bait to capture

Peter Pan. Back in Neverland, Peter easily rescues Jane, and flies off with her. There are some changes on the island—there are no Indians in evidence, for example. And Tinker Bell, it is immediately apparent, has undergone some alterations over the decades, including breast reduction surgery and liposuction on her derriere. Her dress has been stretched as well. What has not changed is her jealousy of female rivals like Jane, whom the fairy proceeds to knock down. Peter shrugs his shoulders and explains, "All girls get like that around me." After a tour of the island, Jane meets the Lost Boys, who remind her of her own little brother. The Lost Boys have the same reaction to Jane as they did to Wendy—they want her to stay and be their mother. Yet Peter notices something odd about Jane—she acts like a grown-up. For one, she is a list maker, the prototypical sign of impending adulthood, and she wants to go home, because her family in London needs her. So she builds a raft, which promptly sinks. Peter offers to teach her to fly, but the pixie dust is not enough; she lacks faith and trust, and so does not believe she can fly. "I don't believe any of this," she says, stalking off. "And I especially don't believe in fairies." This last is inexplicably wounding to Tinker Bell, who seems to fall ill as her light begins to fade. The sprite needs Jane to believe in her, or she will die.

Temptation comes calling, as it often does at this point in Disney features, this time in the person of Captain Hook. He feigns despair to Jane, saying he needs his pilfered treasure to get back to his dear, sweet mother, who is ailing. If only Jane will help him recover it, he will gladly use his ship to take her home. Desperate to get back, she is ripe for both flattery and rationalization. Hook says Peter will not listen to reason, because "he's not sensible, like you and I. He's just a boy who'll never grow up." Jane justifies the betrayal on two grounds, beginning with self-interest. She'll never be able to fly home—which she must do to honor her promise to her father—because she lacks faith. And, if what Hook says is true, the treasure is rightfully his—and the carefree Peter has no use for it anyway. She agrees, on condition that Hook swears, in writing, that he will not harm Peter if the pirate gets the treasure. "You're doing the right thing," Hook assures her. "I'm your only way out."

When she finds the treasure, she is to blow on the ship's whistle to summon the pirates.

Without Jane's belief in her, Tinker Bell is near death, and for an instant she folds her hands in supplication. So Peter and the Lost Boys go looking for the girl and, despite her bargain with Hook, Jane loosens up, singing that she should become a Lost Boy. Stumbling onto the treasure, she contemplates blowing the whistle, but thinks better of it and tosses it away. Peter proclaims her a "Lost Girl." But a Lost Boy, not knowing what it will mean, picks up the discarded whistle and blows it, summoning pirates. Hook is triumphant and prepares to kill Peter; the captain has no intention of keeping his bargain with Jane. Outraged, Peter accuses the girl of being a traitor, and of lying to him. Worse, he says, "because you don't believe in fairies, Tinker Bell's light is going out." Distraught, Jane flees to the Lost Boys' lair to find Tinker Bell. She kneels beside the tiny, inert figure, as if she is praying, weeping, and asking for forgiveness. Jane reprises her song from the beginning, this time singing, "Now I have to believe all those precious stories," that the world is made of faith, trust, and pixie dust. Sparkling dust emerges from the girl's hands, landing on Tinker Bell, who is revived.

On the pirate ship, Peter and the Lost Boys prepare to meet their fate, as Hook volunteers that he loathes children, confirmation of his undiluted villainy. Peter is not afraid to die, urging his young friends to be brave as well and not to let the pirates see them cry. Hook savors the moment, telling Peter to say *his* prayers. Then, in a role reversal from both the original film and the early part of the sequel, Jane now comes to Peter's rescue—although at first Hook is not impressed by her arrival. "Run for your lives," he exclaims facetiously, no doubt insulting many of the film's viewers. "It's a little girl!" This little girl is quick to free the Lost Boys and, when the pirates approach, to fly. Because she now believes, she can fly. Jane and Peter destroy the ship, and send the pirate crew flailing away in a lifeboat.

Now, at last, Jane can fly home, although the Lost Boys protest that they will miss her. "But there's someone back home who needs me. And besides, now I've got great stories to tell him about

Peter Pan and the Lost Boys." Jane and Peter fly back to London and, as Big Ben tolls, Jane awakes on the window seat. She runs to her mother, apologizing for her disbelief and confirms that Peter is indeed remarkable. Daniel, in the doorway, interrupts them, saying that he has had a bad dream. Wendy and Jane agree to tell the boy stories together. Later, Wendy and Peter are reunited. He says she has changed. "Not really," she says, "not ever." Wendy, Jane, and Daniel watch from the balcony as Peter flies off. "I'll always believe in you, Peter Pan," Jane says, just as a truck pulls up below and her father emerges.

In an extremely muted way, *Return to Neverland* makes the same point as the live action film *Life is Beautiful*. In that movie, a father attempts to protect his son from the grotesque realities of a concentration camp by telling him stories and creating a fantasy world. Anne Frank pasted photos of American stars on the wall of her hideaway in Amsterdam. For children, fantasy is a valid retreat, a legitimate refuge, in times of terror. Jane learns that stories can, for a time, mediate reality. Although tragedy and suffering can certainly eradicate childhood innocence, it need not always be the case. In hospital wards for seriously ill young people, in special camps and various programs such as the Make-a-Wish Foundation, children often ask for visits from cartoon characters or trips to Disney theme parks. Durable fantasies, many based on animated features, can give joy and sustain hope, regardless of life's hardships.

Chapter Thirty-Five

Brother Bear (2003): Primitive Predestination

*M*ore than any other of Disney's animated features, *Brother Bear* is a movie infused by spirituality and focused on quest, transformation, and redemption—from beginning to end. In the opening sequence, an old man begins a tale from the world of the Pacific Northwest 10,000 years ago at the end of the Ice Age. Around a campfire, as sparks fly up, the storyteller sketches this Native American cosmos, a world full of magic. The multicolored northern lights are a supernatural force, he explains, the great spirits of their ancestors that have the power to make changes in lives and to transform one thing into another. Greatest of these is the story of a boy who wanted to be a man, he says.

With no solid documentation for what human society was like at the time in a religious sense, the Disney writers relied on stories found in many cultures around the world. Chuck Williams, a development executive and producer at Florida Animation Studio, said he and cowriter Aaron Blaise created the original story after "reading a lot of Native American myths and transformation stories," according to the film's production notes. "We discovered that practically every culture around the world had some kind of story about people transforming into animals. Many of them were about boys changing into bears as a coming of age ritual. Some of the stories even had humans pretending to be bears for a period of time and then they'd come out and be considered men of the tribe." Blaise added, "The transformation myths were designed to teach life lessons and that's why they were passed down all these years by different cultures. They're structured in ways that are unlike Western storytelling, with the idea that you could go from one culture to another, meaning one animal world to the human world."

Of course, as the production notes acknowledge, *Brother Bear* is an idealized portrayal of this place and period—everyone seems well fed, healthy, and happy, with full sets of teeth. An opening song, played over magnificent vistas of land, mountains, water, and ice, explains how in this world humans and nature live side by side, in harmony, "brothers all the same." All beings look to the sky to fill their hearts and souls, and to give thanks for what they have been given. At this moment, a family of three brothers is preparing for a communal ceremony in which the youngest, named Kenai, is to receive his totem. This small carved animal worn around the neck—a symbol revealed to the old shaman Tanana by the Great Spirits—will guide the young person entering adulthood through life. Years earlier, Kenai's oldest brother Sitka received an eagle, signifying guidance; the next in line, Denahi, was given a wolf, for wisdom. So the young boy is understandably disappointed when Tanana gives him an amiable bear, the sign of love. This disappointment is only magnified after the ceremony when Kenai's older brothers tease him about the "unmanly" totem.

Before the ceremony, Kenai has been told by Sitka to make certain to tie a basket of fish high into a tree to keep it out of reach of bears. But the boy is so excited about the gathering that he does not take care to secure the basket before leaving for the campfire. When the brothers return for a celebration, they see that it has fallen and that some animal has made off with it. Now even more embarrassed, Kenai chases off to recover it, only to find that a seven-foot grizzly has destroyed the basket and eaten his fish. Having made one mistake, the boy now compounds his error. Enraged—and overmatched—he throws pieces of wood at the retreating bear. The grizzly is startled, but seems not to want to respond. Still, she understands she must defend herself from the human. Kenai soon calls for help, and his brothers come running. In the ensuing fight, Sitka sacrifices his life to save his two younger brothers, and is transformed by the light spirits into a living, glowing version of his totem, a bald eagle.

However, in the struggle, the bear has escaped, and Kenai vows to kill the animal. Denahi tells his younger brother that he does not blame the bear for Sitka's death, and he reminds Kenai that killing the bear will not bring Sitka back. Doing so will only upset the spirits, he says. Assembled again at the communal campfire, the shaman Tanana bids Sitka a symbolic farewell, saying he left his family and his friends too soon. Kenai tosses his totem into the dying fire, leaves to track the bear and soon kills it with his spear. As his brother Denahi predicted, this act upsets the harmony of their existence, and thus upsets the spirits. The sacred lights surround Kenai and transform him into the bear he has killed. At this moment, Denahi arrives on the scene. He sees the bear on the ground near Kenai's clothes and assumes that another of his brothers has been lost to the beast. But before Denahi can take his vengeance, Sitka's spirit materializes. Transformed into an eagle, he lifts and carries Kenai away. Denahi ties his brother's totem— recovered from the fire by Tanana—to his spear and sets off in deadly, determined pursuit.

When Kenai wakes, he is with Tanana, and the old woman informs him that he has become a bear, and why. Sitka wants his younger brother to achieve a new perspective on life, to make up for what he did wrong. To do so, she tells him, Kenai must find Sitka on the "mountain where the light touches the earth." However, Kenai is not ready to accept that he made a mistake, much less that he has been transformed into a bear. He stumbles into a rope snare and is freed only with the help of a motormouth bear cub named Koda, who needs a companion to help him find the annual salmon run. Kenai is not interested in helping Koda—until the cub informs him that the run is in sight of the mountain where the sacred spirits touch the earth. With Denahi tracking them, Kenai and Koda journey toward their common goals.

As they travel and together overcome obstacles, Kenai and Koda are trailed—or guided—by an eagle, the spirit of Kenai's brother Sitka. Along the way, the pair pass through an abandoned village, where they see a cave painting of a human hunting a bear with a spear. Each sees a "monster" in a different image, one responsible for the death of a loved one, and each wonders why there is hatred between the species. Beneath the surface, it is another of Disney's misleading symmetries. The humans hunt bears when they need food; bears attack humans in self-defense. At the salmon run, the other bears embrace Koda and welcome Kenai as a member of their family. They accept him into the community of feasting and storytelling. Kenai says it is the most peaceful place he has ever been to. But as Koda tells the bears his story of seeing his mother fight the men, Kenai realizes that the bear he killed was Koda's mother and that she only fought the three human brothers to defend her offspring. Kenai is overcome by remorse for what he has done and flees the bears. Kenai sees the mountaintop where he must go to find the spirit of his brother Sitka, and he begins to climb. Koda comes with him.

Now finally transformed into a mature being, Kenai is compelled to confess to Koda. "I did something wrong," he tells the cub, "and I am so sorry." The revelation that Kenai killed his mother shatters the young bear, causing him to run away. Sitka the eagle appears to guide his youngest brother to the sacred summit—and to his destiny. But the middle brother, Denahi, has tracked the bear to the mountaintop as well, still bent on deadly revenge. This time, it is Koda who returns to save his friend, attacking Denahi before he can plunge his knife into Kenai. Sitka then reappears in glowing, human form to greet his two brothers. Koda's mother, also glowing, is reunited with her cub. Kenai must now decide what his incarnation will be—a return to human form, or to the large bear. He realizes that, because he wrongly killed Koda's mother, it is his responsibility to take care of the cub. Kenai makes the right choice, fulfills his destiny, and *becomes* his totem. The spiritual balance is restored. Denahi assures him, "You'll always be my little brother." This is the story of "a boy who became a man by becoming a bear," Denahi tells us. Before the credits roll, we see the two bears being accepted by the humans at their campfire, as Kenai adds his large, clawed paw prints to the handprints of the others on the cave wall.

If, as seems possible, *Brother Bear* turns out to be one of the last predominately hand-drawn animated features produced by Walt Disney Studios, it is one that writers, producers, and artists can be proud of. True, another mother is killed at the outset, and there is only one other female character of substance. Yet, wholly outside the Judeo-Christian construct, the movie communicates all the central messages about love and responsibility and tolerance of differences that Walt Disney wrote into early hits such as *Dumbo* and *Pinocchio,* as well as the studio's later triumphs such as *The Lion King.* And if this is to be a swan song for the genre, it has the perfect sound track. The music and lyrics are written by Phil Collins and Mark Mancina but performed by a diverse and eclectic array of artists, including Tina Turner, the Blind Boys of Alabama, Jeremy Suarez, and the ethereal Bulgarian Women's Choir, who sing in the Native American Inuit language. When Turner first read the lyrics to Collins's "Great Spirits," she thought it was a prayer, with a gospel undercurrent, according to the production notes. "There is a real spiritual quality to it and the message is about love and care and coming together," she said. The instrumentation runs the gamut from Japanese Taiko drums to those from Native American cultures, as well as Hopi instruments and woodwinds made from drilled animal bones—all together with Western instruments.

In making *Brother Bear,* Disney's Chuck Williams told the Greek newspaper *Kathimerini* that the studio wanted to make a film that would showcase its entire history of animated features. "We tried to make something timeless," he said. "We didn't want a movie just about animal rights—the bears are a metaphor for humans. Kenai hates humans because he is disappointed by them and he hates bears because he holds them responsible for his brother's death. We wanted to show Kenai looking at things from a different perspective, showing some understanding for the other side of the argument." To that end, the producers sent the film's writers a note—while *Brother Bear* was still evolving as a project—that the central message they wanted to convey was, "We are all equal in the eyes of the Spirits," according to H. Clark Wakabayashi, in *Brother Bear: A Transformation Tale.*

When I saw *Brother Bear* in its opening week at an upscale, suburban multiplex, the audience response was restrained, and, while profitable, the film was no blockbuster. But months later, shortly before it was released on DVD, I returned for another look, this time to a bargain theater that charges $2.50 a seat. It was an early evening show on a holiday weekend, and, to my surprise, there were forty to fifty people in the theater. They were mostly young children with parents and other family members, many of them Latino or African American. Throughout the film they paid rapt attention, laughing at all the right places, and when the film ended they applauded. They practically bounced out of the theater, repeating punch lines to each other. These children, and their parents, clearly received and understood *Brother Bear*'s messages—love, forgiveness, brotherhood—from a culture far different from their own. This is the realization of Walt's dream, to communicate lessons to children across cultures. For the company's founder, the first tales (and thus the prisms) were in the Western tradition, American and European, and only the audiences were from different cultures. For Disney's successors, the features themselves have become cross-cultural, as well as the audiences.

Part Three

Disney and American Culture

Chapter Thirty-Six

The Theme Parks: American Pilgrimage

The day Disneyland opened in 1955, Walt stepped to the microphone and said he hoped his creation would be "a source of joy and inspiration to all the world." Like Disney's animated features, the company's theme parks in California, Florida, Paris, Tokyo, and (soon) Hong Kong transmit and reinforce values to millions of children each year. Kids who encounter cast members dressed as characters, especially those portraying Mickey Mouse, assume the padded figures have stepped down off the screen—if not from somewhere higher. "If anything is more irresistible than Jesus, it's Mickey," Carl Hiassen wrote in his slender, caustic book, *Team Rodent: How Disney Devours the World*. Dave Barry, Hiassen's *Miami Herald* colleague, had a similar reaction as the parent of a young child. "Our three-year-old daughter loves Disney World," the humorist wrote in 2003, "because she gets to meet Mickey Mouse in person. She sometimes gets to meet Mickey three or four times a day, and he always acts thrilled and surprised to see her, as if he didn't remember that he just met her 45 minutes earlier. Mickey's a little slow, if you ask me."

The parks and their ethos are the subject of some excellent book-length studies and academic articles, which discuss everything from how the rides and characters are intertwined with the animated features, to their role in Disney's relationship with local governments. For Disney, the parks are "the Vatican with mouse ears," wrote Richard Foglesong, professor of politics at Rollins College and author of *Married to the Mouse: Walt Disney World and Orlando*. Italian novelist Umberto Eco called Disneyland "America's Sistine Chapel." In an article for the April 1980 issue of *Anthropological Quarterly,* Alexander Moore described Disney World as "bounded ritual space," as well as a "playful pilgrimage center." Thomas Ryba, theologian in residence at the St. Thomas Aquinas Center in West Lafayette, Indiana, wrote in a paper delivered at the American Academy of Religion meeting in Orlando in 1998 that in the theme parks, "Walt Disney has succeeded in creating an architectural and mechanical artifact by means of which millions of visitors (both Americans and foreign nationals) are introduced to the logic of American hope."

One of the most comprehensive, if challenging, looks at the theme parks came from Michael R. Real in his book *The Disney Universe: Morality Play.* Real studied two hundred visitors to Disneyland, characterizing the experience as "a morality play" that takes place within "the quasi-sacred interior of the park." Ultimately, he wrote, "the Disney universe seems to compete with religious, educational, political, economic and familial forces in setting ultimate standards for reality and behavior. . . . As a morality play of secular American values, Disneyland utilizes entertainment, education, mythology, and utopianism to typify, strengthen, and spread a patriotic American's idealized version of nation and world, of the past, the present and the future. The central idea of Disneyland shows through as 'happiness,' and the achievement of happiness has long been the goal of classical Western ethical systems." Sometimes, according to Thomas Ryba, the theme parks' morality plays are explicitly religious. For example, "the denizens of the Haunted Mansion have not heeded the teaching of the Gospels and have died willfully fixed in their avarice, their punishment being that they are tied ectoplasmically to their material wealth for eternity." While "it's not the intention of Disney to tell us the stories of Jesus, to disclose to us the revelation of God" at the theme parks, the Reverend Michael Catlett told members of McLean Baptist Church in McLean, Virginia, in his sermon, "I think we see some gospel truth mixed in with the entertainment that is offered."

If cleanliness is next to godliness, then Disneyland and Disney World certainly constitute sanctified ground. As the evangelist

Tony Campolo observed, "There are a number of values in the religion of Disney that must not be ignored. And one that hits anybody that ever goes to any of the theme parks is the pristine cleanliness of the place. It grows out of the Protestant work ethic." In the early days of Disneyland, according to longtime company executive Richard Nunis, the world famous evangelist Billy Graham was on a VIP tour of the California park. At the end of the day, Nunis ushered him over to a bench, where Walt himself—disguised in an old baseball cap—was sitting. Graham, hoping to strike up a conversation with a compliment, said, "Walt, you have a great fantasy land here." But Walt was having none of it. "Oh, you preachers get it all wrong," he replied. "This is reality in here. Out there," he said, gesturing beyond his Magic Kingdom, "is fantasy."

Reality? There are no churches in any Disney theme park, apart from a small historical chapel on display at the Norway Pavilion at Epcot, and regular Sunday services at Disney World hotels for visiting (and working) Protestants and Catholics were ended, after twenty-eight years, in 2002. However, there are several wedding chapels, available for a fee, where hopeful couples can try to begin their marriages with a jolt of Disney optimism—and pixie dust. (The Catholic Church does not sanction such services.) Attitudes have changed over the years. As far back as the mid-1970s, Disney officials were "uncomfortable" when "Jesus rallies" and rock concerts were held on vacant land adjacent to the park, according to the Reverend Alex Clattenberg, who organized them. Now there are annual nights devoted to Christian music in both Florida and California parks. For more than a decade, Disney World has hosted "Nights of Joy" each September, drawing tens of thousands of young people with the biggest names in contemporary Christian music. In Anaheim, youth evangelist Greg Laurie has hosted a similar event at Disneyland. Of course, these are *commercial* endeavors, and they have become so lucrative, at least in Orlando, that the competition—Universal Studios Florida—started a similar event scheduled for the same weekend. The musical lineups are almost interchangeable, with performers moving between the parks from year to year. However, the primary difference between the two events is that the Disney World event does not permit evangelists to speak from the various stages. Universal has no such prohibition. (In Disney World's Animal Kingdom there is a "Tree of Life," although it is doubtful that the company's creative designers called "Imagineers" had the Hebrew prophets' *aytz hayim* imagery in mind.)

Christians are not alone in having special times at Disney theme parks. Given their appreciation of fantasy and performance, it is not surprising that members of the gay and lesbian community began gravitating to the parks, both as employees and visitors. An annual event at the Magic Kingdom, called "Gay Days," began as an informal, one-day gathering in 1991 in Orlando. Since then, the event has grown in popularity, leading to a book, *Queens in the Kingdom: The Ultimate Gay and Lesbian Guide to the Disney Theme Parks*. By the early 2000s, the event had grown to three days and all of Orlando's theme parks, drawing more than 100,000 participants. However, Gay Days also provoked considerable controversy, which will be discussed more fully in chapter 37. Unsuspecting straight guests, whose visits unwittingly coincided with Gay Days, said they were surprised and in some cases offended. In June 2003, a group called the Christian Action Network said they were "going undercover" at Gay Days, equipped with cameras and disguised as tourists, to capture "the reality behind 'Gay Days.'" Their goal, according to a press release, was to document "public lewdness and sex acts, and even open drug use," said Martin Mawyer, the group's president. He predicted horrifying events, from "Disney's characters themselves portraying sexual acts openly to large crowds to the homosexual movies shown on the Disney transportation systems." None of the group's outrageous claims were proven or documented.

However, there are some real serpents in this Eden. Allegations by Christians and others about the theme parks have been documented in a book that reprints police reports and other court filings. In *Disney: The Mouse Betrayed,* Peter and Rochelle Schweizer charged that the theme parks are "a magnet" for perverts, pedophiles, and peeping toms, and that Disney officials have been lax in screening, disciplining, and reporting employees acting in this way. The company did not begin running criminal checks on prospective employees until 1998. As recently as April 2, 2004, a Disney World worker who plays the character Tigger, from Winnie-the-Pooh, was arrested on charges of fondling a thirteen-year-old girl and her mother as they posed for a picture with the costumed cast member at the park. In the days that followed the report, more than two dozen more women made similar complaints about Tigger, dating back at least four years.

Because Disneyland was just twenty-five minutes from our home when we lived in Southern California in the late 1980s and early 1990s, we began making regular visits to the park when each of our children hit the age of two. Later, in Orlando, living forty minutes from Disney World, the visits continued until Asher and then Liza became adolescents and lost interest in going. On both coasts, our homes were often landing zones for family and friends from around the country making park visits with their children. We—and they—were not alone. Whenever a multimillion-dollar football player whose team has just won the Super Bowl is asked in a television commercial what's next, he quickly answers, "I'm going to Disney World." Of course, the quarterback won't be paying for the trip, but even so, he's making enough money to afford it if he had to. For many of the lower- and middle-income tourists who mob area theme parks and make them profitable, the name-brand experience is a serious financial strain. Still, for millions of these Americans, the trip to a Disney theme park has come to represent an inelastic cultural demand, regardless of the cost. "It seems that it's something every self-respecting middle class family owes its children—a trip to Disney World—if only as a once-in-a-lifetime thing," said Richard Foglesong. And not just middle-class families. Taken together, the Disney theme parks are thought to be the world's fourth most visited "shrine," behind Mecca, the Vatican, and the Taj Mahal.

Numerous writers and critics have compared this to a religious pilgrimage to Mecca for Muslims. The theme parks are a "quasi-religious Mecca," wrote Margaret J. King in her 1975 paper, "Disneyland and Walt Disney World: Traditional Values in Futuristic Form." Bruce David Forbes, of Morningside College in Sioux City,

Iowa, wrote, "Annual or once-in-a-lifetime pilgrimages to Walt Disney World have much of the character of the Haj in Islam or pilgrimages to Christian sacred sites," in a paper entitled, "And a Mouse Shall Lead Them: An Essay on the Disney Phenomenon as Religion," delivered at a November 2000 conference on Disney at Florida Atlantic University. "How exactly had a visit to Disney World become such an obligation, such a hajj?" wrote author Samuel Freedman for salon.com on August 23, 1999. The answer is complicated, but the process began when Walt envisioned his first weekly television show as an advertising vehicle for his new theme park, and continues to this day with the Disney Channel, the Family Channel, and ABC-TV.

This obligation to pay homage has even been validated by otherwise cynical and cold-eyed journalists. In his April 4, 2003, syndicated column, humorist Dave Barry admitted, "Every year, we return to Orlando. Instinct makes us do this. We are like the salmon who must swim upstream to spawn, and then die. They are lucky. We must go to theme parks." *San Jose Mercury News* columnist Mike Cassidy felt the same way about his family trip to Disneyland in 2003. "They don't call it the Magic Kingdom for nothing," he wrote on August 17 of that year. "Disneyland has the magical power to make you lose your senses. At least when it comes to fiscal responsibility. Whoever said money can't buy happiness hadn't considered the Happiest Place on Earth, where joy comes at a price. . . . Disneyland, it turns out, is not just a vacation. It's a childhood memory, a gigantic expectation, a deep desire to ensure that one's children find the Magic Kingdom every bit as magical as the generation that came before."

In 1996, the working-class family featured on the (Disney-owned) ABC television series *Roseanne* brought nine adults to Orlando for a fictional, four-day tour of the entertainment giant's theme parks. When a character commented on the cost of the excursion, estimated at more than $5,000, the father responded, "Nobody should be worrying anything about money this whole trip!" In 2003, on the competing Fox network, the Simpsons—by then television's best-known *schleppers* (freeloaders)—made their pilgrimage, providing several opportunities to skewer the Mouse.

More realistically than Roseanne's brood, the Simpsons made it by virtue of a free trip to Orlando and a theme park called "EFCOT." In the episode, the family wins their visit to the futuristic park after son Bart nominates his fourth-grade instructor for a Teacher of the Year Award—a competition that sounds a lot like Disney's annual American Teacher Awards. Daughter Lisa explains to the family that EFCOT was designed by people in 1965 who imagined what life would be like in 1987. "It's even boring to fly over," Homer complains from the plane. After the ceremony, Homer announces that he has had enough of EFCOT and is going to Disney World. He attempts to scale a wall topped by barbed wire dividing EFCOT from what is clearly the Magic Kingdom. Despite a warning from a squeaky, Mickey Mouse-like voice to "step away from the wall," he is undeterred. Homer marvels at the park's beauty until he is shocked by an ugly reality at Disney's notoriously overpriced refreshment stands: a sugary Mexican pastry called a *churro* going for fourteen dollars. As Homer likes to say, it's funny 'cause it's true.

Would it really have been so difficult, or so jarring, to put a church in a theme park, as Disney claims? Just look up the freeway from Disneyland to Knott's Berry Farm in Buena Park, the roadside fruit stand that grew into a theme park. Walter Knott, who founded the attraction, was a religious man who was said to have taught Sunday school on the train that still runs through the grounds. In 1955, he saved a country church in Downey, California, from demolition, according to Amy Wilson, in the *Orange County Register* of May 1, 2003. A Baptist congregation founded around the time of the California Gold Rush built the simple, clapboard sanctuary in 1876. Over time, it became an Episcopal church. Knott had the church taken apart piece by piece and reconstructed in the Old West section of Knott's Berry Farm, naming it the Church of the Reflections. Today, it is evangelical and interdenominational, with two Sunday morning services, an early one for park employees and a later one for guests. Worshipers pray while an old-fashioned stagecoach drives by, and the old building sometimes shakes, not with religious fervor, but because of its proximity to the Jaguar roller coaster.

While there is no church at any Disney theme park, there is now a church on Disney-developed property, built with the help of Disney family money. Not far from Disney World in Orlando is the company's planned community of Celebration. The town is a cross between an upscale version of Marceline, Missouri, where Walt spent part of his youth and on which he based Main Street, U.S.A., and his original plans for Epcot, Experimental Planned Community of Tomorrow. From the beginning, Celebration made provision for houses of worship, setting aside land in and around the prosaic town center. The first two-acre plot was offered to the Catholic Diocese of Orlando, which rejected it because it was not large enough. It was plenty of room for a church of the mainline Presbyterian Church (U.S.A.), however. When ground was broken on the site in 1999, the Reverend Patrick Wrisley, the congregation's founding minister, proclaimed, "The kingdom of God has been planted in the shadow of the Magic Kingdom."

The Walt Disney Company made no direct contribution to build the $3-million, 21,000-square-foot structure on Celebration Avenue, but there was indirect help. Disney officials, including Chairman Michael Eisner, approved the design of Community Presbyterian Church, which included a 450-seat sanctuary and a traditional steeple with a 126-year-old bell salvaged from a rural church in Iowa. Dorothy Puder, a niece of Walt and Roy Disney, and her husband, Glenn, a retired Presbyterian minister, of Bakersfield, California, contributed $300,000 of Disney stock left to the couple by Dorothy's uncles. "It's our way of remembering Walt and Roy," said Glenn Puder. "It's a great fit as far as we're concerned. The money is coming full circle."

In early 2004, when the Walt Disney Company announced the closing of its Orlando animation unit—and with it the likely end of hand-drawn features for the foreseeable future—there was a modest amount of dismay, mainly from film critics and serious Disney fans. But this was nothing compared to the reaction to Comcast Corporation's bid to take over Disney a month later. Article after article quoted people concerned about what any change of ownership might mean for their beloved Disney theme parks. "I hope it's not going to happen, but if it does, it won't be Disney," Tonjia Woods, a marketer for Sam's Club in Altamonte Springs, Florida, told the *Orlando Sentinel,* in an article published on February 15, 2004. "Even though it would be Disney World, it would be different." Already there had been complaints from frequent visitors that Eisner's cost-cutting at the parks may have improved the company's bottom line, but resulted in a shopworn, down-at-the-heels feel. On March 27, the *Sentinel* published a feature documenting the deterioration at the Magic Kingdom called "The Old Park," by Jean Patteson and Linda Shrieves. But even those dismayed by the decline were concerned that Disney World might become Comcast World. No more animated features was one thing, but no Disneyland or Disney World was quite another. Why? I think it is because watching a DVD or video or movie on television is something a child might do alone, or with one or two family members, for just over an hour. And, regardless of what technologies emerge in years to come, the library of features will remain.

By contrast, visiting a theme park is usually an extended family experience (what Disney marketers like to refer to as "Magical Gatherings"), sometimes involving both parents and grandparents, and usually lasting for days. It also tends to be an indelible time for a young child. Should the parks be sold off or, worse, closed, that experience would be lost to future generations. That explains the visceral and fiercely proprietary reaction to the possibility—however remote—that the theme parks would somehow go away, or be drastically changed.

Functional, intact, multigenerational families living in close proximity are increasingly rare in America. A gathering at a Disney theme park offers the opportunity to recreate that experience, if only temporarily. This is something Walt would have understood when he set out to build "the Happiest Place on Earth." For adults it may be just an overpriced illusion, created artificially, but for children it is often a cherished memory that lasts forever.

Chapter Thirty-Seven

The Baptist Boycott: Culture Clash

*T*he greatest clash between the Walt Disney Company and American Christians began with a movie, although not with an animated feature. In 1994, Miramax, a highly regarded independent studio acquired by Disney, released a controversial film called *Priest,* which dealt with gay and angst-ridden Catholic clerics. The picture, together with the subsequent (and short-lived) ABC television series *Nothing Sacred,* also about a priest, outraged several Catholic organizations. The Knights of Columbus announced that it was dumping $3 million in Disney stock in protest. A New York–based group called the Catholic League for Religious and Civil Rights called for a nationwide boycott of all Disney parks and products. How many Roman Catholics the League speaks for has always been a matter of considerable debate, but its call for a Disney boycott attracted the attention of another pressure group, the Tupelo, Mississippi–based American Family Association (AFA), headed by a Methodist minister named Donald Wildmon. Formerly known as the National Federation for Decency, the AFA had previously focused most of its attention on sex, violence, and profanity on commercial television, and on one occasion it had attacked the NBC show *The Magical World of Disney.* Now that Disney had acquired ABC, the company presented Wildmon with a target of opportunity.

While the Walt Disney Company's animated features were not at the center of what was to become the most significant confrontation between the company and many of the nation's conservative evangelicals and fundamentalist Christians, growing unease with these movies was one of the less-noticed predisposing factors.

From the first releases in the 1930s and 1940s, some Christians were critical of the use of magical—rather than divine—intervention in the stories. In the April 1934 issue of *Photoplay* magazine, an article asked "Is Walt Disney a Menace to Our Children?" In the article, writer David Frederick McCord criticized the studio for its "overemphasis on magic as a way of solving problems." Later, with the development of freeze-frame technology, others were able to confirm (if only in their own minds) the long-held suspicions that animators were inserting naughty—some said obscene—animated cells in the features. But, as Ward Kimball, one of Disney's Nine Old Men, noted in an interview with Walter Wagner in *You Must Remember This,* this tradition was more a matter of postadolescent mischief making than attempts at subliminal seduction or Satanism:

> Animation is a complex thing. Sometimes it can get very dull. There are twenty-four frames a second in a cartoon. One frame can take fifteen minutes to draw, and it appears on the screen for only a fraction of a second. There's no other way to do it—it just takes time. So to relieve the monotony, we'd do things like, well, on *Snow White* we'd draw porno things. That happened all the time. . . . A lot of those drawings found their way out of the studio. . . . Perhaps the reason for this sort of thing is that everything seemed so perfect and dreamlike in Disney's world. That led to the urge, I know it did with us, to make these drawings. It was something we had to relieve ourselves of.

The raunchy atmosphere among the animators in Disney's early years, many veterans recalled, was that of a college fraternity house.

As recently as June 2003, a guest on televangelist Benny Hinn's broadcast, Alice Smith, of Houston, Texas, railed against occult images in Disney's animated features. Notwithstanding these complaints from the fringes of Christianity, for more than half a century, America's religious community and the Walt Disney Company existed in a symbiotic relationship. While religion was never at the center of Disney's animated features, faith was often the unseen framework, although the Judeo-Christian context was more explicit while Walt was alive. Believers saw in Disney's movies—and later its books, television programs, and theme parks—an exemplary marriage of moral instruction and popular culture for their children, providing entertainment that supported traditional family values.

Of course, in the 1950s and 1960s, some Southern Baptists grumbled that Disney's Sunday evening television show undermined faithfulness by tempting young people to stay at home rather than returning to church for training and worship. But the Reverend Richard Land, who would later play a leading role in the Disney boycott, recalled that he never had a problem with the Walt-era animated features in theaters. "They were clean. They didn't attack the family. They didn't so much undergird or teach Judeo-Christian values as much as they didn't seek to erode or mock them. They presented themselves as good, clean, family entertainment." Disney, in turn, prospered as a result of the patronage of the faithful. Yet during the late 1980s and 1990s, as America seemed to become more polarized on religious and cultural issues, some Christians became disenchanted with Disney, and especially with animated features such as *Pocahontas*. Just as more conservative and fundamentalist elements of the evangelical movement were gaining political momentum and Americans seemed to become more religious, the Disney movies created during the regime of Michael Eisner and Jeffrey Katzenberg were becoming more humanistic, politically nuanced, and multicultural. At the same time, more racy (and profitable) live action comedies such as *Splash* and *Ruthless People* were offending this core audience, even though they were produced under the company's Touchstone and Hollywood Pictures brands, rather than under the Disney name.

Numerous recent studies, including one October 2002 survey done by evangelical pollster George Barna, found that most Americans profess a "smorgasbord of religious beliefs." The nationwide survey indicated that a large share of the people who attend Protestant or Catholic churches have adopted beliefs that conflict with the teachings of the Bible and with their church. "Over the past 20 years we have seen the nation's theological views slowly become less aligned with the Bible," Barna found. "Americans still revere the Bible and like to think of themselves as Bible-believing people, but the evidence suggests otherwise. Christians have increasingly been adopting spiritual views that come from Islam, Wicca, secular humanism, the eastern religions and other sources. Because we remain a largely Bible-illiterate society, few are alarmed or even aware of the slide toward syncretism—a belief system that blindly combines beliefs from many different faith perspectives."

Rather than losing touch, Disney may in its animated features have been a trailing indicator, tracking the beliefs of American mainstream. Thus, some have argued, the political influence and prominence of conservative religious groups may *not* be an accurate barometer of the nation's theological center of gravity. Such surveys suggest that the Disney gospel, as it has evolved in recent animated features, is not out of step with America, but is simply reflecting it. "The Disney films are trying to represent the predominant, shared values of the community," said Dennis Campbell, former dean of the Duke University Divinity School. Disney filmmakers are facing the same dilemma of people in the larger society, according to Campbell. "I think the trouble is that the shared values have increasingly broken down. What we are seeing now in society is real confusion of values."

Attacks on Disney by small but vocal groups such as the Catholic League and the American Family Association were one thing. But when the Southern Baptist Convention, the nation's largest Protestant denomination, decided to take on the entertainment giant, it was quite another. The collision of these two titans was a dispute deeply rooted in a disconnect of politics, culture, and geography. In retrospect, it is an encounter that might have easily been predicted. Walt Disney, a son of Middle America who moved to Los Angeles, chose Orlando as the site for his second theme park. Had he lived ten or fifteen years longer, he might have been more at ease with a corporate foot in each of these two camps—and on the two coasts. Yet, given Walt's own ambivalent feelings about organized religion, it isn't likely.

There are approximately 16 million Southern Baptists in the United States, in about 40,000 congregations. The small group of leaders who control the denomination—and generally reflect the views of a majority of the membership—are theologically fundamentalist, politically conservative, and increasingly amenable to a closer involvement between church and state. Because they believe the Bible is inerrant—without error, literally true in every word—many Southern Baptists support creationism over evolution, and they are unrelenting in their zealous and categorical opposition to homosexuality. Their heritage is rural, although many of the members in this generation have migrated to the Sun Belt suburbs.

The nation's Baptists split North and South over slavery at the time of the Civil War. In the early 1980s, Southern Baptists fought another internal battle—equally brutal, if less bloody—that left hard-line conservatives in control of the denomination. Still largely white and culturally insular, the Southern Baptist Convention did not get around to apologizing for its support of slavery, and for the denomination's morally reprehensible silence during the civil rights movement, until its annual summer gathering in Atlanta in 1995. For the present leaders of the denomination, "tolerance" in the post-9/11 era has become a detested code word for acceptance of other faiths as equally valid. The Reverend Albert Mohler, president of the Southern Baptist Theological Seminary in Louisville, Kentucky, has in numerous broadcast interviews criticized Catholicism as a false religion and a cult. A rising star in the denomination, Mohler has also supported the views of other Southern Baptist leaders such as Franklin Graham that Islam is an evil faith. At a pastors' conference at the Southern Baptist Convention in St. Louis in 2002, the Reverend Jerry Vines, a former denomination president, referred to the Prophet Muhammad as a "demon possessed pedophile." Jerry Falwell called Muhammad a "terrorist."

In stark contrast, the corporate culture at Disney's Burbank headquarters is highly cosmopolitan. Jews, atheists, and agnostics all mix easily with committed Protestants and Catholics. Company officials say there are many Christians at the company, including Disney Studios Chairman Dick Cook, one of Hollywood's best-known evangelicals, described by BusinessWeek Online as "The Nicest Guy in Disney's Jungle." The Burbank sensibility is urban, West Coast, secular and, at least on lifestyle issues, liberal. Its multiplicity of brands and products, marketed globally, gives it an expansive worldview. For company executives, the primary (and yes, zealous) mission is to make money for their shareholders, not to save the world, or the world's souls. Its deity of choice and its allegiance, in biblical terms, is to Mammon and not to God. Thus, when the clash with Baptists came, Michael Eisner was not about to defer to the provincial sensibilities of people whose views he did not respect. After the shareholders, the CEO's first loyalty has been to the company's diverse workforce of more than 100,000, and especially to the creative community in Southern California that enables the company to work its magic.

A significant (no one knows precisely how significant) percentage of Disney's workforce, including its top-level executives, is gay. An article in the May 1995 issue of Los Angeles-based *Buzz* magazine on the gay presence at Disney was titled "Will the Mouse Come Out?" In it, writer Steven Gaines named half a dozen high-level executives as gay, most involved in the animated features, and he quoted an unnamed company source estimating that as many as 40 percent of Disney employees are gay. Senior Vice President Tom Schumacher said in the article that gays may be drawn to Disney by the message contained in the animated features. "Thematically, the animated films promote the right to be who you are," he said in the article, "and not to change for anyone else. The characters make their own family. They bond and have close friends. They grow up and grow old together. Anyone who is disenfranchised is touched by that." Schumacher, cited in Peter and Rochelle Schweizer's *Disney: The Mouse Betrayed,* said that, as an openly gay man, "he was concerned about being accepted when he joined the company [in 1988]. Today, however, he said that for homosexuals the Mouse offers a 'supportive environment.'" Lower-level workers at parks on both coasts were also quoted in *Buzz,* echoing Schumacher's opinion.

In early October 1995, following a three-year study by top management (and a three-year campaign by the company's Lesbian and Gay United Employees, LEAGUE), Disney revealed that it would extend health benefits to partners of gay and lesbian employees and their dependent children, effective January 1, 1996. "An employee wanting to claim the benefit must sign an affidavit affirming that he or she is living with the person who will receive the benefit and prove their financial interdependence," according to an October 19, 1995, *Los Angeles Times* story by Don Lee. "The benefit . . . was quietly disclosed by Disney in an employee newsletter." Unmarried, heterosexual couples were not eligible for coverage. Such health coverage had, by that time, become commonplace in the entertainment industry, and, according to the *Times*, "more than 200 public and private employers have extended domestic partner benefits," including companies such as Microsoft, Levi Strauss, Xerox, and institutions such as Stanford University.

While the policy change passed virtually without notice in Los Angeles, in other communities it was a different story. "When Disney gave in to gay lobbying forces and extended health benefits to partners of homosexual workers, North America's religious community was generally dismayed," according to Perucci Ferraiulo, in *Disney and the Bible*. Dr. Bob Brooks, an infectious disease specialist from Winter Park, Florida, and then a freshman Republican in the state legislature, asked the nonprofit, Tampa-based Florida Family Council, an affiliate of the American Family Association, to draft a letter of protest on his behalf to Eisner. The two-page document was then signed by thirteen other Republican legislators and one Democrat, and faxed by the Florida Family Council to news media throughout the state. Legislators characterized the benefits policy as "antifamily" and at odds with Disney's reputation for "wholesome, family-oriented entertainment." It was, the lawmakers wrote, "a big mistake both morally and financially," likely to backfire among the company's devoted customer base. "We wonder what Walt Disney himself would think of your decision if he were alive today?" they asked. "We are inclined to believe he would be quick to pull the plug on such antifamily company policies" that mock "the sanctity of marriage."

In Burbank, Disney spokesman John Dreyer was asked to comment on the letter, which he said he had not yet seen. But the vice president for corporate communications was unabashed, setting the tone for the company's response in the months and years to come. "The decision was made and we intend to stick to it," he said. The announcement was "in line with our corporate non-discrimination policy" based on race or sexual preference, Dreyer told the Associated Press, and Disney had no intention of changing its decision. "This is about providing health benefits for our employees and nothing more."

For their part, the legislators said they had no plans to pursue the matter beyond sending the letter to Eisner and the Disney board. But the Reverend Arthur Rathje of Marianna, a town in the Florida Panhandle, had a different idea. The Southern Baptist minister prepared a resolution on Disney for the annual meeting of the Florida Baptist Convention, to be held in November in Tampa. He felt, he said later, that Disney officials "need to turn from the non-traditional values they are displaying. If they're going after the almighty dollar and don't care about traditional family values, they need to say so. . . . They need to make a decision to go one way or another." Speaking for Florida's one million Southern Baptists, Rathje's resolution threatened to punish the Walt Disney Company at the cash register for disregarding "traditional family values." The motion claimed that "Disney's corporate integrity and moral leadership have been eroded." It called on its members to "prayerfully reconsider their continued purchase and support of Disney products." However, the resolution stopped short of calling for a boycott of the theme parks, films, and merchandise by the state's 2,000 Baptist congregations.

"By openly acknowledging and accepting shifting values in the United States that included homosexuals as normative rather than deviant, Disney betrayed the Southern Baptist Convention," wrote Darlene Juschka in her paper "The Wonderful Worlds of Disney and Fundamentalism," delivered to the American Academy of Religion in Orlando in November 1998. The denomination's notion of the family "more properly belongs to a nostalgic fantasy, a fantasy clearly depicted in Disney productions throughout the '50s, '60s and

'70s. The fantasy of Walt Disney had come to act as a nostalgic memory of fundamentalist history. Hence their sense of betrayal."

The debate in Tampa among the 1,400 delegates—called "messengers"—opened a vein of antipathy for Disney that extended well beyond the new benefits policy. Baptists and other religious conservatives were also angry at Disney because they said the company encouraged gays and lesbians to congregate at the Magic Kingdom each spring for "Gay Days." Similarly, the company was also criticized for promoting combination cruise and theme park vacations involving such companies as Carnival Cruise Lines, which the resolution claimed promoted the use of liquor and gambling—both of which are forbidden by Baptists. "There's been a lot of concern among the Baptist community on a national level," said the Reverend Jim Henry, pastor of the First Baptist Church of Orlando, "a sense that Disney has stepped backwards to some of its commitments to what was previously the image of Disney." On November 15, 1995, after a twenty-minute debate, the resolution passed unanimously.

No deadlines were set for Disney to respond in the Florida resolution, nor were there specific demands. However, there were some enforcers in the final draft. The Florida Baptist Convention called on the state's Baptist churches to "cease promotion" of the annual evenings of contemporary Christian music at Orlando's Disney World called "Nights of Joy." After passing the resolution, the group voted to send it on to the Southern Baptist Convention meeting in New Orleans in June, with the aim of taking the drive national.

John Dreyer, Disney's spokesman, did his best to strike a measured note in responding, not wanting to let a small fire spread, while acknowledging that the complaints had gone beyond the benefits policy. "We have not departed from family values," he said. "The standard against which to measure our family values is the . . . entertainment that we produce and the fact that we are the world's leader in terms of producing family entertainment of all kinds."

But the sparks were already spreading. A month after the Tampa meeting, on December 15, 1995, a woman named Janet Gilmer filed a lawsuit in Fayetteville, Arkansas, charging that videos of

The Lion King and *The Little Mermaid* concealed subliminal sexual messages. According to the class action complaint, the videos "contained drawings and animated scenes that depicted sexual messages or other material unsuitable for young children." Gilmer said that on the cover of the *Little Mermaid* videotape case there was a drawing of an erect penis nestled among the spires of the underwater castle and, during one scene in *The Lion King*, a cloud of dust spelled out the word "SEX" in the sky. She also claimed that in *The Fox and the Hound* there was a subliminal scene in which a character gives "the finger" to the camera. Disney denied the charges—and the rumor that the *Little Mermaid* drawing was an artist's prank. (The suit was resolved in 1997 in what one of Gilmer's attorneys said was "a little bit of a settlement," which neither party would disclose.) Earlier, in March 1995, a group called the American Life League, based in Stafford, Virginia, made similar charges against Disney, mailing out one million postcards urging a boycott. The group also charged that there were subliminal audio messages in the videos, including one in *Aladdin* in which the title character whispers, "Good teenagers, take off your clothes." According to the script, the line is, "Scat, good tiger, take off and go."

(Years later, when the furor subsided and conservative investigators looked into these charges, they were dismissed out of hand. In *Disney: The Mouse Betrayed*, one of the most anti-Disney books in recent years, authors Peter Schweizer and Rochelle Schweizer quoted Tom Sito, whom they described as "a straight talking animator." Sito told them that the letters in the clouds in *The Lion King* actually spell "SFX," short for special effects. "Someone on the animation team wanted to leave a little 'calling card' in the film," they wrote. "Animators insert the images as an inside joke to be shared with their colleagues." The Schweizers also concluded that the dialogue in *Aladdin* is easily mistaken and "hard to distinguish even when you know what to listen for.")

Although I was born in Miami, at the time of the Tampa meeting I was new to the *Orlando Sentinel* and Central Florida, and was returning to the religion beat after an absence of several years while at the *Los Angeles Times*. It became apparent that the possibility of a Baptist boycott of the Walt Disney Company would be an enormous story for my newspaper. Disney is the largest employer in Orlando, with a workforce of 55,000. Southern Baptists represent the largest religious group in our circulation area and, at the time of the proposed action against Disney, Jim Henry of First Baptist Church of Orlando was then serving as national president of the Southern Baptist Convention. Many Baptists—including members of Henry's large congregation—work for Disney, so there was great potential for both strife and economic damage in Central Florida if the confrontation took hold. For all these reasons, I had the distinct impression that, after the Tampa action and the Arkansas suit, the Disney resolution would be quietly consigned to oblivion, and would never make it to the floor when the Southern Baptist Convention met in New Orleans in June 1996. Fortunately, I never committed this impression to newsprint. I still had a great deal to learn about Southern Baptists.

On a national level, the Southern Baptist boycott against the Walt Disney Company unfolded in two acts. In New Orleans, the Baptists cocked the hammer; a year later in Dallas they pulled the trigger. Despite a conciliatory meeting in Orlando between representatives on both sides of the issue, boycott talk was strong when the delegates arrived in New Orleans on June 11. Jim Henry, finishing his second and final one-year term as president of the Southern Baptist Convention, predicted that "somebody will probably ask for a boycott, and the convention will have to deal with it, either in the form of a resolution or in a motion from the floor." Disney's Dreyer was reluctant to comment on boycott prospects, other than to warn darkly that any economic impact would spread beyond the gates of Disney's theme parks and into Orlando's tourism-based economy. There might be larger consequences for the entertainment industry as well, beyond Disney. "To a certain extent they're cutting off their noses to spite their faces. If they are going to boycott or call for a boycott of the most family-friendly media company in the world, they're sending a very strange message to the rest of the entertainment community."

As the convention's leaders met behind closed doors to plot

strategy, the bill of particulars against Disney was growing. In addition to the benefits policy, support for marketing "Gay Days," and the cruises through travel agents and the Internet, attention was turned to content produced by various Disney divisions and subsidiaries. These included a number of controversial books (*Heather Has Two Mommies* and *Growing Up Gay* from Hyperion) and live action films (*Priest* and *Kids,* although the latter was not, as widely thought, from Miramax, a Disney subsidiary). The Reverend Richard Land, president of the denomination's Christian Life Commission, criticized the company for what he said was its support of "Gay Days." "Do they expect Mickey to leave Minnie and move in with Donald?" Land asked convention delegates, to gales of supportive laughter. "That's Goofy!" But behind closed doors denomination leaders drafted an official resolution that, after listing its specific concerns with Disney, did *not* call for a boycott of Disney's theme parks and products. Bill Merrell, a vice president of the denomination and staff liaison with the resolutions committee, said that the resolution the committee was drafting "comes as close to calling for a boycott as the English language permits without actually using the word."

An official news release said the word *boycott* was avoided because using that term "might be misunderstood by Southern Baptists, and could make the denomination look foolish." But not all of the leadership agreed with this strategy. For his part, Richard Land said that if the resolution were to be changed on the floor to seek a boycott, he would vote in favor of the move. "Usually the only thing that people respond to is pressure in the secular world," he said. The Princeton graduate, a large, hefty man given to booming oratory, was prescient—or perhaps more.

On the morning of June 12, just as officials of the Southern Baptist Convention felt they had achieved a delicately balanced and carefully crafted resolution on Disney, along came the Reverend Wiley Drake, a gravel-voiced gadfly who was also serving as California state director of the American Family Association. Drake, pastor of the First Baptist Church of Buena Park, California, and a boycott backer, took care to position himself in the Louisiana Superdome where the convention's sessions were held. "I made sure I was in the hall and near a microphone." When the floor was opened for debate, he was right there, offering an amendment that mandated a boycott if Disney did not mend its ways. "We need to have the word 'boycott' in there. Disney doesn't care about Baptist concerns for morality. The Walt Disney Company understands one thing—money," Drake told the roughly 13,000 convention delegates in the hall. The wave of resentment and sense of betrayal set in motion by denomination leaders would not be denied. Drake's motion, which mentioned no timetable for compliance, passed overwhelmingly. There were no torches or pitchforks in evidence on the convention floor, but the emotions were undeniable. After the delegates cleared the hall, Drake said he got a call from the American Family Association congratulating him for his work.

Among the names of Baptist leaders suggested to meet with Disney in the wake of the New Orleans vote was Jim Henry, since he had strong connections with both sides in the dispute. Henry, a compact, soft-spoken man, had been an upset winner in the denomination's presidential race when the Southern Baptist Convention met in Orlando in 1994. As a result, he was never part of the denomination's inner circle of leadership. As a conservative—but also a recognized conciliator—Henry said he would be happy to join a Southern Baptist delegation to speak with Disney, or to serve as a go-between. "I'm willing to do anything to reconcile some differences and help people talk to each other and not shout at each other," he said, urging Disney to "send some sign that they've heard us and they hear our concerns."

While Henry was offering Disney a carrot, others were sharpening the stick. Within twenty-four hours of the vote, other Southern Baptist Convention leaders outlined a timetable for implementing a boycott against the Walt Disney Company, giving the entertainment giant up to a year to change policies that represent "a gratuitous insult to Christians."

In reaction to the worldwide firestorm of publicity provoked by the vote, the Walt Disney Company issued a terse statement: "We find it curious that a group that claims to espouse family values would vote to boycott the world's largest producer of wholesome family entertainment. We question any group that demands that we deprive people of health benefits, and we know of no tourist destination in the world that denies admission to people as the Baptists are insisting we do." But after a series of such bland, corporate reactions, Michael Eisner finally shot back, telling the *Los Angeles Daily News* on June 24, "We think they're a very small group of the Southern Baptists that took a very extreme position which we feel is foolish."

None of the top leaders of the denomination I spoke with in the year following the New Orleans vote—on or off the record—seriously expected that Disney would change its policies or products in response to the resolution. What the Southern Baptists wanted, as they said repeatedly, was to be given a respectful hearing by top-level Disney officials. If this meeting was not with Michael Eisner himself, then they wanted it to be with someone near him in the company's hierarchy. There were a number of efforts to make such a meeting take place, on both the East and West Coasts, which fell through. Disney executives are famously tight-lipped, so it is difficult to know why they reacted as they did. The executives may have felt that such a meeting would be pointless. Eisner may have calculated that even if he conferred with Disney's critics, and thus gave them some credibility, they would go ahead with the boycott anyway, thus sandbagging the company.

In any event, as the months passed, the debate between the two sides grew increasingly harsh, hardening into a barely suppressed meanness. As a result, the religious boycott also appeared to be gaining momentum. On August 14, 1996, the governing body of the 2.5-million-member Assemblies of God denomination voted to join, declaring that Disney had abandoned its "commitment to strong moral values." Yet in Orlando, the Reverend Clark Whitten, of Calvary Assembly of God, the denomination's largest church in the area, anticipated the actions of some Southern Baptist churches in Central Florida. Whitten said that, although he had criticized Disney, he would not support the boycott or urge his parishioners to do so. Like Jim Henry, Whitten had a relationship with Disney. The congregation passed along surplus clothing donated by the company on its short-term mission trips abroad.

As the Dallas meeting of the Southern Baptist Convention neared in June 1997 and there seemed little doubt that a Disney boycott was inevitable, some in Florida began to have second thoughts. Jim Henry, who had been leaning in favor of a boycott, announced that, after "a lot of praying," he had decided to oppose it, and would urge other Southern Baptists to do the same. "I don't think it's the right thing to do," he explained, clearly anguished. "I personally will not support a boycott of theme parks, and will urge my fellow Baptists not to support a boycott."

Looking back at the boycott in its December 2001 issue, the Christian magazine *Charisma* found "many Christians among the 50,000-plus employed across Disney's Orlando-area attractions, from those selling souvenirs and snacks along the boardwalks to those making major decisions in the boardrooms." Derrick McKenzie, a former China missionary, worked as an assistant special effects animator on *Lilo and Stitch* at the Orlando facility, where he took part in a lunchtime Bible study. "What better place for a Christian to be than out in the world," singer David Wise told the magazine. When not performing as part of the Four for a Dollar quartet at the Disney/MGM Studios, Wise was a member of the contemporary Christian music group Return2Zero.

In Texas, at the Dallas Convention Center, Jim Henry's successor as president of the denomination, the Reverend Tom Elliff, made plain that a new regime had taken charge, and that it was in no mood to be conciliatory. (The steely Oklahoma preacher had a family history with Baptist controversy. His brother-in-law was the Reverend Bailey Smith, a previous denomination president best known for his pronouncement that "God almighty does not hear the prayers of a Jew.") Elliff said, "I think a boycott is a Christian response," characterizing Disney as a "purveyor of pornography" and predicting the boycott resolution would pass. Elliff compared watching Disney-owned ABC television (then also under fire for *Ellen*'s coming-out episode) to spending time with a prostitute. He said that if Disney's entertainment philosophy did not change, employees should "give some serious thought" to quitting their jobs. The pastor of First Southern Baptist Church of Del City,

Oklahoma, said in his presidential address that Disney was part of "a culture that has failed." There was still work to be done, he said. Especially when corporations such as Disney "look at the almost 16 million members of our Southern Baptist churches and question whether we are people of our word, whether we really mean what we say, and whether we are actually willing to sacrifice the enjoyment of their products, performances or media presentations."

Richard Land said Disney had "studiously ignored" the Baptists' New Orleans resolution, apart from some "unofficial back and forth. On good days the Disney company ignored us," Land said. "On bad days they contemptuously gave us the back of their hand." On the eve of the boycott vote, Land then referred to a famous remark attributed to Joseph Stalin when he was warned about Catholic opposition to some Soviet outrage. "How many divisions has the pope?" the dictator asked. Disney, Land told the 13,000 cheering convention delegates, doesn't think Southern Baptists are significant. "I suspect that tomorrow when you vote to refrain from giving of your resources to any of Disney's enterprises that . . . Disney is going to find out just how many regiments and just how many divisions of godly people Southern Baptists have."

The boycott resolution passed, with an estimated 85 percent of delegates voting in the affirmative. Because Disney "has not only ignored our concerns, but flagrantly furthered this moral digression in its product and policies," the denomination urged members to "refrain from patronizing" the diversified entertainment giant. Following the vote, a list of Disney's numerous subsidiaries was made available to delegates. Denomination officials said no mechanism had been set up to measure the success of the boycott.

Disney officials would not comment individually on the Dallas boycott vote, but issued a statement: "We are proud that the Disney brand creates more family entertainment of every kind than anyone else in the world." In July, Eisner named the Reverend Leo J. O'Donovan, president of Georgetown University, to the Disney board. The priest, who is also a theology professor, told the Associated Press that the timing of his appointment was "utterly accidental." Whatever the intent of the appointment, support for the boycott continued to spread, at least among evangelical Protestants. On August 27, James Dobson announced in a radio broadcast that his organization, Focus on the Family, was urging its four million contributors not to buy any Disney products or visit any of the company's theme parks. "The Disney organization has utter disdain for those who hold traditional moral principles and conservative family values," he told listeners on 1,900 stations. "Year after year, its leaders have insulted a large segment of the population by producing films, television, and music that contradict cherished beliefs." This time Disney seemed to be reeling under the attack. "We will continue to do the best we can," the company said in a statement.

The critics were in no mood for patience. By late October 1997, Richard Land's renamed Ethics and Religious Liberty Commission joined the American Family Association to produce a thirty-minute video called *The Disney Boycott: A Just Cause.* In the crudely put-together tape, Land said, "Disney is the same as any other entertainment conglomerate in the secular world. Perhaps it's even worse, because they are the custodians and the guardians of the powerful emotional images we grew up with." Lulled by this reputation, he said, "we have not inspected Disney's product the way we have inspected other products before we allow our children to see them." In the video, Land asked more than 90,000 Southern Baptist pastors to have their members write Michael Eisner and pledge support for a boycott of the entertainment company. Fliers mailed to the pastors included a form letter to Eisner, promising to withhold at least $100 of the amount the sender otherwise would spend on Disney products. The ministers were also asked to distribute copies of the flier during services, but larger Baptist churches in Central Florida said they had no plans to do so. Land also cowrote a book about the boycott, *Send a Message to Mickey: The ABCs of Making Your Voice Heard at Disney,* for the denomination's publishing arm, Broadman & Holman. In the slim volume, Land referred to an animated feature to make a point: "The heart of Disney management now seems to have more in common with the evil, jealous stepmother in *Snow White* than it does with the moral purity of the heroine." Readers searching for an alternative to the animated films were urged to go to the chain of retail stores operated by the Southern Baptists and to choose an alternative from the VeggieTales collection.

Disney again chose not to respond to these latest attacks, other than to point to record theme park attendance, movie revenues, and stock prices as evidence that the boycott hadn't worked. Company spokesman John Dreyer did take the opportunity to address Disney's values in a more explicit way. "We always try to promote moral ideologies in our programming," he said. "We remain committed to certain values in our everyday life, values that include tolerance and compassion and respect for everyone."

Finally, on November 19, 1997, Land and Eisner faced off on CBS's *60 Minutes*. Actually, the two men were never physically together. Correspondent Lesley Stahl did the interviewing, and editing and cutting created the sense of a debate. "The all-American, family-loving, Bible-quoting Southern Baptist Convention, the nation's largest Protestant denomination, and the Walt Disney Company, the world's largest producer of family-friendly programs and products, seem like a match made, well, in heaven," she said in her introduction. In a film clip from an earlier convention meeting, Land charged that by doing things like renting Disney's animated features or seeing them in theaters, Baptists were subsidizing materials in other venues that constitute "an attack on your values and your beliefs."

"That's ridiculous," Eisner scoffed. "We're not pushing any agenda. We are pushing, in our corporate marketplace, tolerance and understanding, expansiveness. We are totally onto an ethical compass, a moral compass." He told Stahl that the Baptists targeted his company because "we're large, and when somebody attacks us, it gets their agenda into the news."

Stahl then began to have some fun with the two men. She asked Land, "What was wrong with *The Little Mermaid*? That's a sweet little movie." Admitting that he hadn't actually seen it, the Southern Baptist leader replied, "I am told from those who have seen it and who have watched it carefully that there was the suggestion that a—a clergyman became sexually aroused while he was performing a marriage ceremony." Speaking over a clip from the film, Stahl said, "the allegedly offending bulge goes by in less than a second. But if you were to slow down a few frames of this scene, you might think the preacher was, indeed, more than happy to see Ariel. There. Right there, right there, right there. OK." Eisner did not agree. "It's completely untrue. You know it's untrue. I know it's untrue. . . . It is clearly his knee. Everybody knows it's his knee. It's just people spending too much time looking for things that aren't there." (Disney's Tom Sito, who drew the wedding scene, told the authors of *Disney: The Mouse Betrayed* that "the protrusion you see is his knees.")

The discussion then moved to *Pocahontas*, as a clip from that film played. Land said that the problem with that feature was that it was an example of how Disney attempted to "twist history," in this case by leaving out of the movie the fact that Pocahontas converted to Christianity. Why? "Disney does not want to have positive portrayals of orthodox Christians." By this time, Eisner was having a difficult time controlling himself. "Because I'm on *60 Minutes*, I have to act proper and not get crazy and excited and annoyed, but that is just ridiculous," he said. *Pocahontas* "is one of the most pro-social movies made in the 75 years of the history of the Disney Company. It's about an American legend. It's about a Native American. It's pro-environment. It's about the Earth. It's about respecting one another. By the way, she didn't become a Christian in the legend until after our story ended." Goaded repeatedly by Stahl about what he thought about the Baptists' interpretation of *Pocahontas*, Eisner let loose: "I say inside deep down, they're nuts. They really are." At the same time, he acknowledged that his company was not flawless, that it sometimes made mistakes and did inappropriate things.

Switching subjects, Stahl asked Land for the Southern Baptist view of sexual orientation. "We detest homosexuality, as does the Bible, as—as does God," he replied. Their view of Disney's granting of health benefits to partners of gay employees? "We're gonna deny, or do the best we can to deny the normalization of a lifestyle that we believe is abnormal, deviant, unhealthy, and dangerous."

Next came Jim Henry's turn, after Stahl noted, "In a recent independent poll, 55 percent of Southern Baptists disagreed with the Disney boycott." The Orlando minister was shown at his church, asking members to pray for Eisner. Later, in an interview, he asked, "What do I tell our people who work at Disney? Quit?" Henry said some members even warned him, "If you all are gonna do this, if this is what you're about, don't invite me to church anymore. I don't want to hear about it, and anything you say, I'm not interested in, if this is what you're about." However, Henry did not give Disney a free pass. "It comes across as being arrogant when you got millions of people with deep concerns and there's no response, or very little response." A single meeting was held between boycott representatives and a Disney executive in Washington, D.C., Stahl said, but it didn't go well.

Stahl asked Eisner if he would be willing to meet face-to-face with leaders of the Southern Baptist Convention to talk about the issues troubling them. "I will meet with anybody at any time, when it is presented in a rational and non-media-hyped way," he said. "So my answer is, absolutely." If he didn't take the boycott seriously, Eisner said, he wouldn't be appearing on *60 Minutes,* although he denied the boycott was having any financial impact on the company. Then the CEO extended what was for him an olive branch, with a flag attached. "I think we're the wrong—the wrong group to go after. But the one thing that's great about this country is they have the right to do it, and they're doing it the right way. They have the right to do letter-writing campaigns. They have the right to hold back their wallets. They have the right not to go to our property. I love that. I respect that."

Reviews of the *60 Minutes* confrontation were mixed, and split along predictable lines. James Dobson, founder of boycott supporter Focus on the Family, charged in a statement from his Colorado Springs headquarters that Stahl served up "softballs" to Eisner. Instead, the Disney chairman should have been asked, "How does the glorification of brutal violence, homosexuality, drug abuse, and teen sex, and the mockery of Christian beliefs reflect Walt Disney's philosophy of family entertainment?" Dobson said Eisner's comments were disparaging to the Christians who opposed his company's products and policies. "He ridicules those with deeply held religious beliefs who are genuinely concerned about the direction the Disney company has taken in recent years," Dobson said. "Mr. Eisner says he is willing to sit down and talk with those participating in the boycott. If that is now true, why has he never made such an offer to this point? I challenge him to live up to this newly proclaimed openness. So far, Disney has given a deaf ear to our concerns. Its communications department has told our constituents that Disney will not even respond by letter to consumers who send letters of concern on this issue. I hope that Disney will become more receptive to the views of millions of families who would like Disney to return to the legacy of Walt himself."

Cary McMullen, religion writer for *The Ledger* of Lakeland, Florida, offered a contrary view from the state's Southern Baptist heartland. "I can hear the screams from Anaheim to Washington that the report was biased against Baptists," he wrote on November 29, 1997, "that CBS was too easy on Eisner, that it gave him much more camera time than it gave Richard Land." Really, though, the pairing of the two men was "a natural public relations mismatch, on the order of, say, Nebraska vs. South Weekiwachee Tech." McMullen said he did not doubt Land's leadership skills, or his ability to bring thousands of Baptists to their feet with his thundering oratory. "But what did the American public see on their TV screens Sunday night?" he asked. "Here was Land, combed-over hair, jowls down to his collarbone, solemnly drawling that Disney is 'pushing a Christian-bashing, family-bashing, pro-homosexual agenda.' He looked and sounded for all the world like a character from a Tennessee Williams play. Then there was Eisner, a guy who could appear witty and charming while taking out the trash." Because the Disney head appealed to common sense and good taste, even when defending the lesbian kissing episode of *Ellen*, "Eisner (and therefore Disney) looked cultured, modern and progressive, while Land (and therefore the Baptists—or those favoring the boycott) looked like backward, intolerant hicks. I'm not saying any of this is accurate. I'm simply saying that's what it looked like. Nor can responsibility be given entirely to CBS for making it look that way. A boycott is more of a public relations battle than an economic battle. The object is to make your opponent seem contemptible and your own cause righteous. In Sunday's skirmish, the Baptists got routed."

Eisner's position won him some support from unlikely quarters. "That Disney is defying the morality police is a positive sign, one that somewhat softens my visceral antipathy toward Team Rodent," novelist Carl Hiassen wrote in his 1998 nonfiction book *Team Rodent.* "Given a choice between intolerant moralizers and unflinchingly ruthless profiteers, I'll have to stand with the Mouse every time. Many publicly held corporations would have caved at the first throaty outcry from the fundamentalists, but Disney continues to stand firm. Obviously, the Gay Day promotion makes enough dough and generates enough goodwill that Team Rodent can afford to ignore the Bible-thumpers. . . . Remember also that the company's granite base of consumers is a prosperous and relatively open-minded Middle American. . . . Team Rodent knows the tolerance level of its audience because it *raised* its audience. The fundamentalists' 'boycott' of Disney is doomed to flop because Middle America isn't participating and doesn't, if you'll pardon the expression, give a rat's ass."

In the months and years following the boycott vote and the ensuing controversy, essentially nothing happened. The denomination, as some within it feared—and warned—appeared to be an economic paper tiger. Through the late 1990s and early 2000s Disney's fortunes did decline dramatically. Logically, and with some justification, Southern Baptist leaders claimed at least a portion of the credit. Yet, since no comprehensive studies were ever done to quantify the impact of the religious boycott, it is impossible to know how much of a role the boycott had. And no reputable financial analyst credited the boycott for Disney's difficulties—even marginally. A poll published in 1998 in the *Orlando Sentinel* found that only 30 percent of Southern Baptists had participated in the boycott. The factors most commonly cited for Disney's downturn were: ABC-TV's dismal ratings, sluggish sales at Disney's retail outlets, the recession, terrorism, and the failures of the studio's animation unit. Frank Rich, writing in the Arts and Leisure section of the *New York Times* on June 22, 2003, called the religious boycott an "utter flop," and said that, as a result, no other media company would fear such action in the future.

Even some Baptists agreed. "The Southern Baptist Convention is trapped," said Robert Parham, director of the Baptist Center for Ethics in Nashville, and founder of ethicsdaily.com. "It cannot declare victory. It can't end the boycott. Consequently, its strategy is to pretend it doesn't exist. That is, don't mention it and hope everybody will forget about all the threats and bombastic talk."

There was some benefit. Despite fears that the boycott would make them look like backwoods, knuckle-scraping yokels—as some feared when the boycott was first proposed—Southern Baptist leaders found that this publicity *helped* them. In the domestic religious marketplace at least, their controversial stands established and burnished their own brand as *the* conservative, family values denomination. Richard Land, in particular, profited from his role in the Disney boycott. His Christian Life Commission got a new name, the Ethics and Religious Liberty Commission, and a much higher profile, landing him on media's "Golden Rolodex" and guaranteeing him considerable exposure. (The Reverend Albert Mohler, of Southern Baptist Theological Seminary— Land's glib, telegenic rival in the denomination—also did well, becoming a favorite of CNN's Larry King.) Land launched a nationally syndicated radio show, *For Faith and Family*, heard daily on 600 stations. Oddly, Land has engaged in some revisionism about the boycott, perhaps to accommodate more compassionate attitudes about AIDS. At a recent meeting of the Southern Baptist Convention in the early 2000s, he chastised me for saying that the boycott had been sparked by Disney's decision to grant health benefits to partners of gay employees. The boycott was never about that, he snapped.

Although they are still loath to admit it, the conservative Christian critics who took up their cudgels against Disney were really complaining about what has made America what it is today: global capitalism and the market economy. As a modern, multinational entertainment conglomerate, Disney does what it does to maximize profits. Yet the boycotters argued that Disney was somehow under some special obligation to serve some higher purpose—even if it meant rejecting the popular tastes of their customers—because of Walt Disney's legacy of producing uplifting, family-friendly fare. This is a sentimental notion—naive at best and disingenuous at worst. If people's tastes in entertainment are becoming more depraved—in a media environment that offers a multiplicity of choices, including cable television, the Internet, and dozens of film studios—whose responsibility is that? Singling out Disney for blame was like blaming one brand of thermometer for causing a raging fever. Disney, the cultural critics said, should be held to a higher standard than, say, Universal or Viacom or Rupert Murdoch's News Corp., which turn out a greater quantity and percentage of decadent content than Disney. Why?

The fallacy of this argument is that Walt Disney created his animated features to entertain people and to make money—not to evangelize. If in the process, Disney made the world a better place, that was a fine but unintended by-product. His company was never a philanthropic undertaking. Arguably, that is still the company's philosophy. As the country's attitudes toward religion, values, and culture have shifted, Disney's animated features—its historic corporate center of gravity—have shifted to accommodate them. It's just business.

Chapter Thirty-Eight

Conclusion: Questions and Answers

Walt Disney steadfastly refused to interpret his own work, expecting his animated features to speak for themselves. "We make the pictures and then let the professors tell what they mean," he said many times. Yet the company's founding father was also aware of his responsibility in creating his movies. In 1947, appearing before the House Committee on Un-American Activities, he was asked if he ever permitted his films—apart from those he made for the government during World War II—to be used for propaganda. "We watch so that nothing gets into the films that would be harmful in any way to any group or any country," he testified. "We have large audiences of children and different groups, and we try to keep them as free from anything that would offend anybody as possible. We work hard to see that nothing of that sort creeps in."

Many have disputed that point, some vociferously, and it hasn't always been easy. Janet Wasko, in *Understanding Disney,* asked, "How has Disney developed and maintained such a sacred aura that many refuse to criticize? It has something to do with the link to childhood and innocence. Disney products typically become a part of every child's life, in one form or another (at least in the USA). Thus, they are intimately and strongly associated with childhood and retain a special place in people's memories of childhood." The company's status in the eyes of the American people is so exalted that, at least until the Baptist boycott, criticizing Disney was "a kind of secular sacrilege," according to Elizabeth Bell, Lynda Haas, and Laura Sells in *From Mouse to Mermaid.* "There is such a large aura of religiosity around the Disney name and product that they are almost invulnerable to effective criticism, so far as the majority of moviegoers are concerned," William McReynolds wrote in his paper "Walt Disney in the American Grain."

All of this has not been a deterrent to many, on the Left and the Right. "Disney, in all of its manifestations—theme parks, movie production, and so forth—appears to be simultaneously a manifestation of and a propagandistic ode to American capitalism," William Arnal wrote in "The Segregation of Social Desire: 'Religion' and Disney World," which appeared in the March 2001 issue of the *Journal of the American Academy of Religion.* For Matt Roth, in "A Short History of Disney-Fascism," in *Jump Cut,* the full-length animated features represented thinly veiled propaganda for the company's "reactionary views of the world." And from the Right: "New Age thought, homosexuality, Buddhism, black magic, occultism, Greek mythology, Satanism—it appears that Disney is the antithesis of everything Christians believe and hold dear," wrote Perruci Ferraiuolo, in *Disney and the Bible.*

Susan Lochrie Graham, in "Some Day My Prince Will Come," wrote that the animated features implicitly supported values such as faith, hope, and love associated with belief in Jesus as a redeemer. "For children, especially the church-going children of the 1950s, the images of Walt's fantasy films provided an important intertext for understanding these Christian concepts." So are the animated features of the Walt Disney Company good for today's young children? The short answer is basically yes. The longer answer? Some movies are clearly better than others and, at least on initial viewing, they should be watched with a morally informed adult, preferably a close relative. These films are studded with valuable life lessons, often reflecting the lives of men who made them, from Walt and Roy Disney to Michael Eisner and Jeffrey Katzenberg. At the same time, the earlier features do put forward a dangerously unrealistic view of what life holds in store for children, and some include troubling stereotypes. For the most part, they also equate physical beauty with goodness. Do the animated features support paganism, pantheism, and the occult? Not in any systematic way. Yet they are in no specific way—apart from peripheral details and images and their general sensibility—identifiably Judeo-Christian films. And they are certainly not evangelical by any interpretation, in part because some are based on pre-Christian myths, magic, and fairy tales. The strength of the more recent features is the growing assertiveness with which they portray girls and young women, perhaps reflecting the growing number of women writers, producers, and executives at the studio, and the respect they give to other ethnic groups, religions, and nationalities. And I cheer the occasional shots they take at capitalism's excesses and developers in particular. To be sure, this has a great deal to do with reflecting the changes in the culture at large. And, frankly, it probably has at least as much to do with Disney's identification of its target market for such movies. More recent animated films, now aimed at a slightly older group of youngsters, are infused with a certain amount of realism.

In the end, even the most hard-edged and hard-boiled of Disney's critics and observers tend to make their judgment by drawing on their experience as parents. Donald E. Fadner, of the University of Wisconsin, cited his eleven-year-old son in his paper, "Disney Gets Religion," delivered in Orlando at the American Academy of Religion meeting in 1998. "My son has learned from *Aladdin* that it is a mistake to pretend to be something he is not in order to get others to like him, that he should 'be himself' and trust that there will be others who will like him for that. He has learned from *Pocahontas* and *Mulan* to like and appreciate girls who are active and accomplished; the kind who spend their time trying to be petite and pretty pale by comparison."

"The question of whether Disney's animated films are good for kids has no easy answer and resists simple analysis," wrote Henry A. Giroux in *The Mouse That Roared*. "I soon found that for my children, and I suspect for many others, these films possess at least as much cultural authority and legitimacy for teaching roles, values, and ideals as more traditional sites of learning, such as the public schools, religious institutions, and the family. Disney films combine enchantment and innocence in narrating stories that help children understand who they are, what societies are about, and what it means to construct a world of play and fantasy in an adult environment. The authority of such films, in part, stems from their unique form."

Mike Thomas, my colleague at the *Orlando Sentinel,* wrote in a July 13, 2003, column about the dilemma Disney's animated features pose for parents like him. "I know Disney is a money-grubbing multinational corporation that has cursed us with a low-wage service economy," he wrote. Yet, he did not begrudge letting Mickey Mouse pick his pocket for films such as *Finding Nemo,* a Pixar production distributed by Disney. "I give to him gladly because money is the best positive reinforcement for this rodent, and I want more Disney movies." His young daughter Carly's top ten movies are all Disney animated features, and each teaches her a lesson:

> When she has been afraid of the dark shapes in her room at night, I remind her of Snow White imagining all sorts of scary things when running through the woods. It turns out they were nothing but trees, logs, shadows and friendly animals. From *Beauty and the Beast,* we learned people could change. From *Lilo and Stitch,* we learned that even two people can make up a family—a bond that squabbles, fights and a crazed alien can't break. Disney can be a child's first introduction to the cruelties of the real world. It puts them up there on the big screen and forces you to talk about them. Death. Loss of a parent. Struggle. . . . Say what you will about Disney, and I have. But when it comes to kids' movies, nobody does it better.

I have to admit that my own children were never inordinately enamored or affected by Disney's animated features, and there is relatively little company merchandise and memorabilia in the Brown-Pinsky household. (*The Simpsons* is another matter.) Yet I always felt comfortable when the kids watched the films, as long as either my wife Sallie or I sat with them the first time around. In matters of popular culture, we take nothing on faith. *Atlantis,* in 2001, was the last Disney feature all four of us went to the theater to watch. At age ten and age thirteen, had my kids just outgrown these movies? There was some of that, I suspect, but the popular culture and media environment were also in transition. Computer generated animation, combined with more edgy and ironic story-telling, had produced competitors such as DreamWorks's *Shrek* and Fox's *Ice Age.* Video games and the Internet provided more alternatives.

When the time came to screen *Brother Bear* for this book, I had to go to the theater alone—the rest of my family was long over Disney's hand-drawn animation. (By the way, if you don't think it is a little uncomfortable to be a man in his mid-50s sitting by himself in a Disney animated feature, think again.) And there is some evidence at the box office that much of the American movie-going audience feels the same way. Given the high production and labor costs of creating these works of art, this era and the genre of two-dimensional features may be ending. On January 12, 2004, the month after Roy Disney resigned from the board, company exec-utives announced that its feature animation unit at Disney-MGM Studios in Orlando was being closed, and that 200 of the 250 ani-mators would be laid off. The rest would be offered jobs at Disney headquarters in Burbank. During the fifteen years the Orlando stu-dio had been in operation, as many as 400 animators were on the payroll, turning out features such as *Mulan, Lilo and Stitch,* and, finally, *Brother Bear.* Elvis Mitchell, writing in the January 16, 2004, *New York Times,* called the studio's closing an "exercise in corporate short-sightedness." On April 3, 2004, Disney announced that it would close its Japanese animation unit in June, laying off 100 workers. Thirty of those were being transferred to Burbank.

In an *Orlando Sentinel* commentary, published a day before the announcement, film critic Roger Moore described Disney as "the company that rode to glory on the colorful, animated backs of a mouse and seven dwarfs." As a result of these cuts, he wrote, there would be "no more Fantasia hippos in tutus, dancing with caped alligators, given their fluid, comic dimension by painstaking, cell-by-cell drawing and painting.

"No more little elephants who can fly or little Hawaiian girls who go their own way, breaking our hearts because feelings trans-mit better when they go straight from hand to page, without a sil-icon chip in between. . . . [N]obody goes to a cartoon for the realism. We want the abstract, the whimsy, the personality and humanity that rendering figures by hand, frame-by-frame gives us. Disney [is] the studio that invented and perfected the 'classic' hand-drawn animated feature film."

For all such eloquent valedictories, it is likely that these beloved movies will live eternally, preserved for future generations of young children in the amber of DVD and succeeding technologies. But you—and your grandchildren—may not find them in darkened theaters. While I will miss them, I predict a return of the beloved Disney animated feature in some form, perhaps digital. Admittedly, *Home on the Range,* officially the last hand-drawn Disney release, was a disappointment. Yet at about the same time that film opened, the studio announced that it had purchased the rights to a touching story about birds written by a British grocer, called *One for Sorrow, Two for Joy.* Begun as a bedtime story for Clive Woodall's young children, it's the story of a plucky robin that saves his fellow birds from genocidal magpies—a perfect tale for a Disney animated film.

Acknowledgments

*L*ike writing a book, this part of the process is easier the second time around, with some new names added to some of the old ones.

As always, I begin by thanking my family, for indulging my moods and storms and "hibernations" in preparing this work: daughter Liza, son Asher, and my wife, Sallie (the photographer Sarah M. Brown). My children will probably cringe for some time at my use of them as touchstones and points of reference, but in this I make no apologies. They return the favor manifold by reminding me that, despite what some articles and interviewers suggest, I am not *that* smart.

Next I want to express my gratitude to my editor, David Dobson, of Westminster John Knox Press, whose skills I think I taxed even more with this book than with *The Gospel according to The Simpsons*. He was right, as usual, in discerning where more was needed, and where less. Kelly Hughes, of DeChant Hughes and Associates, has done a superb job on my behalf. From the time I first encountered her on the phone, while covering religion for the *Los Angeles Times* more than fifteen years ago, I knew that if I ever wrote a book she was the one I wanted to publicize it. Prospective authors take note.

Although many are cited in the text, I would like to acknowledge my great collective debt to scores of Disney scholars and critics who pioneered this field, beginning in the late 1930s. Their work made this book possible, and I hope I have not poached too much. Numerous times, while typing quoted citations, I said to myself, "I wish I had written that."

Many readers of this manuscript have contributed to whatever coherence and insight it offers, and they bear no responsibility for its faults or errors. Three in particular helped shape it. Jay Boyar, film critic for the *Orlando Sentinel* and a frequent lunch partner, argued his points about Hollywood, animation, and Disney with great conviction, in addition to offering incisive suggestions regarding the text. Rusty Wright, my old-new friend of more than thirty years, provided the same kind of excellent advice for setting the tone of this book as he did with *The Gospel according to The Simpsons.* Mark Matheis, a longtime Disney cast member and expert on the animated canon, caught a number of factual errors and took the trouble to go back and review some of the features to make certain of his points.

Other perceptive manuscript readers, including the Reverend Ernie Bennett, my reliable guide to all things Episcopalian and Anglican, also provided some excellent guidance. Valuable research assistance came from Professor David Steinmetz and Deborah Marcuse, both of Duke University, and Professor Terry Lindvall, of Regent University.

David Buckna, creator and author of the excellent feature *Pop Gospel,* which appears in the *Calgary Herald,* continues to monitor the Internet for material with a skill that mystifies me. On the subject of cyberspace and Web sites, I wish to thank Mark Naghsh, Dana Fasano of the *Orlando Sentinel,* and Brian Peterson for their assistance.

My writing colleagues in the features section of the *Orlando Sentinel* have endured much of my book promotion with good spirit— at least within my earshot. They are subject to my sometimes-mordant worldview, my bad language (unforgivable for a religion writer), and my repetitious and self-serving radio interviews. In particular, nearest neighbors Harry Wessel (who persists in seeing the good in everyone, including those with whom we all disagree), Greg Dawson (our indomitable precinct captain), Linda Shrieves (who often gets stuck with my stories when I am out of the office), Mark Matthews ("Mark the Younger," whose desk and floor space I am always encroaching on), the ever stylish Jean Patteson, and the forever young Jim Abbott. Critics Roger Moore (whose tongue and pen are even sharper than my own) and Hal Boedeker (another regular lunch companion) have been extremely supportive. Among *Sentinel* editors, I owe particular thanks to Nancy Pate, to my good friend Peter Brown, to Matt Palm, and to Mark Andrews. For moral support, I must recognize kindred spirit Dean Johnson, a.k.a. Commander Coconut and a real doodle. Chief among my *Sentinel* colleagues I wish to thank is my long-suffering editor, Loraine O'Connell; the list of things she has done for me, and endured on my behalf, is long.

I am also fortunate in community support, beginning with my friends and neighbors along Trotters Drive in Maitland, Florida. Dr. Eddie Waldheim, a healer of body and spirit, helped put me back together whenever I started to fall apart. Rabbi Steve Engel and his family, together with the larger family of the Congregation of Liberal Judaism in Orlando, have provided a strong community of faith for our family. The Maitland Public Library continues to be a valuable resource in my research, as were the staffs at the Olin Library at Rollins College in Winter Park and the University of Central Florida Library in Orlando. The Hardaway and Dey families were generous in their loan of Disney tapes and DVDs, and the two Blockbusters of Winter Park were helpful in locating some of the more hard to find. The night crew at the Winter Park Kinko's came through for me again. Despite my habit of breezing in thirty minutes before closing for a twenty-five-minute workout, the friendly folks at the Lakemont Avenue YMCA in Winter Park were always welcoming.

In the larger sense of community, I must again cite my friends and colleagues of the Religion Newswriters Association. We make each other look good, to the benefit of our readers.

Former Disney spokesman John Dreyer was a reliable, accessible, and helpful source of information for me, within the constraints of his position. Our relationship was one of mutual respect, for which I am grateful.

My old comrade of more than three decades, Clay Steinman, provided some excellent late-innings assistance.

Bibliography

Behlmer, Rudy. *America's Favorite Movies: Behind the Scenes.* New York: F. Ungar Publishing Co., 1982.

Bell, Elizabeth, Lynda Haas, and Laura Sells, eds. *From Mouse to Mermaid: The Politics of Film, Gender, and Culture.* Bloomington: Indiana University Press, 1995.

Bryman, Alan. *Disney and His Worlds.* New York: Routledge, 1995.

Budd, Mike, Steve Craig, and Clay Steinman. *Consuming Environments: Television and Commercial Culture.* New Brunswick, N.J.: Rutgers University Press, 1999.

Byrne, Eleanor, and Martin McQuillan. *Deconstructing Disney.* London: Pluto Press, 1999.

Canemaker, John. *Nine Old Men and the Art of Animation.* New York: Hyperion, 2001.

The Complete Fairy Tales of the Brothers Grimm. Translated by Jack Zipes. New York: Bantam Books, 1992.

Collins, Jim, and Jerry Porras. *Built to Last: Successful Habits of Visionary Companies.* New York: HarperBusiness, 2002.

Culhane, John. *Aladdin: The Making of an Animated Film.* New York: Disney Editions, 1993.

———. *Walt Disney's Fantasia.* New York: Abradale Press, 1983.

Dowling, Colette. *The Cinderella Complex: Women's Hidden Fear of Independence.* New York: Summit Books, 1981.

Edgerton, Gary, and Kathy Merlock Jackson. "Redesigning Pocahontas," *Journal of Popular Film and Television* 24 (1996).

Eisner, Michael. *Work in Progress.* New York: Random House, 1998.

Eliot, Marc. *Walt Disney: Hollywood's Dark Prince.* Secaucus, N.J.: Carol Publishing Group, 1993.

Epstein, Jeffrey, and Eddie Shapiro. *Queens in the Kingdom: The Ultimate Gay and Lesbian Guide to the Disney Theme Parks.* Los Angeles: Alyson Publications, 2003.

Ezell, Lee. *The Cinderella Syndrome: Discovering God's Plan When Your Dreams Don't Come True.* Ann Arbor, Mich.: Vine Books, 1994.

Fadner, Donald E. "Disney Gets Religion." Paper presented at the American Academy of Religion meeting in Orlando, November 1998.

Feild, R. D. *The Art of Walt Disney.* New York: Macmillan, 1942.

Ferraiuolo, Perucci. *Disney and the Bible: A Scriptural Critique of the Magic Kingdom.* Camp Hill, Pa.: Horizon Books, 1996.

Field, Rachel. *Ave Maria: An Interpretation from Walt Disney's Fantasia.* New York: Random House, 1940.

Foglesong, Richard E. *Married to the Mouse: Walt Disney World and Orlando.* New Haven, Conn.: Yale University Press, 2001.

Forbes, Bruce David. "And a Mouse Shall Lead Them: An Essay on the Disney Phenomenon as Religion." Paper delivered at a Disney conference at Florida Atlantic University, 2000.

Giroux, Henry A. *The Mouse That Roared: Disney and the End of Innocence.* New York: Rowman & Littlefield, 1999.

Gitlin, Todd. *The Twilight of Common Dreams: Why America Is Wracked by Culture Wars.* New York: Henry Holt, 1996.

Graham, Susan Lochrie. "Some Day My Prince Will Come: Images of Salvation in the Gospel according to St. Walt." Paper presented at the American Academy of Religion meeting in Orlando, November 1998.

Griffin, Sean. *Tinker Belles and Evil Queens: The Walt Disney Company from the Inside Out.* New York: New York University Press, 2000.

Herberg, Will. *Protestant—Catholic—Jew: An Essay in American Religious Sociology.* Chicago: University of Chicago Press, 1983.

Hiassen, Carl. *Team Rodent: How Disney Devours the World.* New York: Ballantine, 1998.

Jackson, Kathy Merlock. *Walt Disney: A Bio-Bibliography.* Westport, Conn.: Greenwood Press, 1993.

Juschka, Darlene. "The Wonderful Worlds of Disney and Fundamentalism." Paper presented at the American Academy of Religion meeting in Orlando, November 1998.

Land, Richard D., and Frank D. York. *Send a Message to Mickey.* Nashville: Broadman & Holman Publishers, 1998.

Maltin, Leonard. *The Disney Films.* New York: Bonanza Books, 1973.

Masters, Kim. *The Keys to the Kingdom: How Michael Eisner Lost His Grip.* New York: William Morrow, 2000.

McGilligan, Patrick, and Paul Buhle. *Tender Comrades: A Backstory of the Hollywood Blacklist.* New York: St. Martin's Press, 1997.

McReynolds, William I. "Walt Disney in the American Grain." PhD diss., University of Minnesota, 1971.

Mosley, Leonard. *Disney's World.* New York: Stein & Day, 1985. First Scarborough House paperback edition, 1990. Reprinted 1992.

Pinsky, Mark I. *The Gospel according to The Simpsons: The Spiritual Life of the World's Most Animated Family.* Louisville, Ky.: Westminster John Knox Press, 2001.

Real, Michael R. *The Disney Universe: Morality Play.* Englewood Cliffs, N.J.: Mass-Mediated Cultures, 1977.

Schickel, Richard. *The Disney Version: The Life, Times, Art, and Commerce of Walt Disney.* New York: Simon & Schuster, 1968.

Schweizer, Peter, and Rochelle Schweizer. *Disney: The Mouse Betrayed.* Washington, D.C.: Regnery, 1998.

Shaheen, Jack. *Reel Bad Arabs: How Hollywood Vilifies a People.* New York: Interlink, 2001.

Smith, Dave, comp. *The Quotable Walt Disney.* New York: Disney Editions, 2001.

Thomas, Bob. *Building a Company: Roy O. Disney and the Creation of an Entertainment Empire.* New York: Hyperion, 1998.

———. *Walt Disney: An American Original.* New York: Simon & Schuster, 1976.

Wagner, Walter. *You Must Remember This.* New York: Putnam, 1975.

Wakabayashi, H. Clark. *Brother Bear: A Transformation Tale.* New York: Disney Editions, 2003.

Ward, Annalee R. *Mouse Morality: The Rhetoric of Disney Animated Film.* Austin: University of Texas Press, 2002.

Wasko, Janet. *Understanding Disney: The Manufacture of Fantasy.* Malden, Mass.: Blackwell Publishers, 2001.

Watts, Steven. *The Magic Kingdom: Walt Disney and the American Way of Life.* Boston: Houghton Mifflin, 1997.

Wilmington, Michael. *The American Animated Cartoon: A Critical Anthology.* New York: E. P. Dutton, 1980.

Zipes, Jack. *From Mouse to Mermaid: The Politics of Film, Gender, and Culture.* Bloomington: Indiana University Press, 1995.

Index

Abdel-Meguid, Esmat, 152
abortion, 167
    in *Lilo and Stitch*, 208
absent father, in *Treasure Planet*, 214. *See
    also* parents missing
acceptance
    in *Bambi*, 46–47
    in *Dumbo*, 40
Acquino, Reuben, 140
action, characters transformed by, 86–87
adventure capitalism, 198
adversity, in *Snow White*, 23
aesthetics, in *Beauty and the Beast*, 146
Africa, without Africans, 185
African American women, first positive
    Disney portrayal of, in *Hercules*, 175
Africans, historical prism for viewing *The
    Lion King*, 159
African themes, in *The Lion King*, 154
AIDS, *Beauty and the Beast* as allegory
    for, 146
Akedah, 22–23
Aladdin, 148–53, 264
    alternative lyrics for offensive material,
    148
    charge of subliminal audio messages in,
    247
    Eisner writing on, 127–28
Aladdin: The Making of an Animated Film
    (Culhane), 148
Aladdin's Lamp, 150
Alice in Wonderland, 57–60
Al-Marayati, Salam, 151
alternative religious tradition, in *The Lion
    King*, 154, 159
Alwaleed Bin Talal Bin Abdulaziz, 152
America, maturing of, in *Lady and the
    Tramp*, 69, 73

*American Animated Cartoon: A Critical
    Anthology, The* (Wilmington), 43
American capitalism, Disney as ode to,
    263
American Family Association, 238, 241,
    250
American Jewish Committee, 136–37
American Jewish Congress, 111
American Life League, 247
American optimism, 42
American Original, 110
Americans
    civic religion of, 7–8
    religious beliefs, 240–41
American virtues, threat to, in *101 Dalma-
    tians*, 80
*America's Favorite Movies: Behind the
    Scenes* (Behlmer), 26
Anderson, Kerby, 163
Andrews, Mark, 77
animal rights, 79
    in *Brother Bear*, 224
animals, 69–72
    anthropomorphic treatment of, 50–51
    befriending, in *Snow White*, 23
    dead and dying on-screen, in *Beauty
        and the Beast*, 146
    treatment of, in *Robin Hood*, 94
animated features, winning formula for, 150
animism, perceived in *Pocahontas*, 163
anticapitalism, in *Atlantis*, 199, 202
anti-Catholic undertones, in *The Hunch-
    back of Notre Dame*, 173
anti-Semitism, 111–13
    associated with Walt Disney Company,
    121
    Eisner family's experiences with, 124,
    126

anti-Western message, in *Atlantis,* 199, 202
appearances, affecting perceptions, 147
Arab-Muslim proposed Disney boycott, 152
Arnal, William, 263
arranged marriages, 155
Art of Walt Disney, The, 37
Ashman, Howard, 148
Assemblies of God, decision to join call for Disney boycott, 251
Atlantis, 194–202, 209
"Ave Maria" (*Fantasia*), 37–38
Ave Maria: An Interpretation from Walt Disney's Fantasia (Field), 38

bad boys, attraction to, 140
Baehr, Ted, 134, 172
Baerwald, Susan, 125
Bailey, Pearl, 103
Baker, Jeff, 50
Bakker, Jim, 170
Bambi, ix, 46–51, 102, 187
Baptists, relations with other religions, 173–74, 242
Barna, George, 240
Barrier, Michael, 44, 112
Barry, Dave, 229, 234
beauty
    equated with character in *Pocahontas,* 162
    not required for Disney lead, 208
    unrelated to goodness, in *Beauty and the Beast,* 143, 144
Beauty and the Beast, 143–47, 264
Behlmer, Rudy, 26
believing in self
    in *Black Cauldron, The,* 107
    in *Dumbo,* 44
    in *Mulan,* 181–82
Bell, Elizabeth, 52, 262
Bentsur, Eitan, 152
Bible, in *Johnny Appleseed,* 113–14
Billins, Josh, 69
Black Cauldron, The, 104–8
black crow sequence (*Dumbo*), xiv, 43–44
black magic, 24, 39, 84
Blaise, Aaron, 220–21
Blue Fairy, Virgin Mary reference, 29
Bluth, Don, 115–16
bondage, in *Lady and the Tramp,* 73
boredom, in *Alice in Wonderland,* 57, 60
Boyar, Jay, xiii, 41, 91, 137

boycott of Disney products, 152, 230, 248–55, 259, 260
Brashares, Charles W., 26–27
Bright, Bill, 136
Bright, Vonette, 136
Brooks, Bob, 244
Brother Bear, 220–25
Brother Bear: A Transformation Tale (Wakabayashi), 224
brotherhood, in *Brother Bear,* 225
Brown, Dan, 139
Bruns, George, 93
Bryman, Alan, 15
Buddhism, in *The Lion King,* 158
Buhle, Paul, 55
Building a Company: Roy O. Disney and the Creation of an Entertainment Empire (Thomas), 1, 15, 18, 19
Built to Last: Successful Habits of Visionary Companies (Collins and Porras), 129
Burroughs, Edgar Rice, 185
Bustany, Donald, 151
Buzz, 243
Byrne, Eleanor, 140, 167, 169, 170, 176, 182–83

Calloway, Cab, 110
Camp (Eisner), 126
Camp Keewaydin, 125–26
Campbell, Dennis, 241
Campbell, Joseph, 178
Campolo, Tony, 4, 8–9, 231
Canemaker, John, 38, 44, 115
caricatures, in *Fantasia,* 33
Carnival Cruise Lines, Disney's copromotions with, 246
Carnochan, John, 36
Carroll, Lewis, 60
cartoon characters, Disney's detractors using, for symbolic value, ix
Cassidy, Mike, 234
Catholic-Baptist relations, 173–74
Catholicism, 29, 38
Catholic League for Religious and Civil Rights, 238, 241
Catlett, Michael, 11–12, 45, 171, 230
Celebration (Fla.), 236
celebrity, in *Hercules,* 177
character, in *Hercules,* 177
Charisma, 252
childhood lost, 48–49
children, growing up too quickly, in *Return to Neverland,* 215–16

China, experience with women leaders, 179
Chinese values, in *Mulan,* 182
Chopra, Deepak, Eisner unimpressed by, 128
Christ, saving work of, suggested in *Lady and the Tramp,* 72–73
Christian Action Network, 232
Christian Film and Television Commission, 164
Christian imagery, in *Sleeping Beauty,* 77–78
Christian message, in *The Small One,* 114–17
Christians. *See also* conservative Christians, conservative evangelicals, fundamentalists, Southern Baptist Convention
    critical of *Hercules,* 175
    critical of presence of magic in Disney animated features, 239
church, portrayal in *The Hunchback of Notre Dame,* 167–68
churches, not present in Disney theme parks, 2, 231, 236
Cinderella, 52–56, 77
Cinderella Complex: Women's Hidden Fear of Independence, The (Dowling), 56
Cinderella Syndrome: Discovering God's Plan When Your Dreams Don't Come True, The (Ezell), 56
civil rights era, 91–92
class politics, in *Robin Hood,* 97–98
Clattenberg, Alex, 231
cleanliness
    at Disney theme parks, 230–31
    in *Snow White,* 24
Clements, Ron, 175
cloning, in *Lilo and Stitch,* 203, 208
Collins, Jim, 129
Collins, Phil, 185, 186, 188, 224
colonialism, 159
    in *Peter Pan,* 63
Colonna, Jerry, 60
Complete Fairy Tales of the Brothers Grimm, The (Zipes, trans.), 26
concern for others' feelings, in *Snow White,* 24
Confucianism, in *Mulan,* 180, 183
Congregation of Liberal Judaism (Orlando, Fla.), 127, 135
Conrad, Joseph, 187

conscience, 28–29
    in *Atlantis,* 200
    in *Emperor's New Groove, The,* 190, 192
conservative Christians
    criticism of *Pocahontas,* 163–65
    giving up on Disney's animated features, 178
conservative evangelicals, nonembracing of *The Hunchback of Notre Dame,* 173
conservatives, political, criticism of *Pocahontas,* 166
Consuming Environments: Television and Commercial Culture (Steinman), 199
Cook, Dick, 149, 242–43
Corliss, Richard, 5
courtship, in *Bambi,* 49
Cox, Penny Finkelman, 134
crisis of faith, in *Cinderella,* 54–55
cross, symbolism of, in *Sleeping Beauty,* 77
crows
    in *Dumbo,* compared to vultures in *Jungle Book,* 92
    as ominous symbol, 48, 51
Culhane, John, 4, 38, 111, 117, 148
culture wars, 6–7

damnation, in *The Hunchback of Notre Dame,* 170
"Dance of the Hours" (*Fantasia*), 36–37
Da Vinci Code, The (Brown), 139
Davis, Jim, 170
Davis, Marc, 62, 64
death, in *Bambi,* 48–49
Deconstructing Disney (Byrne and McQuillan), 140, 167, 169, 171, 176, 182–83
defense industry, criticism of, in *Lilo and Stitch,* 208
Deja, Andreas, 145, 157
de la Tour, George, 139
deleted (unfilmed) material
    from *Fantasia,* 36
    in *Peter Pan,* 62
    in *Snow White,* 24, 26
    from *Sword and the Stone, The,* 83
Depression, defiant mood reflected in shorts, 110–11
Desmond, Norma, 140
destiny, in *Brother Bear,* 223–24
determination, in *Bambi,* 49
deus ex machina, 4

Disney. *See* Disney *listings*, Walt Disney
   Company
Disney, Elias, 15–18
Disney, Flora, 16, 17
Disney, Herbert, 16
Disney, Lillian, 18
Disney, Patricia Dailey, 19
Disney, Raymond, 16
Disney, Roy, 3
   adapting movie based on St. Peter, 18
   ambivalence to organized religion,
      17–18
   death of, 19
   early years, 15–17
   recycled biographical information
      about, 15
   response to complaints about portrayals
      of Jews, 111
Disney, Roy Edward, 17, 19, 88, 266
   dispute with Eisner, 129–30
Disney, Ruth, 16
   on *Fantasia,* 33
   hiring Eisner, 127
Disney, Sharon, 18, 111, 113
Disney, Walt, 3
   on *Alice in Wonderland,* 57
   Alice in Wonderland's disappointing
      box office, 60
   ambivalence to organized religion,
      17–18
   ambivalence toward Peter Pan, 62
   aversion to religious movies, 18
   avoiding religious content, 1–2, 3–4
   on *Cinderella*'s assertiveness, 55
   commissioning special lyrics for "Ave
      Maria," 38
   concern about legacy, 19
   creating new genre of feature films with
      Snow White, 27
   death of, 19
   dwarfs referred to as "little men," 24
   early years, 15–17
   fears of offending and excluding, xiii
   influence of, 5
   influence on *Jungle Book,* 88
   intentions for *Fantasia,* 33, 37
   looked to for support in civil rights era,
      91
   opening of Disneyland, 229
   perceiving theme parks as reality, 231
   philosophy of faith, 20
   pseudoreligious aura around, 21
   purpose of animated features, 261
   realization of dream, 225
   recycled biographical information
      about, 15
   refusal to interpret own work, 262
   Small One, The, not reflective of philos-
      ophy, 116, 117
   social contract with, 27
   theme parks of, goals for, ix
   thoughts on prayer, 20–21
   Tramp representing aspect of, 73
   use of anthropomorphous animals, 50–51
   value system of, 8–9
   viewed as anti-Semitic, 111–13
   viewing animated features as message
      films, 2
   violating mission to entertain, 39
   writing in *Guideposts,* 20–21
Disney animated features
   approach to good and evil, 7
   changes in, over time, 264
   changing female portrayals in, 142
   competition for, 265–66
   conservative Christians giving up on,
      178
   considered too frightening for children,
      50
   early films reflecting Disney's human-
      ism, 7
   endurance stories, 10
   financial success of, 5–6
   growing sophistication of, evident in
      Beauty and the Beast, 146–47
   harsh view of magic vs. religion in, 6
   historical context for, xii–xiii
   house religion of, 10
   impact on children's lives, 2–3, 12
   lessons in, for children, 263–64
   lessons and values in, consistency of,
      xi–xii
   Lion King, The, as critical juncture for
      religious portrayals, 159
   magic featured in, 4–5
   through parent's eyes, x
   potential end of hand-animated fea-
      tures, 266
   pregnancy first shown, in *The
      Emperor's New Groove,* 190
   religious leaders' ambivalence toward,
      11
   Robin Hood as '60s movie, 98
   Scripture citation in, 92
   shifting to accommodate contemporary
      culture, 261

Disney animated features *(continued)*
　theological dimension to choosing
　　magic over religion, 4–5
　theological vocabulary in, 1
　tracking American mainstream beliefs,
　　241
　variety of families in, 12
　young man at center of narrative, 209
*Disney and the Bible: A Scriptural Cri-
　tique of the Magic Kingdom* (Fer-
　raiuolo), 38–39, 54, 109, 123, 244
Disney Boycott: A Just Cause, The, 254
Disney family, 15–18
Disney Films (Maltin), 43
Disney gospel
　faith, trust, and pixie dust, 62
　Snow White as template for, 22
Disney and His Worlds (Bryman), 15
Disney: The Mouse Betrayed (Schweizer
　and Schweizer), 145, 148, 168, 232,
　243, 247
Disney products, as safe haven, 3
"Disney's America," 166
Disney's World (Mosley), 16–17, 112
Disney theme parks, 2, 229–37
　as academic subjects, 229–30
　allegations about, 232–33
　churches absent from, 2, 231, 236
　in China, 184
　cleanliness of, 230–31
　expected effect on, of Comcast
　　takeover, 237
　Gay Days at, 232
　"Nights of Joy," 231, 246
　religion at, 231–32
　role in children's memory, 237
　visit to, portrayed as religious pilgrim-
　　age, 233–34
Disney Universe: Morality Play, The,
　(Real), 230
*Disney Version: The Life, Times, Art, and
　Commerce of Walt Disney, The,*
　(Schickel), 5, 27, 42, 60, 91, 110,
　111
diversity, in *Atlantis,* 195–96
Divine, 140
Dobson, James, 254, 257–58
dogs, smarter than humans, 82
domestic partner benefits, available for gay
　Disney employees, 243–45
Dowling, Collette, 56
Drake, Wiley, 249–50
drama, magic used in, 4–5

dreams, in *Hercules,* 175
DreamWorks SKG, 131, 132–34
Dreyer, John, 173, 245, 246, 248, 255
drunkenness, 43
Dubov, Sholom, 135
Duke, James B., 184
Dumbo, xiv, 40–45, 92, 224
Duricy, Michael P., 29

Easterbrook, Gregg, 122
Eco, Umberto, 229
Edenic themes
　in *Bambi,* 49
　in *Snow White,* 25–26
Edgerton, Gary, 162
Edington, Howard, 135–36
education, importance of, in *The Fox and
　the Hound,* 100
ego, in *Alice in Wonderland,* 58
Eisenhower, Dwight David, 8
Eisner, Bertha Weiss, 123
Eisner, Jane Breckenridge, 126–27
Eisner, Lester, 124–25
Eisner, Margaret Damman (Maggie), 124,
　125, 127
Eisner, Margot, 124
Eisner, Michael, 7, 19, 121, 122–23
　appearance on *60 Minutes,* 255–59
　approving design of church in Celebra-
　　tion (Fla.), 236
　change in tone of movies during regime
　　of, 240
　changing female portrayals in Disney
　　features, 142
　conflict with conservative Christian
　　groups, 131
　dispute with Roy Disney, 129–30
　handling of Epcot Jerusalem contro-
　　versy, 152, 153
　hired at Disney, 127
　leading Disney beyond Western, Judeo-
　　Christian constructs, 159
　loyalty to shareholders and employees,
　　243
　more Walt than Walt, 129
　refusing Katzenberg's promotion,
　　130–31
　religious and moral identity, 124–25
　response to criticism of *Pocahontas,*
　　164
　response to Southern Baptist Conven-
　　tion boycott, 250–51
　silent on own religion and philanthropic

practice, 127–29
upbringing and early life, 123–26
Eisner, Sigmund, 123–24, 153
elderly, reverence for, in *Snow White*, 25
Eliot, Marc, 17, 112
Elliff, Tom, 252
Emperor's New Groove, The, 189–93
empowerment, 181
Engel, Steven, 135
environmentalism
    in *Bambi*, ix, 46
    in *Lilo and Stitch*, 208
Epcot, proposed "Journey to Jerusalem"
    pavilion, 151–52
Ethics and Religious Liberty Commission,
    260
ethnic cleansing, in *The Hunchback of
    Notre Dame*, 171
ethnocentrism, in *Aladdin*, 148
euthanasia, 167
evangelical Christians
    DreamWorks forging relationships with,
        135–36
    view of Disney, 123
evil
    in *Cinderella*, 53
    in *Snow White*, 26, 27, 53
evil stepmother, 52–53
evolution, "Rite of Spring" as lesson in,
    35–36
exploitation, in *Pinocchio*, 30
Ezell, Lee, 56

fable, Disney's attraction to, 50–51
Fadner, Donald E., 159, 164, 168, 170,
    264
Fain, Sammy, 62
fairy godmother, 54–55
faith
    Disney's philosophy of, 20
    importance of, in *Peter Pan*, 66–67
    root of American civic religion, 7–8
    in *Tarzan*, 185, 187
    unseen framework for Disney animated
        features, 239–40
For Faith and Family, 260
faith, trust, and pixie dust
    in *Peter Pan*, 62
    in *Return to Neverland*, 216, 217, 218
Falwell, Jerry, 133–34, 242
family, in *Bambi*, 46
family, intact. *See* parents missing
    in *Mulan*, 179

in *Peter Pan*, 61
family values activists, positive response
    to *The Hunchback of Notre Dame*,
    171–72
family virtue, in *101 Dalmatians*, 80
Fantasia, 33–39, 85
fantasy, valid retreat in times of terror, 219
fate, in *Pinocchio*, 28
Father Noah's Ark, 109
Feder, Don, 164
female passivity
    in *Cinderella*, 55, 56
    in *Snow White*, 25
female rescue fantasies, 77–78. See also
    *Cinderella, Sleeping Beauty, Snow
    White*
female sexual attraction, in *Bambi*, 49
Ferraiuolo, Perucci, 38–39, 54, 104, 109,
    244, 263
Feild, R. D., 37
Field, Rachel, 38
Finn, Will, 168
Florida Baptist Convention, resolution to
    reconsider support of Disney prod-
    ucts, 245–47
Florida Family Council, 244
Flowers and Trees, 109
Focus on the Family, 254
Fogelsong, Richard, 229, 233
Forbes, Bruce David, 35, 233–34
Ford, Henry, 113
forgiveness, in *Brother Bear*, 225
Fox and the Hound, The, 99–103
    charge of subliminal scene in, 247
Frank, Anne, 219
Freedman, Samuel, 234
friendship, struggling against natural law,
    in *The Fox and the Hound*, 99–102
Friendship in Vienna, 127
*From Mouse to Mermaid: The Politics of
    Film, Gender, and Culture* (Bell,
    Haas, and Sells, eds.), xvi, 46, 52,
    91, 140, 147, 262
Full Court Miracle, 127
fundamentalists
    consulted for *Prince of Egypt*, 134
    giving up on Disney's animated fea-
        tures, 178
    nonembracing of *The Hunchback of
        Notre Dame*, 173

Gaines, Steven, 243

gama honza, in *The Lion King*, 158
Garner, James, 198–99
Gay Days, 232
gay narcissism, 145
Geffen, David, 131, 132
George, Hazel, 19
Gilkyson, Terry, 93
Gilmer, Janet, 246–47
Giroux, Henry A., x, 148, 264–65
Gitlin, Todd, 134
global capitalism, 260
God
    belief in, in *The Hunchback of Notre
        Dame*, 167
    invoking name of, in *The Hunchback of
        Notre Dame*, 167
    referred to in *The Small One*, 117
Goddess of Spring, 109
Gold, Stanley, 127, 129
Golden Touch, The, 110
Goldwyn, Sam, 2
gospel, in *The Hunchback of Notre Dame*,
    170
The Gospel according to the Simpsons
    (Pinsky), xi
gospel message, mixed with entertainment
    at theme parks, 230
Graham, Billy, 231
Graham, Franklin, 242
Graham, Ruth, 67
Graham, Susan Lochrie, 66–67, 72–73, 263
greed, in *Pocahontas*, 161
Greek mythology, 109
    in *Fantasia*, 36
    in *Lion King, The*, 157
Green, Howard, 116
Greene, Katherine, 18, 113
Greene, Richard, 18, 113
Griffin, Sean, 157
Groening, Matt, 50
group, mutual benefit of, in *Jungle Book*,
    89
Grove, Lloyd, 131, 132
Growing Up Gay, 249
guardian angel, 113, 114
Guideposts, Disney's publication in, 2,
    20–21
gun control, in *Bambi*, ix, 46

Haas, Lynda, 52, 262
Haddock, Shelley, 12
Hahn, Don, 173
hardship, turning into advantage, in

Dumbo, 44–45
Harris, Phil, 90, 93
Hattenstone, Simon, 123, 126
Hays office, 36
Heart of Darkness (Conrad), 187
Heather Has Two Mommies, 249
Henry, Jim, 246, 248, 250, 257
Herberg, Will, 7–8
Hercules, 175–78
heroine, Disney formula for, in *Cinderella*,
    53
Hetrick, Paul, 172
Hiassen, Carl, 229, 259
Hindu tradition, in *The Lion King*, 154
Hodge, Tim, 116–17
Holocaust, 171
Home on the Range, 267
hope
    in face of adversity, in *The Fox and the
        Hound*, 103
    in *Hercules*, 175
    in *Robin Hood*, 96
hospitality, 143
House Committee on Un-American Activi-
    ties, 262
Hugo, Victor, 167
human nature, 93
humans
    as barbarians, in *The Little Mermaid*,
        138, 140
    harboring good and bad, 188
    presence of, signaling trouble, 49, 187
Hunchback of Notre Dame, The, 37,
    167–74
Hunt, Robert, 164

Ice Age, 266
imperfections, mocking in others, 41
inclusion, in *Snow White*, 24
infant baptism, in *The Lion King*, 154–55
innocence, myth of, 176
intermarriage, in *The Little Mermaid*, 138,
    141–42
Internet, 60
intolerance, in *Pocahontas*, 162
Isaac, sacrifice of, 22–23

Jackson, Kathy Merlock, 4, 5, 24, 44, 50,
    110, 162
jealousy
    in *Peter Pan*, 64–65
    in *Return to Neverland*, 217
Jeffords, Susan, 147

Jesus, parallels in *Hercules,* 178
Jews
    cultural divide among immigrants, 131
    cultural identity of, 121
Jiminy Cricket, ix, 28–30
Johnny Appleseed, 113–14
Jonah, 10–11
"Journey to Jerusalem" pavilion, 151–52
Judeo-Christian framework, in *The Lion King,* 157
Jump Cut, 144, 155, 263
Jungle Book, The, 88–93
Juschka, Darlene, 123, 245–46

karma, in *The Lion King,* 157
Katzenberg, Jeffrey, 121, 122, 129
    change in tone of movies during regime of, 240
    changing female portrayals in Disney features, 142
    concern over *Aladdin,* 153
    concern over offending gays with *Aladdin,* 148
    instructions for portrayal of Pocahontas, 165
    leading Disney beyond Western, Judeo-Christian constructs, 159
    leaving Disney, 130–31
    making of *The Prince of Egypt,* 131–37
    move to DreamWorks, 131
    religious profile of, 136–37
    upbringing, 130
Keane, Glen, 165
keeping to one's own kind, in *Jungle Book,* 93
Keys to the Kingdom: How Michael Eisner Lost His Grip, The, (Masters), 124, 125
Kill Bill, 122
Kimball, Ward, 19, 36, 44, 112, 239
King, Margaret J., 233
Kipling, Rudyard, 88
Knight, Robert, 7, 136, 172
Knights of Columbus, 238
Knott, Walter, 235
Knott's Berry Farm, 235
knowledge, route to nobility and civilization, in *The Sword and the Stone,* 83, 84, 85–86
Kong Min, 184
Kristof, Nicholas D., 8
Kundun, 184

Lady and the Tramp, 69–73, 150
land development, in *The Emperor's New Groove,* 189
Land, Richard, 134–35, 171–72, 249, 253, 260
    appearance on *60 Minutes,* 255–59
    expressing Southern Baptists' view on homosexuality, 256
    no problems with Walt-era animated features, 240
Lapin, Daniel, 133
Laurie, Greg, 231
Lawrenceville School, 126
learning, boredom with conventions, in *Alice in Wonderland,* 57
least of these, 47
Lee, Don, 244
Leviathan, description of, quoted in *Atlantis,* 196
Life Is Beautiful, 219
Lilo and Stitch, 203–8, 264
Lion King, The, 154–59, 191, 224
    charges of concealed sexual messages in, 247
    Hindu tradition in, ix
Little Mermaid, The, 138–42
    charges of concealed sexual messages in, 247, 255–56
    intermarriage and, ix
Little Mermaid II: The Return to the Sea, 142
Londy, Alan, 135
love
    in *Bambi,* 46, 49
    in *Brother Bear,* 224, 225
    conquering all, in *Sleeping Beauty,* 74, 75
    lower-class characterization, in *Peter Pan,* 63
Lund, Lori K., 12
lying, in *Pinocchio,* 30

magic
    as feature in drama, 4–5
    in *Sleeping Beauty,* 74–76, 77–78
    in *Sword and the Stone, The,* 85
Magic Kingdom: Walt Disney and the American Way of Life, The (Watts), 21, 80
Majoribanks, Duncan, 166
Malinowski, Bronislaw, 4–5
Maltin, Leonard, 4, 37, 43, 117
man, disruptor and destroyer, in *Bambi,*

48, 51
Mandela, Nelson, 159
market economy, 260–61
marriage
    American paradigm of, in *Sleeping Beauty,* 76
    egalitarian model of, 67–68
Marty, Martin, myth in Disney, 9–10
Masters, Kim, 124, 125
Matheis, Mark, 41
Matrix, The, 60
Mawyer, Martin, 232
McCord, David Frederick, 239
McGilligan, Patrick, 55
McKenzie, Derrick, 252
McMullen, Cary, 258
McQuillan, Martin, 140, 167, 169, 171, 176, 182–83
McReynolds, William I., x, 21, 32, 44–45, 80, 262–63
Medved, Michael, 133, 134, 173
Merrell, Bill, 249
Mickey Mouse
    epitome of Walt Disney Company, 9
    Fantasia image as central company icon, 35
    symbolism of, 6
Midas story, 110
middle-class family, in *Peter Pan,* 61
Middle East politics, 151–53
Miller, Diane Disney, 2, 17, 18, 111–12
Miller, Ron, 115
Miller, Susan, 91
Minkoff, Rob, 154
miracle, promise of, in *The Sword and the Stone,* 83
Miramax, 238
misogyny. *See also* women, negative characterizations
    in *Atlantis,* 197
    in *Emperor's New Groove, The,* 193
    in *Snow White,* 24
Mitchell, Elvis, 266
Mohler, Albert, 242, 260
Moore, Alexander, 229–30
Moore, Roger, 266–67
moral hypocrisy, 168
moral instruction
    for children, 3
    in *Pinocchio,* 28, 29
morality, essence of Disney religion, 32
morality play, visit to theme parks characterized as, 230

Moses narrative, 131–32
Mosley, Leonard, 16–17, 112
mother love
    in *Bambi,* 46, 47
    in *Dumbo,* 40–45, 46
    in *Peter Pan,* 61, 65
Mouse Morality: The Rhetoric of Disney Animated Film (Ward), xiii, 53, 157, 162, 166, 182
Mouse That Roared: Disney and the End of Innocence, The, (Giroux), x, 148, 150, 264–65
Movieguide, 164
Mulan, 179–84, 264
Murdoch, Rupert, 184
Murphy, Eddie, 44
Murray, Cecil, 122
Museum of Tolerance, 136
Musker, John, 175, 177
Muslims, offended by *Aladdin,* 148, 151
mythology, 175
    Disney's invention of, 9–10
    reflected in Disney products, 3
    transformation myth, 220

National Federation for Decency, 238
Native Americans
    criticizing *Pocahontas,* 165
    positive portrayal of, in *Pocahontas,* 160
Native American spirituality, in *Brother Bear,* 221
Nativity, 46
natural law, friendship struggling against, in *The Fox and the Hound,* 99–102
nature
    amorality of, 51
    cruelty of, in *Bambi,* 48
    Disney's view of, apparent in *Jungle Book,* 88–89
    enemy of, in *Bambi,* 48
    good and bad within, 188
    as ideal state, in *Bambi,* 51
Nawrocki, Mike, 10–11
New Republic, 50
News Corporation, 184
New Testament, Disney animated features as anathema against, 6
New York Times, 149
"Night on Bald Mountain" (*Fantasia*), 37–38
Nine Old Men and the Art of Animation (Canemaker), 115

Noah story, 109–10
Nothing Sacred, 238
nuclear family, 48. *See also* parents missing
necessity of, undermined, in *Lilo and Stitch,* 208
slim hopes for survival of, in Disney features, 209
Nunis, Richard, 231
nurture, trumping nature, in *The Fox and the Hound,* 103

occult concepts, in *The Black Cauldron,* 104–8
occult images, 239
O'Donovan, Leo J., 253–54
Ohana, 203, 206, 207, 208
Once and Future King, The (White), 83
One for Sorrow, Two for Joy, 267
101 Dalmatians, 79–82
Orlando (Fla.), 248
Our Crowd (Birmingham), 124

parentage, in *Bambi,* 47
parents, critics viewing Disney animated features through lens of, 264–65
parents missing
in *Atlantis,* 194
in *Beauty and the Beast,* 143
in *Emperor's New Groove, The,* 189
in *Hercules,* 176
in *Jungle Book,* 88, 92
in *Lilo and Stitch,* 205, 207
in *Little Mermaid, The,* 139
in *Peter Pan,* 63
Parham, Robert, 260
Parr, Walter, 16
Passion of the Christ, The, 173
Pastoral Symphony, 36
patriarchy, as ideal, in *Bambi,* 51
Patteson, Jean, 237
Payne, David, 46
Pearlman, Cindy, 132
Penitent Magdalene, The (de la Tour), 139
Peter Pan, 61–68
faith and, ix
foreshadowed in *Fantasia,* 33
Peter Pan syndrome, 67
"Pink Elephants on Parade" (*Dumbo*), 43
Pinocchio, 1, 3–4, 28–32, 74, 205, 224
Pinsky, Asher, 45
Pinsky, Liza, 45
Pocahontas, 109, 160–66, 264

Christian disenchantment with, 240
covered on *60 Minutes,* 256
Pocahontas, conversion to Christianity, 163–65
Pocahontas II: Journey to a New World, 164
politicians, in *Alice in Wonderland,* 57–58
Pontius, Larry, 19
populism, in *The Hunchback of Notre Dame,* 169–70
pornographic drawings in animation, 239
Porras, Jerry, 129
prayer
in *Lilo and Stitch,* 205
in *Peter Pan,* 66
in *Snow White,* 24, 25
Precker, Michael, 148, 149
pre-Reformation Catholicism, 167
Priest, 238
Prima, Louis, 91, 93
Prince of Egypt, The, 131–37
profane-sacred, struggle between, 37
Protestant–Catholic–Jew: An Essay in American Religious Sociology (Herberg), 7–8
Providence, 10, 11
Puder, Dorothy, 16, 17, 236
Puder, Glenn, 17, 236

Queens in the Kingdom: The Ultimate Gay and Lesbian Guide to the Disney Theme Parks, 232
quest, in *Brother Bear,* 220
Quotable Walt Disney, The, 20

race relations, pre–civil rights era, 102–3
racial stereotypes, 36. *See also* stereotypes
in *Dumbo,* 40–41, 43–44, 45
Native Americans, in *Peter Pan,* 63, 64
in shorts, 110
racism
condemned in *The Hunchback of Notre Dame,* 167
in Disney movies, x
in *Pocahontas,* 162
Rafferty, Max, 5
Rapf, Maurice, 55, 112
Rather, Dan, 146
Rathje, Arthur, 245
Real, Michael R., 230
redemption
in *Brother Bear,* 220

in *Cinderella*, 56
Reel Bad Arabs: How Hollywood Vilifies a People (Shaheen), 133
religion
    explicit treatment of, in *Fantasia*, 37–38
    off-limits in shorts, 109
    portrayal of, in movies, xiii
    refusal to admit serious role for, 168
religious hypocrisy, 168
religious syncretism, in *Hercules*, 175
responsibility, in *Brother Bear*, 224
resurrection
    in *Black Cauldron, The*, 106, 107
    in *Pinocchio*, 31, 74
    in *Sleeping Beauty*, 74, 78
    in *Snow White*, 74
Return to Neverland, 215–19
reverence, in *Treasure Planet*, 214
Rich, Frank, 259–60
righteousness, weapons of, in *Sleeping Beauty*, 77
"Rite of Spring" (*Fantasia*), 35–36
Robin Hood, 94–98
Rode, Greg, 91
Roseanne, 234
Roth, Matt, 144–45, 155, 263
Ruthless People, 240
Ryba, Thomas, 230

sacrifice
    in *Beauty and the Beast*, 145–46
    in *Mulan*, 181
salvation
    in *Peter Pan*, 67
    through works, in *Pinocchio*, 31–32
Satan, in *Fantasia*, 37, 38–39
Sayers, Frances Clarke, 5
Schickel, Richard, 5, 27, 36, 42, 60, 91, 110, 111
Schiesel, Seth, 128
Schuller, Robert, 7, 42, 164
Schumacher, Thomas, 148, 162, 177, 181, 243
Schweizer, Peter, 145, 168, 232, 243, 247
Schweizer, Rochelle, 145, 168, 232, 243, 247
Scripture citation, in *Jungle Book*, 92
secular 'toonism, 6–7
secular humanism, 6
self-confidence, in *Treasure Planet*, 209
self-reliance, in *101 Dalmatians*, 81
Sells, Laura, 52, 262
Send a Message to Mickey; The ABCs of

Making Your Voice Heard at Disney (Land), 254–55
Sevaried, Eric, 21
sexual attraction, in *Jungle Book*, 93
sexuality, different portrayal of, beginning in *Beauty and the Beast*, 146–47
Shaheen, Jack, 133, 149–50
Shapiro, Merrill, 135
Sharia law, portrayed in *Aladdin*, 150
Sheldon, Lou, 6, 133, 164, 172
Sherman, Richard, 83, 93
Sherman, Robert, 83
shorts, 109–17
Shrek, 147, 266
Shrieves, Linda, 237
Silly Symphonies series, 110
Simon, Jeff, 137
the Simpsons, 234–35
sin
    in *Pinocchio*, 30–31
    in *Snow White*, 22, 26–27
Sito, Tom, 166, 247, 256
60 Minutes, 255–60
Skeleton Dance, 109
Sleeping Beauty, 74–78, 176
Small One, The, 114–17
Smith, Alice, 239
Smith, Bailey, 252
Smith, David, 2, 20, 116
Snow White and the Seven Dwarfs, 3, 22–27, 53, 74, 77, 193
    pornographic drawings on, 239
social gospel, in *Robin Hood*, 94, 97–98
Some Day My Prince Will Come (Graham), 72–73
songs, used to shape moral identity, 53
"The Sorcerer's Apprentice" (*Fantasia*), 34–35, 85
Southern Baptist Convention, xi, 67, 241–42
    boycott against Disney, 248–55
    Ethics and Religious Liberty Commission, 134
    notion of family, 245–46
    results for denomination, of boycott, 260
    threatening boycott, 171
Southern Baptists, complaints about Sunday evening television show, 240
Spielberg, Steven, 29, 131–32
spirit, in *Fantasia*, 34
spirituality, in *Brother Bear*, 220
spiritual realm, off-limits in shorts, 109

Splash, 140, 240
Stahl, Lesley, 255–57
star, for wishing
  in *Lilo and Stitch,* 205
  in *Peter Pan,* 61
  in *Pinocchio,* 28
Steinman, Clay, 199
stereotypes. *See also* racial stereotypes
  in *Aladdin,* 149–50
  in Disney movies, x
  end of era of acceptance, 149
  in *Fantasia,* 33
  gay, 144–45, 157
  of Jews, 111
  in *Jungle Book,* 90–91
St. George, battle with dragon reenacted in
  Sleeping Beauty, 77
still, small voice, 28–29
straight-to-video sequels, toning down
  offensive aspects of *Aladdin,* 151
Stravinsky, 35
submission, in marriage, 67
supernatural, in *Snow White,* 22
supernatural powers, gone awry in *Fantasia,* 34–35
surrogate salvation, in *Pinocchio,* 28
Swaggart, Jimmy, 170
Sword and the Stone, The, 83–87
syncretism, 241

Tarzan, 185–88, 209
Taylor, Deems, 34, 35, 37, 38
*Team Rodent: How Disney Devours the
  World* (Hiassen), 229, 259
teen alienation, in *Treasure Planet,* 209–10
television, presence in Disney films, 80,
  81–82
temptation
  in *Pinocchio,* 29–30
  Return to Neverland, 217
  warnings about, in *The Hunchback of
    Notre Dame,* 170
Ten Commandments, The, 131–32
*Tender Comrades: A Backstory of the Hol-
  lywood Blacklist* (McGilligan and
  Buhle), 55, 112
Thomas, Bob, 1, 15, 17, 18, 54, 110
Thomas, Mike, 265
Three Little Pigs, The, 110–11
Time, 5, 6, 44
*Tinker Belles and Evil Queens: The Walt
  Disney Company from the Inside Out*
  (Griffin), 157

tolerance
  in *Brother Bear,* 224
  detested code word for Southern Bap-
    tists, 242
  in *Dumbo,* 40, 224
  in *Pinocchio,* 224
totalitarianism
  in *Alice in Wonderland,* 59–60
  in *Lion King, The,* 156–57
Towbin, Mia Adessa, 12
traditional religious faith, in *The Hunch-
    back of Notre Dame,* 167
Traditional Values Coalition, 6
transformation
  in *Alice in Wonderland,* 57
  in *Brother Bear,* 220
Treasure Island, 209
Treasure Planet, 209–14
Turner, Tina, 224
twitterpation, 49, 50, 93
tyranny, revolt against, 94, 96

Ugly Duckling, The, 206–7
unconditional love, in *Lilo and Stitch,* 203
underclass, in *Dumbo,* 41
*Understanding Disney: The Manufacture
  of Fantasy* (Wasko), 15, 138, 165,
  262
universality, in *Dumbo,* 40
Universal Studios Florida, 231
Updike, John, 9
urban gangs, perceived in *The Lion King,*
  155
U.S. foreign policy, in *Atlantis,* 194
U.S. Holocaust Museum, 128

vegetarianism, in *Snow White,* 24
VeggieTales, 255
Vines, Jerry, 242
violence, explicit, 171, 188
Virgin Mary, Blue Fairy as possible refer-
  ence to, 29
Vischer, Phil, 10–11

Wainer, Alex, 91
Wakabayashi, H. Clark, 224
Waking Walt (Pontius), 19
Walt Disney: An American Original
  (Thomas), 17, 54
Walt Disney: A Bio-Bibliography (Jack-
  son), 5, 44, 110
Walt Disney Company
  anti-Semitism associated with, 121

Walt Disney Company (continued)
  boycott of, proposed, 238
  breaking sequel strategy for Return to
    Neverland, 215
  Burbank headquarters, corporate culture
    of, 242–43
  clash with American Christians, begin-
    nings of, 238
  closing animation units, 266–67
  closing Orlando animation unit, 236
  Comcast's proposed takeover of,
    236–37
  debate in society over values of, 5
  designs on Chinese market, 183–84
  features becoming cross-cultural, 225
  gays in workforce, 243–44
  interaction with faith community, xi
  irony in naming Pleasure Island, 31
  lack of entertainment material dealing
    with Jewish experience, 127
  link to childhood and innocence, 262
  making money as central ideology, 199
  not controlled by immigrants in early
    days of Hollywood, 122
  post-Aladdin clashes with Islam and
    Arab world, 151–52
  reasons for financial downturn, 259–60
  refusing comment on motivation for
    Hunchback's religious content, 173
  religiosity surrounding name, 262–63
  response to protests about Aladdin,
    148–49
  response to Southern Baptist Conven-
    tion call for boycott, 250–52
  social contract with, 27
  standard held to, 261
  symbiotic relationship with American
    religious community, 239–40
  transfer of power in, 122–23
  Treasure Planet as financial disaster for,
    209
  viewed as interested only in money,
    122–23
Walt Disney: Hollywood's Dark Prince
  (Eliot), 17, 112
Walt Disney's Fantasia (Culhane), 38
Walt Disney World, 151–53

Ward, Annalee R., xiii, 53, 157, 162, 166,
  182
Warren, Bill, 152
Wasko, Janet, 15, 138, 165, 262
Watts, Steven, 21, 80
Weber, Jonathan, 184
Weinstein, Harvey, 122
Wells, Frank, 122, 130
Western cultural imperialism, in Atlantis,
  194
White, Gayle, 173
White, T. H., 83
Whitten, Clark, 6, 251–52
Wildmon, Donald, 238
Williams, Chuck, 220, 224
Williams, Robin, 150
Wilmington, Michael, 43
Wilson, Amy, 235
Wise, David, 252
Wise, Stephen, 124
wishing, element of Disney's theology, 28,
  55, 61, 205
Wolpe, Daniel M., 28–29, 141–42
women
  changing roles of, in The Little Mer-
    maid, 138, 142
  portrayal as independent, in 101 Dal-
    matians, 82
women, negative characterizations
  in Emperor's New Groove, The, 190,
    193
  in Little Mermaid, The, 140–41
  in 101 Dalmatians, 80–82
women warriors, 179
Woods, Tonjia, 237
work ethic, in Snow White, 23
Work in Progress (Eisner), 121, 128, 131
Wrisley, Patrick, 236
Wynn, Ed, 60

yoga, as indicator of eccentricity in
  Atlantis, 195
You Must Remember This (Wagner), 239

Zimmerman, Toni, 12
Zipes, Jack, xvi, 26